"This 'field guide' for Christian educators is distinguished by its holistic approach. Addressed especially to those who are new to Christian higher education, it sets that enterprise in its cultural and historical contexts, and provides valuable guidelines for integrating faith and learning in classrooms and scholarship, and for engaging the wider culture. Beyond those more intellectual concerns, it adds wise advice for engaging in Christian education as part of a balanced Christian life that includes concerns for community, joy in one's vocation, principles for leadership, and the value of worship and rest."

—**George Marsden**, University of Notre Dame, author of *The Outrageous Idea of Christian Scholarship*

"John Henry Newman once said that 'a university is . . . knowing her children one by one, not a factory, or a mint, or a treadmill.' With firm conviction that all truth is Gods truth, the contributors to *The Soul of a Christian University* offer helpful suggestions and practical arguments that help transform the mundane classroom into an atmosphere of incarnational, interactive exchange that begins to restore John Newman's ideal. The suggested reading and endnotes are worth the price of the book."

—**Jay Kesler**, President Emeritus, Taylor University

"In this fine volume, Stephen Beers and his colleagues succeed in surveying the scope of Christian higher education. The book offers both inspiring and helpful strategies for application for the practitioners who make the institutions of the CCCU places of Christ-centered excellence."

—**Kimberly C. Thornbury**, Vice President for Student Services and Dean of Students, Union University, Jackson, Tennessee

The Soul of a Christian University

A Field Guide for Educators

The Soul of a Christian University

A Field Guide for Educators

STEPHEN T. BEERS, EDITOR

THE SOUL OF A CHRISTIAN UNIVERSITY

ISBN 978-0-89112-520-4

Library of Congress Control Number: 2007942391

Printed in the United States of America

Cover design by Rick Gibson
Interior text design by Sandy Armstrong

For information contact:
Abilene Christian University Press
1648 Campus Court
Abilene, Texas 79601

1-877-816-4455 toll free
www.abilenechristianuniversitypress.com

08 09 10 11 12 13 / 7 6 5 4 3 2 1

Contents

Contributors

Jane Klosterman Beers is an instructor of biology at John Brown University. She has a gift for working with first-year students in introductory courses, specifically cell biology and biological science. She works diligently to find new and creative ways to encourage the students' love for creation and the Creator. Her teaching has spanned fifteen years on two different campuses. She has a B.A. in Biology and an M.S. in Science Education.

Stephen T. Beers has served ten years as the Vice President for Student Development in addition to being the director of the graduate program emphasis in higher education at John Brown University. Previously he served at Taylor University and Northwestern College (Iowa). Steve has been active in the leadership of the Association of Christians in Student Development and has continued to write and speak on issues pertaining to Christian higher education. Steve holds an Ed.D. from Ball State University in Higher Educational Leadership.

Brian Clark is a student in the John Wesley Honors College at Indiana Wesleyan University double-majoring in Philosophy and History. He currently serves his university's student government as Vice President of Academic Affairs and works as an undergraduate research assistant.

Norris Friesen is Vice President and Dean at Huntington University. Prior to his role in academic affairs, Norris served for seventeen years as Vice President for Student Development at Huntington University. He is a graduate of Tabor College (Kansas), Kansas State University, and Purdue University (Ph.D.). Norris has an interest in peace and justice issues and currently serves on the boards of Huntington County Habitat for Humanity and Education for Conflict Resolution. He also maintains a high level of contact with students and has lead several spring break mission/service projects in Jamaica and Central America.

Tim Herrmann is Director of the M.A. program in higher education & student development at Taylor University. Tim has also served in several other roles including Dean of Assessment, Associate Professor of Psychology, and Associate Dean of Students. A past-president of the Association for Christians in Student Development and co-founder/co-editor of *Growth Journal*, Tim earned a B.A. from Taylor University, an M.A. from Ohio State University, and a Ph.D. from Indiana State University.

Eileen Hulme is Executive Director of the Noel Academy for Strengths-Based Leadership and Education and associate professor of Higher Education and Organizational Leadership at Azusa Pacific University. Prior to joining APU in 2005, Hulme served as vice president for student life at Baylor University and George Fox University. Eileen received her Ph.D. from the University of Texas–Austin and is a 2001 Fulbright Scholar. She is passionate about the integration of faith into the national higher education dialogue.

Thomas Jones is Dean of Arts & Sciences at Taylor University and has served as a member of the history department faculty and Director of the Center for Teaching & Learning Excellence. He has received the Alumni Council's Distinguished Professor award twice during his seventeen-year career at Taylor. His teaching interests are focused on U.S. diplomatic history and social studies education. He has also served as minister of Center Christian Church for thirty-six years.

Paul Kaak is Assistant Professor of Organizational Leadership at Azusa Pacific University. He is also the Assistant Director of the Noel Academy for Strengths-Based Leadership and Education and the Program Coordinator for APU's Leadership Minor. Paul has a Ph.D. in Leadership from Andrews University where he is a member of the Faculty Community, teaching a course in worldview formation. Paul mentors leaders from various domains both nationally and internationally. Prior to his work in higher education, Paul pastored in three churches and continues to equip "organic church planters."

Kina Mallard is Academic Dean at Gordon College in Wenham, Massachusetts. Prior to moving north, she worked as chair of the communication arts department and Associate Provost at Union University in Jackson, Tennessee. Kina enjoys leading faculty development workshops on teaching and learning, scholarship, faith integration, balance of work and life, and related topics. She contributes regularly to *The Department Chair* on academic leadership issues and serves as Council for Christian Colleges and Universities Senior Fellow for Faculty Development.

Rick Ostrander, Academic Dean at John Brown University, holds a Ph.D. in American Religious History from the University of Notre Dame. As a scholar of American religion and an academic administrator, he maintains an active interest in Christian higher education. His publications include *The Life of Prayer in a World of Science* (Oxford, 2001), *Head, Heart, Hand: John Brown University and Evangelical Higher Education* (University of Arkansas, 2003), and "Spirituality and the Discipline of History," in *Searching for Spirituality in Higher Education* (Peter Lang, 2007).

Todd C. Ream (Ph.D., Pennsylvania State University) is the Associate Director of the John Wesley Honors College and Assistant Professor of Humanities at Indiana Wesleyan University. Along with Perry L. Glanzer, he is the author of *Christian Faith* *and Scholarship: An Exploration of Contemporary Debates* (Jossey-Bass, Association for the Study of Higher Education Report Series).

Mark Sargent is Provost at Gordon College; previously, he served at Spring Arbor College and Biola University. After his Ph.D. at Claremont Graduate School, he was a Fulbright Scholar at the University of Utrecht in the Netherlands. For his research he received the Walter Muir Whitehill Prize in Colonial History, and recently has chaired the chief academic officers commissions for the CCCU and the Council of Independent Colleges.

Darryl Tippens serves as Provost of Pepperdine University where he is also professor of Early Modern literature. For over two decades he has taught courses in the literature of Christian spirituality. His publications include *Pilgrim Heart: The Way of Jesus in Everyday Life* (Leafwood Publishers, 2006), *Shadow & Light: Literature and the Life of Faith*, co-editor (Abilene Christian University, 2004), and many essays on literature, film, spirituality, and contemporary culture. He and his wife Anne live in Malibu, California.

Wendy Soderquist Togami is in her ninth year as the Director of Leadership Development at the Soderquist Center for Leadership and Ethics at John Brown University. Wendy brings over seventeen years of leadership experience to her work with the emerging leader population and the Center's work with the not-for-profit industry. Wendy continues to play a vital role in the Center's mission and vision, providing research, speaking, and facilitation across industries. Wendy's experience includes eight years of student leadership development at Taylor University. She is a graduate of Taylor and received her M.A. in Higher Education from Ball State University.

Mark Troyer is Vice President for Student Development at Asbury College. He has worked in Christian higher education for over twenty years. His work and research interest have been primarily in the area of leadership development, both creating co-curricular programs and teaching at the undergraduate level. His programs have been selected for national best practices awards from the Templeton Foundation and Florida State Center for Study of Values in Student Development. Mark has spoken widely on the theme of leadership development. Mark holds a Ph.D. from the University of Kentucky.

Skip Trudeau is Dean of Student Development at Taylor University. Skip holds an Ed.D. from Indiana University, Bloomington, and has served in a variety of student affairs related positions. In addition to his administrative role, Skip also teaches in the Masters of Higher Education and Student Development program at Taylor. He has been active in professional organizations and has held several leadership roles, including President, of the Association for Christians in Student Development.

Acknowledgements

The genesis for this book came from a late night conversation at a conference for educational leaders. The conversation focused the need for a text that communicated the essential components of the Christian college experience in a language usable for educators. Those present—Paul Blezien, Ron Coffee, Tim Herrmann and Skip Trudeau—"blessed me" to take the lead in pulling together such a book. They have continued to be supportive in this labor of love.

The authors of this text have spent their lives shaping Christian colleges and universities. I appreciate how they have carved time out of busy days to research and "journal" for all of us their knowledge and wisdom. They have done a wonderful job translating their topics into understandable and practical formats.

We wanted responses from many voices on this project, so beyond the normal readers we field tested the text at several universities. We sent preliminary copies to seven Christian colleges and universities which used them in ways that provided important feedback for our final edit. Thanks to the many educators at Asbury College, Azusa Pacific University, Gordon College, Huntington University, Indiana Wesleyan University, John Brown University, Taylor University, and William Jessup University for their help.

To collect and organize writings from different authors and to edit them in an artful and coherent way was a challenge. Our editor Leonard Allen assisted me in ways that provided direction and support. His willingness to assist such a large group of writers, stretching across the country, has made this project possible.

Thank you to my children Jacob, Sarah and Jonathan. I pray that your Christian college experience will continue to impact you for the rest of your lives. Finally, thanks to my wife who coauthored a chapter and supported me in the editing process. Her commitment to integrating faith and learning in and out of her classroom has provided inspiration for this book.

I pray that this volume, along with prayer and meditation on scripture, will assist educators at Christian colleges and universities as they carry out the mission of Christian education and thus further the kingdom of God.

Stephen T. Beers

Introduction

Stephen T. Beers

Sarah entered her new office on the second floor with the first of her many boxes of text books. These books had been her "friends" to which she had committed the last five years of her life. They were all now a few thousand miles away from their former home. After lunch, and many wrestling matches with the oversized front doors, the U-Haul striped cardboard boxes began to stack up in the corner. The trips up and down the stairs, the balancing act of managing excitement, loss, and fear, and the sweltering heat of early August slightly sapped her spirits. However, the reality of her new, first office provided the counterbalance.

Her attention was diverted when she spotted a note from her division chair penned on the university's sturdy card stock. The postcard-sized note proudly carried the university's logo on one side, printed in the university color, crimson red. She studied the logo for a moment, surprised that it was not some generic medieval crest or a replica of an East Coast Ivy league school's. At the center was the Latin phrase *Deus est lux*, "God is Light." It was prominently displayed on every document that the university printed, and she realized then that it heralded a foundational description of how this community of educators viewed the world.

The phrase immediately invigorated her mental and physical state, for she was one of them. "Finally!" she thought out loud, she would be able to share her faith openly. Not that she had hidden it before, but this phrase, so prominently displayed by these scholars, would empower her to boldly acknowledge her beliefs. As she pondered this phrase and the boldness of its display, she flipped over the card to find a handwritten greeting from Dr. Blezien. It was a simple note wishing her the best as she started her new job. But in the salutation, after the invitation to "give me a call if you need anything," he had penned a portion of a Bible verse.

Sarah had been a Christian for most of her life. She had attended church and committed her life to God as a young girl, but she had never so boldly mixed her faith with her work. Sure, she believed in a creator, but how was she going to manage these new boundary lines between her faith and work? What was an intriguing freedom just a moment ago, now to her bewilderment initiated troubling questions. She wondered, "What would be expected of her?" and "How was she going to be evaluated?" She even wondered if she was "Christian enough."

LEARNING THE CHRISTIAN COLLEGE DISTINCTIVE

Each year over a thousand new Christian educators, made up mainly of professors and student development professionals, join the ranks of faith-based institutions. While these new educators may have pushed the limits of their discipline, most have not experienced or been oriented to the Christian college community and its guiding principles. In addition, most have not had anyone challenge or shape their assumptions about what it looks like to live and work as a healthy Christian educator. The questions that generated this work were, "How do we ensure an opportunity for training and dialogue with new educators about the defining aspects of the Christian college community?" and "Can we provide a framework and a common language for dialogue for first-year educators in these communities?" In other words, "What do new Christian educators need to hear from those of us who have spent our lives in this profession?"

New Christian college faculty and staff receive their training from virtually every major college and university in the United States. This diversity of preparation provides a unique strength to the ethos of each campus, but it may also leave new educators ignorant of the Christian college distinctive. Therefore, the primary purpose of this book is to inform the new educator about the Christian college distinctive and to prepare him or her for long- term success.

A number of recently published books address topics surrounding the Christian college. For example, Wheaton College President Duane Litfin's work, *Conceiving the Christian College,* summarizes the purpose of and vision for Christian higher education. Harry L. Poe's text (Union University), *Christianity in the Academy: Teaching at the Intersection of Faith and Learning,* helps us understand the challenges facing Christian institutions of higher learning. And George Marsden's book (University of Notre Dame), *The Soul of the American University,* gives the academic community a deeper understanding of the transition that colleges in America and specifically Christian colleges have traversed. Furthermore, Christian scholars Cornelius Plantinga Jr. (Calvin College) and Mark Cosgrove (Taylor University) have provided us with specific texts about the challenge of integrating faith and learning and the specifics of how to do it.

Each of these books fills an important role.[1] This book will acquaint the reader with the daily challenges facing Christian college educators and will assist in navigating them.

This book is a collaborative effort by sixteen authors representing eight different Christian institutions. The authors are currently employed at these institutions as professors, student development officers, vice presidents, and provosts. Most, excluding the honor student who assisted with one chapter, have over twenty years of experience in Christian higher education. The group has worked to leverage this rich experience by providing relevant and practical dialogue about each of the chapter topics. This experience-based writing has been beneficial in recording and translating the distinctive aspect of the Christian college and should assist in preparing the new educator for a successful transition. In addition, each chapter ends with a list of discussion questions and suggestions for further reading. Remember: the author's purpose in each chapter is to provide a general overview of the topic, some issues to ponder, and basic applications.

Overview

The book has been organized into two parts. Part One focuses on the core responsibilities of any college or university: student learning and scholarship. Chapter 1 provides an opportunity for the reader to think through the vision and the mission of faith-based institutions. Chapter 2 surveys the history of Christian higher education in America, providing the reader a deeper understanding of the distinctive identity and purpose of these institutions and how that distinctive has been marginalized. The chapter also helps the reader understand why leading scholars like George Marsden have challenged the American academy to make room for Christian scholarship.

The recovery of a strong integration of faith and learning into the college's curriculum is a major aspect of maintaining a Christian college. The authors in chapter 3 provide the reader a baseline understanding of what a worldview-oriented integration of faith and learning is and what it is not. The chapter ends by outlining the practical components of integrating a Christian worldview within the various disciplines.

Most faith-based institutions and virtually all colleges in the Council for Christian Colleges and Universities (CCCU) are primarily focused on teaching and secondarily on research. With this in mind, chapter 4 provides an outline of important shifts in pedagogical theory and research, thus enabling readers to engage in dialogue about their responsibility to facilitate student learning and maximize the student's education.

Chapter 5 challenges all Christian educators to remain engaged in the world of scholarship. Informed and organized by Ernest Boyer's model of educational scholarship (Discovery, Integration, Application, Teaching, Collaboration), the authors provide key insight into what Christian educators can do to sustain the life of the mind.

Part Two focuses on the practical issues of work and life within these unique communities and how each Christian college educator performs his or her daily tasks. Chapters focus on finding joy in work, managing working relationships, taking a leadership role on campus, and finding an appropriate balance between work and rest. The book ends with a challenge to engage the world around us for the sake of God's kingdom. In all, the book is about how to integrate your faith with your life's work.

Chapter 6 continues and expands the previous chapter's discussion on collaboration. Christian educators have the unique opportunity to be leaders in cooperative endeavors between academic affairs and student development programs. The chapter challenges old assumptions about the roles of faculty and staff and provides examples of current collaborative programs that have a proven record of success. The authors provide ample examples of what obstacles can be anticipated along with some practical suggestions for first steps towards collaborative projects.

Chapter 7 asks how we can find and sustain joy in the workplace. The authors organize their discussion of joy in the workplace with three foci: finding joy in "place," in "people," and in "self." They end with practical ways to navigate some stressful experiences, namely evaluation and promotion.

In chapter 8 the reader meets George Newfellow, a new staff member who struggles to balance his work with the rest of his life. The authors then challenge readers to think through what it would mean to live out a Sabbath existence as a way of life.

Each one of us will be called upon in some form to take leadership on our campuses. This is especially true for those who wish to impact more than their specific classes or programs. In chapter 9, after a succinct survey of leadership theory, the author challenges us to see our roles, both formally and informally, as including leadership. Using the lens of Scripture, the chapter looks at our call to be servant leaders.

The final chapter challenges us to move from our cloistered communities into the greater marketplace of ideas. They challenge the Christian college educator to be the salt and light of this world: salt as providing a preserving quality and enhancing flavor and light as illuminating truth and authenticity.

CONCLUSION

After unpacking more of her office decorations that reflected her love for biology, Sarah sat down at her desk and attempted to log onto her dated, university-supplied desktop computer. Awaiting the warm-up script, she looked past her division chair's note and leafed through the institutional mail stacked on the corner of her desk. She was looking for an access code or some sort of pin number that would allow her entrance to the campus system. She contemplated how something that would become so simple and natural was more complicated and daunting the first time through. In time, with a bit of practice and maybe even some assistance, her log on sequence would become second nature.

Sarah represents the latest class of Christian educators. She is characterized by a love of her discipline and a commitment to her faith. We must assist her in making a constructive transition into our communities. We are obliged to help her understand the faith-based learning community and her role within it. In the end, the future of Christian higher education rests less on the shifting sands of the educational landscape than it does with the intentional integrative activities of professionals like Sarah. To sustain the integration of faith and learning in our schools, to incorporate the redemptive power of biblical truth into our disciplines and our lives, to collaborate across the campus in ways that maximize the holistic development of our students is noble—and it is our calling. To do all of these things in ways that are healthy and sustainable—and to find joy in the task—is the challenge before us. The authors hope that this book will provide both support and challenge in this endeavor.

must homogeneity be boring?

The secular university has diversity — but thin on sameness (in some ways)

The Christian university has sameness without enough diversity.

CHAPTER 1

SCHOLARS AND WITNESSES

The Christian University Difference

Darryl Tippens

All scholarship should be witness.
—LUKE TIMOTHY JOHNSON

Invited or not, God will be present.
—INSCRIPTION OVER CARL JUNG'S STUDY

Today there is an ambivalence about, or disenchantment with, higher education.[1] While the reasons are complex, some of the angst lies in the fact that universities appear to have lost their center and sense of direction. Many are saying they have lost their "soul." Even as "the nation has lost its way and must now rediscover the path of truth," in the words of Daniel Yankelovich, our universities have fallen strangely silent on the most urgent questions of the day.[2] Harry R. Lewis, former dean of Harvard College, sounds the alarm in *Excellence without Soul: How a Great University Forgot Education*.[3]

As vagueness about purpose grows, so does a predictable homogeneity. There is irony here. Even as institutional leaders promote diversity, the pressure for sameness mounts. Each month I receive scores of slick publications from the nation's best universities—each one straining to differentiate itself from the pack. But most of these pieces look and feel surprisingly similar. I wonder: if anyone switched the names of the universities in these publications, but left the text essentially untouched, would anyone notice?

What is the problem here? Clark Kerr, former president of the University of California system, has observed that today's university leaders have "no great visions to lure them on, only the need of survival for themselves and their institutions."[4] It seems to me that Christian universities are—or should be—noteworthy exceptions to Kerr's observation. "Purpose" is not merely an outcome for our students, "purpose" lies at the heart of the whole enterprise, coloring and animating everything we do. We are like King Henry as he woos the French princess Katharine in Shakespeare's *King Henry V*:

> Dear Kate, you and I cannot be confined by the weak list of a country's fashion. We are the makers of manners, Kate. (5.2.272)

Rather than be confined by "the weak list" of the academy's fashion, shouldn't Christian universities be "the makers of manners," the ones setting the standards for others to imitate?

If we are to be the makers of our own manners, what should they be? Precisely because we are a university, the answers should be the product of a rich and fervent collegial conversation. Christian universities can play a unique role in higher education in the twenty-first century by virtue of our unique mission and our cultural milieu. Let me begin with some comments about our historical moment.

The Milieu: Disillusionment with the Academy

The first observation about our cultural milieu is this: secular higher education in America today is under judgment. Our society is changing rapidly in many ways, and there is uncertainty as to whether or not the university can be responsive to these changes. Some would argue that higher education has "too many constituencies to satisfy, too many traditions, too many constraints weighing on it to lend it the flexibility—or the political will—to adapt rapidly to the outside world."[5]

Complaints against the academy are not new, of course. Town-gown disputes can be traced to the Middle Ages; yet higher education in the United States has generally enjoyed a comfortable and trusted relationship with the government and its citizens. Americans generally have believed deeply in the gospel of American education—the royal road to a better life. But that conviction is under duress. In the late 1990s Ernie Boyer described "a growing feeling in this country that higher education is, in fact, part of the problem rather than the solution . . . . "[6] Nathan Hatch, president of Wake Forest University, describes the "rising tide of criticism, wave upon wave" that is eroding "the esteem once accorded the academy."[7] Anthony Kronman argues eloquently that our society is in desperate need of universities that will address the question of life's meaning and purpose. Yet, he maintains, the modern university is unwilling or unable to deal with such urgent matters.[8] In the halls of Congress and in the media we hear a chorus of complaints. Universities are too expensive, too arrogant, too easy, too politicized, too unaccountable, or too out of touch.

Such criticism comes not only from the folks in the "town." Those who wear the gown are also saying many of the same things. *The Chronicle of Higher Education* reports that "[u]ndergraduate education in the research university is a project in ruins."[9] Harry Lewis, former dean of Harvard College, says that Harvard's undergraduate curriculum is a "total disunity."[10] David L. Kirp notes an incoherence and uncertainty "about what knowledge matters most."[11] C. John Sommerville, professor emeritus of English history, the University of Florida, in his recent book *The Decline of the Secular University*, maintains that universities today cannot or will not address the most urgent questions that face us, because to do so would require some attention to matters of faith and values—and universities just cannot go there. "Universities are not really looking for answers to our life questions."[12]

There is deep frustration among faculty. Parker Palmer describes professors who enter the university with passion, but end up in pain, "disconnected from their students, from their souls, from each other."[13] The former president of Cornell University, Frank Rhodes, laments the dramatic decline of community in the university: "loss of community is not a mere misfortune," he says. "[I]t is a catastrophe, for it undermines the very foundation on which the universities were established . . . . Our loss of community reflects not a lack of agreement, not even a lack of cohesiveness, but rather a lack of discourse, an absence of meaningful dialogue, an indifference to significant communication."[14] Edward Erickson describes aging faculty members who entered the professoriate in the Sixties with "[e]nergy and high spiritedness," but who "have given way to joylessness, sourness, brittleness. Proclaiming nihilism has led to experiencing exhaustion." These aging activists now have the unhappy task of playing "the conservative role of defending their version of the university's good old days against those they consider the new barbarians at the gate."[15]

> ". . . our society is in desperate need of universities that will address the question of life's meaning and purpose."

The Milieu: New Openness to Faith and Spirituality

A second fact about our milieu is this: even as universities fall under suspicion, in much of the world there is a new openness to religion and spirituality. Whether you call it postmodern, post-secular, or post-Reformation—many observers point to a significant cultural shift. It has been traced empirically by Alexander Astin's research into spirituality in higher education through UCLA's Higher Education Research Institute.[16] A revolution appears to be underway. Students are demanding courses that deal with "the big questions of life."[17] Daniel Yankelovich reports that one of the most significant trends facing higher education in the next decade will be the public's increasing skepticism that science can provide all the answers to our essential questions, coupled with a growing conviction that

> other ways of knowing are also legitimate and important. . . . Americans hunger for religious ways of truth seeking, especially with regard to moral values. By seeming to oppose or even ridicule that yearning, higher education pits itself against mainstream America. Unless it takes a less cocksure and more open-minded approach to the issues of multiple ways of knowing, higher education could easily become more embattled, more isolated, and more politicized.[18]

Given the public's suspicion of higher education, given the growing conviction that "some categories of truth" do not "yield to scientific inquiry,"[19] and given the growing populations of minorities which are overwhelmingly religious (e.g., African American, Hispanic, and Asian), we can reasonably conclude that Christian universities are well placed for important roles on the national and the world stage.

Risk, Opportunity, Vision

The remarks that follow suggest some of the qualities that ought to characterize the vibrant, faithful university of the next generation. Christian universities already possess many of these qualities, but they are in need of *preservation* and *enhancement* if we are to meet the challenges and opportunities before us.

First and foremost, we must articulate a vibrant and distinctive vision. Christianity first became a world religion because it simultaneously presented a convincing account of reality and a compelling way of life. People believed it was true—true not only in some abstract or philosophical way, but true "on the ground," true to human experience. No university can hope to succeed today unless it promises and delivers the good, the true, and the beautiful. According to Robert Benne, the faithful university ought to offer an "articulated account of reality. . . . a comprehensive account encompassing all of life; it provides the umbrella of meaning under which all facets of life and learning are gathered and interpreted."[20] This university will have a compelling story to tell—one that convincingly accounts for what it means to be human, that encourages human flourishing, that addresses life's deepest questions.

Christian universities are well placed for important roles on the national and the world stage.

In 1986 anthropologist Mary Douglas wrote a book called *How Institutions Think*. Normally, we suppose that only individuals "think" or have "minds," but institutions also "think" in certain ways. Institutions "pressure and socialize people to think in specific ways." For example, most Americans think "Americanly," because they have been shaped by certain founding documents—the Constitution, the Declaration of Independence, and by distinctive cultural practices. Americans' thoughts do not range freely, but are bounded by tacit cultural convictions, derived from the national story.

> Non-Christians—and many Christians—don't fully understand what a Christian education should look like or what it is for.

So the question might be: *How does your university think?* What philosophy guides and frames its thinking? Carlin Romano, in a very insightful essay, suggests that it is possible to establish "One University, Indivisible, Under a Coherent Idea."[21] If that were true, what would the "coherent idea" of the Christian university be? How would it be articulated?

Consider just one lively issue that is provoking conversation at many faith-based colleges today: *the relationship between faith and learning.* Jewish scholars have long debated the question under the term *Torah umadda* (law and secular learning). The earliest Christians considered deeply the connection between faith and reason (the logos). For centuries Catholics have wrestled with the question of the relationship of faith and reason (Anselm's and Augustine's "faith seeking understanding" or "I believe in order that I might understand.")[22] The Lutheran and Reformed traditions have robust traditions upon which to draw. Mennonite and Restorationist traditions are engaging these issues in incisive new ways today. With our traditions clearly in view, we must offer a free and friendly space where, in Mark Schwehn's phrase, "spirited inquiry" can occur.

Considering how long Christian colleges have been in business, it may seem passing strange and rather late to be trying to articulate the coherent idea that undergirds and informs our institutions. Yet there is an explanation for the paucity of theoretical (and theological) accounts. When most of them were founded, there was a general cultural (mostly Protestant) consensus and at least the impression, if not the reality, that we were functioning in a Christian society. A Christian worldview was operative and dominant. Much was assumed, and because it was assumed, no one needed to say it, explain it, or justify it. Because the "fundamentals" were givens, then the means to defining the institution were largely external and structural. You had a Christian college when you required religion classes (usually courses in Bible instruction), when you required chapel, hired Christian faculty, and recruited Christian students. It was formulaic and fairly uncontroversial. Today the situation is radically different. The consensus has dissipated. The old convictions are no longer received or honored by the culture at large. Non-Christians—and many Christians—don't fully understand what a Christian education should look like or what it is for. Now is the time for construction and articulation.

In this postmodern moment our work will require us to range freely and broadly through the Christian tradition. We will need to examine Christian traditions, East and West, ancient, classical, and contemporary, in order to compose a *mosaic.* I use the term in two senses: first, like distinct pieces of glass found in a work of art, a living tradition is a collection of disparate influences and features. Mosaics can be both beautiful and enduring. The earliest surviving churches and other buildings of the ancient world contain the remnants of elegant mosaics. Visit the churches of the Middle East or the houses of Ephesus or Pompeii, and you will see how beautiful mosaic patterns can be.

> We cannot write enough policies or bylaws to protect the spiritual legacy that has been entrusted to us.

But church-related higher education is "mosaic" in a second sense: it entails an abiding commitment to moral order, reason, and law. Without faith in the logos, there would be no Christian higher education. Over time, new elements have been added: new disciplines, the methods of the secular research universities, the standards of professional societies and accrediting agencies. But the original design, the deep moral purpose (the *mosaic* pattern) remains. The danger is that, while the institution may contain some wonderfully colorful elements in the design, without periodic review and conscious reflection, the newly added elements may not constitute a pleasing design or a coherent unity.

American colleges and universities are as susceptible to fad and fashion as any other part of the culture. Christian institutions, like their secular counterparts, often scan the horizon for new programs, new "revenue streams," and new ways to increase their "competitive edge," sometimes with little thought to the mission. Things can go wrong when one gets lazy and fails to ask the big questions about what is happening.[23] For example, because secular disciplines and theology are often not brought into conversation, scientific and religious ways of knowing may operate quite independently of one another in what Michael Beaty has called "the two-realm theory of truth." On the one hand, we are faithful believers. On the other hand, we are good scholars; but there may be little meaningful connection between the two domains. This bifurcation leads to divided minds, a confused identity, and a divided existence. It can mean we serve two masters—and neither very well.

The incapacity to articulate a coherent vision may emerge from another cause. As external pressures to conform to secular models of education intensify, and as sponsoring denominations undergo change, links to the university's spiritual heritage may wear thin. Michael Hamilton has noted that denominational colleges face the loss of their identities and "the real possibility of secularization" because "these schools have always thought of their religious identity mainly in denominational terms, rather than thinking of themselves more broadly as Christian colleges. The hard truth is that the old denominational identity that has kept their schools Christian is dying."[24] He cites Southern Baptist institutions as being particularly vulnerable, because their religion is so deeply "intertwined with the distinctive cultural features of the South." "For many, being Southern Baptist was as much about being Southern as it was about being Baptist. . . . As Southern distinctiveness dries up, the cultural foundations of Southern Baptist identity are crumbling from beneath the denomination's schools." These schools face a "stark choice," Hamilton says. "They must either build new kinds of Christian foundations for their schools, or watch the Christian character of their schools fall into disrepair." The leaders of every Christian college and university ought to consider whether this scenario is a plausible one in their respective circumstances; and, if so, what options might prevent the loss of mission and identity.

Serious questions confront us: *If student or faculty loyalty to or knowledge of the sponsoring denomination wanes, what then? If that faith tradition becomes less distinctive and more amorphous, or if the sponsoring denomination goes into decline, what then? What will sustain the institution?*

One possible approach would be to write more rules, adopt a creed, and batten down the hatches. But even creedally based institutions find this "rules" approach inadequate. James T. Burtchaell, former provost at Notre Dame, once observed:

> Notre Dame's character is not guaranteed by its Charter, Statutes, or Bylaws, nor by those who govern it, despite the assertion of our Statutes that it is the "stated intention and desire of the Fellows that the University retain in perpetuity its identity as a Catholic institution." Living traditions live not at all by law and governance if the law and governance do not find their affirmation in the persons who live by them.[25]

We cannot write enough policies or bylaws to protect the spiritual legacy that has been entrusted to us. Though a formal connection to a sponsoring church may be important—a strong ballast against drift—written rules alone will not guarantee the future. We will best sustain our heritage if the members of our community are shaped by a singular, compelling "vision." Robert Benne describes three ways we ensure our future:

"three components of the Christian tradition . . . must be publicly relevant: *its vision, its ethos, and the Christians who bear that vision and ethos*" (my emphasis).[26]

If an institution is to sustain its mission over the generations, it must encourage its best and brightest, whatever their discipline—but philosophers and theologians in particular—to articulate the vision. This is a particularly apt time for doing this, as there is a growing sense that we are entering a post-Reformation moment. Protestants demonstrate a new interest in the great tradition of pre-Reformation thinkers. Catholic leaders today are initiating dialogues with other traditions. A fruitful Jewish and Christian dialogue is certainly underway as well. And through the labor of Philip Jenkins and others many believers are discovering that the church in the global South and East has much to teach us about the nature of Christianity.[27] At such a time, surely it is possible to conceive of a new kind of global Christian university.

A university does not live by endowments and tuition alone. It also lives by *ideas*—compelling, audacious, life-changing ideas. To do our work, we need healthy, robust departments of philosophy, history, and theology which will inspire us to do this original constructive work. All our disciplines need to examine the methodological assumptions that govern their practices. Even our most practical degrees should be overseen by faculty who have a broad understanding of the theoretical issues lying back of their disciplines as well as an appreciation for the urgent issues gripping our society. "The life of the mind" is for all of us; otherwise, we segregate ourselves into intellectual ghettoes—the thinkers from the narrow technicians.

What I am describing is more than a productive life of the mind. It may take us a long time to develop a theological vocabulary, a conceptual repertoire, an agreed upon language and syntax for discussing the relationship of faith and learning. And if we achieve it, we will find that this language is insufficient to the vision. We must also attend to the concrete practices that hold our university together: the social virtues, the practice of hospitality, care of the body, the honoring of time, and so forth—the practices that shape us into a very particular kind of community. So, while we strive for an *intellectual* consensus, we should vigorously pursue an *ethical* consensus that will truly distinguish us.

Part of our work is to return to the sources—both to the sources of the earliest colleges and universities, but also to the sources of Western (and Eastern) rationality and those early practices that shaped both churches and universities. As we enter a post-Reformation era, the old sectarianism wanes. "What no eye has seen, nor ear heard, nor the human heart conceived" (2 Corinthians 2:9) we are now able to see, hear, and conceive in our day. In the words of one of my colleagues: "In general,

Christian educators, like me, value denominational specificity but we want nothing to do with any sectarian exclusivity. We have bigger fish to fry, such as confronting and transforming a post-Christian culture, and this challenge is so large and so complicated that there isn't time to re-fight the battles of the sixteenth century." By transcending the debates of the Reformation, new possibilities beckon.

Robert Louis Wilken, in his elegant and scholarly *The Spirit of Early Christian Thought*, shows how Christianity was persuasive in the ancient world because it constituted "a way of thinking about God, about human beings, about the world and history."[28] It has been cogently argued recently that Christianity was born at a unique historical moment when Judaism encountered Greek rationalism. Both the Septuagint translation of the Old Testament and the New Testament were written in Greek and bear "the imprint of the Greek spirit."[29] In that ancient setting *thinking was a part of believing*; thought and practices were intimately related. The university with soul will explore the necessary connection between faith and reason, thought and practice. So many of our intellectual and moral problems today—concerning epistemology, the problem of authority, the nature of truth, the abuse of human persons, the neglect of the weak and the marginalized, etc.—were first probed by our spiritual ancestors. They thought deeply about the relationship of faith to reason, knowledge to love, and they offered helpful paths that we have largely forgotten.[30]

. . . nothing else counts for much if we don't get the vision right.

Forgive my camping so long on the matter of *vision*, but nothing else counts for much if we don't get the vision right. If there is no vision, the university perishes. Before concluding, I wish to offer four additional theses—essential features of the faithful university.

A Place of Discovery

The faithful academy will demonstrate a passionate commitment to the discovery and transmission of knowledge, for there is no university if there is no discovery and diffusion of learning. Universities by definition "encourage curiosity, discovery, intellectual risk-taking."[31] The Christian college or university will not slavishly imitate the great research universities in this goal, however. The United States has a sufficient number of secular research universities. We rightly refuse to sacrifice our primary service to students in order to discover new knowledge.

However, great liberal arts colleges and professional schools serve their students best by inviting them to join a rich culture of discovery. I emphasize the word *culture*, for the secular university has adopted an exceedingly narrow definition of "discovery," and it has seemingly lost some of its memory of the traditions and practices of the intellectual life which have their roots in the Christian past. For example, excellent scholarship is only possible when grounded in certain virtues (honesty, truth-telling, humility, etc.). Good scholarship is produced by good men and women—people of high ethical character. Scientific reductionism, stripped of transcendent purpose, cannot in the long run sustain the scientific enterprise. The Christian university must be unapologetic about the spiritual foundations of good research.

> Christian universities should possess a natural ease in linking one's intellectual life and work with one's passion for service, love of people, and care for the world.

This requires a robust understanding of the past. The faithful academy will cultivate a community rich in memory. One element of the "restoration" impulse that has been so pervasive in American Christianity is the uncovering of what has been forgotten and passing it on (the *traditio,* i.e., the handing down, the delivery, surrendering of the wisdom of the ages).[32] Yet Americans in general, and our students in particular, are victims of amnesia, blissfully unaware of the riches of the past. Few students know their heritage. "Not to know what happened before you were born is to remain forever a child," said Cicero. "In remembrance lies the secret of redemption," said the Ba'al Shem Tov. The Judeo-Christian tradition invites us to see ourselves as participants in an ongoing historical, purposeful narrative, and Christian universities should be superior at explaining this story. Our strong sense of story will have a strong teleological and hopeful direction. We participate in a narrative of *eternal purpose*.

A Place of Ethical Transformation

The faithful academy will be heart-centered in the classical sense of the term. We will recover the "heart side" of faith and learning. *Heart* in the biblical tradition is a large and resonant term.[33] The heart involves *thinking* as well as *emotion*. It is the zone of "emotion-fused thought," which includes intelligence, mind, wisdom, intention, will, love, sadness and joy.[34] Recent discoveries in science are enabling us to reconsider the vital bond between thought and feeling. After centuries of segregation, many are re-imagining an integration of head and heart, rather like the poet W. B. Yeats:

> God guard me from those thoughts men think,
> In the mind alone;
> He that sings a lasting song
> Thinks in a marrow-bone.[35]

According to the work of Robert and Michèle Root-Bernstein, for example, body orientation and visceral feelings play significant roles in major scientific discoveries. Christian universities should possess a natural ease in linking one's intellectual life and work with one's passion for service, love of people, and care for the world. "The love of learning and the desire for God" will not be seen as competing aspirations, but a single aspiration.[36] The healthy university will reconnect the head-bone to the heart-bone, and we will seek more than knowledge but the *transformation of hearts*.[37]

A Place Where Matter Matters

The faithful university will be incarnational. In this respect, the Christian university's essential difference from the other universities of our day may be most apparent, for this *incarnationalism* (or sacramentalism) will color all our practice and set the agenda in many ways: in our appreciation of mystery as well as reason, in our love of creation, in our commitment to hospitality, and in our devotion to discernment and wisdom. By many accounts, the Enlightenment is over and "desecularization" is underway. According to Peter Berger, "The assumption that we live in a secularized world is false." "The assumption that 'modernization necessarily leads to a decline in religion' has proved to be mistaken."[38] What is desperately needed in this new era (which bears an uncanny resemblance to the pre-modern era) is the capacity to honor a God-infused universe—a sacred reality. The doctrine of the incarnation, which declares that the divine has touched and continues to inhabit material reality, causes us to say with John of Damascus: "I do not worship matter; I worship the Creator of matter who became matter for my sake, who willed to take His abode in matter; who worked out my salvation through matter. Never will I cease honoring the matter which wrought my salvation."[39]

This sacramental understanding of the world leads naturally to a love of creation, the arts, and practical wisdom. There will be a strong appreciation for the arts and sciences at any university where the incarnation is taken seriously. A love of creation will inspire artistic productivity. We will know that a Christian university has matured when it produces a number of artists, musicians, novelists, dancers, screenwriters, and poets. Beauty will abound. We will say with Augustine, "How beautiful is everything, since you have made it, but how ineffably more beautiful are you, the Creator of all this" (*Confessions* XIII.xx.28). Such a sacramentalism will not only inspire the production of "high art." It will also validate all honorable human endeavors: life-enhancing entrepreneurs, devoted school teachers, legendary jurists, and committed public servants.

Because we believe that the Logos took flesh and dwelt among us, we will hold a special love of nature. The university will have a "green" cast to it because its inhabitants will see that one cannot honor the "Maker of heaven and earth" and trash what the

Maker has made. With Simone Weil, everyone will say, "Let us love the country of here below. It is real."[40] And to love it means to protect it, care for it, and renew it.

A Place of Welcome

The institution's incarnationalism will yield a distinctive view of human beings. We will practice a radical hospitality, loving the stranger across class, gender, ethnic, and religious boundaries to a degree rarely seen in the world. Much modern higher education today is the antithesis of hospitality. Parker Palmer reports that "education is a fearful enterprise." "Fear is everywhere."[41] However, if we practice "mere Christianity," "a generous orthodoxy,"[42] our faith will not be coercive or triumphalist, but welcoming, humble, and servant-hearted. Seekers, non-believers, and believers from other faith traditions will feel honored and welcomed in our midst. We will not merely practice "toleration," but something far kinder. Doubters will study beside the faithful in an atmosphere of honesty and charity.

This hospitality will extend to those from the other two-thirds world. It will be open to the new *Southern Christianity*—not of the American South—but of the burgeoning populations of the Southern hemisphere. Recognizing that the majority of Christians no longer reside in North America and Europe and knowing that the world of higher education is "flat," a new internationalism will characterize the hospitality of our institutions. We will consider closely the fact that Christianity was not originally a "Western" religion, and it will be less and less so in this generation.[43] It's worth noting that the growing Hispanic and Asian populations in our country are also predominantly Christian. We will more effectively serve these populations if we acknowledge the increasing multi-cultural complexion of the faith.

The earliest Christians were interested not only in ideas, but in practices—not merely *orthodoxy*, but *orthopraxy*: "immersion in the *res*, the thing itself, the mystery of Christ and the practice of the Christian life. The goal was not only understanding but love. . . . "[44] The earliest "colleges" (monastic schools) were sometimes called "schools of charity." The great Christian universities of the twenty-first century will also be "schools of charity." Love is meaningless if it does not translate to the concrete and the material. We may understand all mysteries and all knowledge, but if these do not lead to loving actions, so says the Apostle Paul, we are "a noisy gong or a clanging symbol" (1 Corinthians 13:1-2). The university with soul will be known for the cultivation of *phronesis* (practical wisdom, the virtues). We will challenge the devastatingly reductive turn taken by higher education when it abandoned its commitment to moral and spiritual formation. The faithful university of the twenty-first century will be committed to the formation of the whole person, as we learn from the great traditions and incorporate new knowledge about how learning occurs.

Because virtue is fostered in community, the faithful university will be committed to communal life to a degree that the secular university cannot. It will challenge the bankrupt North American myth that one find one's "true self" in radical independence from others. Through shared practices, especially shared worship, a flourishing common life will be evident throughout the institution. Students, having experienced a rich *koinonia* (fellowship), will know how to form and sustain communities once they depart alma mater, and loyal alumni will remember with gratitude their years in a soul-forming community.

We will practice a radical hospitality, loving the stranger across class, gender, ethnic, and religious boundaries to a degree rarely seen in the world.

Conclusion: The Role of Educators

But how shall such a university come to be? It will not happen because the provost, the president, or the governing board wills it. It can happen when the faculty and staff wholly embrace the vision. The personal influence of the educator is the single most important element in higher education. If we lose that, we lose it all. As John Henry Newman once warned: "With [faculty] influence there is life, without it there is none. . . . An academical system without the personal influence of teachers upon pupils is an Arctic winter; it will create an ice-bound, petrified, cast-iron University, and nothing else."[45]

Yet even the best academically prepared faculty may not be ready for the unique task of educating in the kind of university we are contemplating, unless we offer them the means to develop in ways different from, and beyond, the reductive traditions of the research university. The formation of educators may well be our most urgent, unfinished (perhaps never-quite-finished) task. James Burtchaell more than thirty years ago commented on the difficulty of sustaining a university's faith mission:

> [I]t is the faculty deliberations within the departments, not in the mind of the University leadership, that [core] beliefs are given flesh. Please understand that this preservation of our corporate strength is nothing that can be accomplished by administrative fiat, or quantitative norms, or official pledges of affirmative action. It is only a conscious conviction and commitment among the faculty that will assure its own continuance.[46]

In 2004 the esteemed biblical scholar Luke Timothy Johnson delivered the Staley Distinguished Lectures at Pepperdine University. In one address, he proclaimed that "*all scholarship should be witness.*" Most academics have been schooled in intellectual traditions that would render this claim either incomprehensible or heretical. In my graduate studies I was instructed to segregate my scholarship from my witness, to conceal my convictions behind a façade of pure disinterestedness. Johnson imagines a different (and more honest) approach to our calling. Our scholarship is necessarily an expression of our core identity.[47]

Today many are coming to see that certain essential questions about life cannot be answered by a sterile, reductive secularism. When Clark Kerr delivered the Godkin Lectures at Harvard in 1963, he enthusiastically envisioned a great future for the multi-versity, "the city of the intellect": "a city of infinite variety . . . held together by a name and . . . related common purposes." Nearly forty years later, Kerr's enthusiasm gave way to something akin to despair. When he wrote a new final chapter for his classic *The Uses of the University*, he was less confident and less positive about the university's future. University leaders, Kerr noted sadly, have, "*no great visions to lure them on, only the need for survival* for themselves and their institutions" (my emphasis).[48]

At the end of a sobering critique of higher education, David L. Kirp, Professor of Public Policy at Berkeley, concludes with this riveting question: "*If there is a less dystopian future [for higher education], one that revives the soul of this old institution, who is to advance it—and if not now, then when?*" (my emphasis).[49] It is the Christian university's destiny to answer the call. And how will we do this? Consider the words of Margaret Mead: "Never doubt that a small group of thoughtful, committed citizens can change the world; indeed, it's the only thing that ever has." The vision of a faithful university will become real when a group of thoughtful, committed faculty members determines that it will be so. It will happen when they say: "*Here we are, poised to restore what has long been disjoined: a comprehensive educational vision which unites knowledge, virtue, faith, and service. At the Christian university knowledge will seek wisdom through love, understanding through faith. That is how we will be purposeful, that is how we will serve the world, and that is how we will be a leader in higher education.*"

The personal influence of the educator is the single most important element in higher education.

Discussion Questions

1. The author suggests that within the halls of Congress and in the media we hear a chorus of complaints: universities are too expensive, too arrogant, too easy, too politicized, too unaccountable, or too out of touch. Does this critique describe your institution to some degree?

2. Discuss what you believe to be the philosophy that guides and frames your university's thinking.

3. Discuss what the author sets out as essential elements of a faithful university—A faithful academy will: demonstrate a passionate commitment to the discovery and transmission of knowledge; be heart-centered; be incarnational.

4. Review the mission statement of your university. Discuss your institution's vision and purpose.

5. If student or faculty loyalty to, or knowledge of, a particular Christian tradition wanes in the coming years, what then? If that tradition becomes less distinctive and more amorphous—which seems likely—what then?

For Further Reading

Benne, Robert. *Quality with Soul: How Six Premier Colleges and Universities Keep Faith with Their Religious Traditions*. Grand Rapids: Eerdmans, 2001.

Henry, Douglas V. and Michael D. Beaty, eds. *Christianity and the Soul of the University*. Grand Rapids: Baker Academic, 2006.

Lewis, Harry R. *Excellence Without Soul: How a Great University Forgot Education*. New York: PublicAffairs/Perseus Books, 2006.

Rhodes, Frank H. T. *The Creation of the Future: The Role of the American University*. Ithaca, N.Y.: Cornell University Press, 2001.

Summerville, C. John. *The Decline of the Secular University*. Oxford: Oxford University Press, 2006.

Chapter 2

The Distinctive of a Christian College

An Historical Perspective

Rick Ostrander

Before considering the unique responsibilities of Christian college professionals, we must understand the Christian institutions to which they are called. And to understand the nature of the Christian college today, we must first consider where these institutions came from. The following narrative, of course, does not characterize in detail every institution of Christian higher education in the United States. Christian colleges in the South, for example, typically did not experience the jarring effects of late-nineteenth-century secularization as did institutions in the North. Moreover, some Christian colleges outside the American Protestant mainstream such as Anabaptist and Catholic institutions followed a different trajectory throughout much of their history in the U.S. Nevertheless, the notion that Christian academic institutions are currently engaged in a recovery project—in rebuilding a robust, academically rigorous, culture-shaping enterprise of Christian higher education—does describe to a greater or lesser extent the Christian college today. In this chapter, therefore, I will attempt to describe the American Christian college's distinctive identity and purpose by briefly tracing its historical trajectory over the past four hundred years.

The Founding and Growth of Christian Colleges, 1600-1860

Among North America's first European settlers was a group of radical English Protestants known as Puritans. Influenced by the theology of John Calvin and champions of religious reform in England, many of them had grown impatient with the moderate Protestantism of Queen Elizabeth and her successor King James I. When the main group of Puritans landed in New England in 1630, they immediately set about building shelter, planting crops, and doing other tasks necessary to survive in a sparsely inhabited wilderness. Not long after that—in 1636, to be exact—they founded Harvard College. One would think that with harsh winters, Indian wars, and religious controversies to preoccupy them, the Puritans would have left founding a college to a later, more secure generation of Christians. Why was a Christian college so important to them?

As Protestant Christians just a couple of generations removed from the Reformation, the Puritans were part of a religious movement that highly valued Christian education, as the career of the Reformer John Calvin indicates. Trained as a lawyer in Catholic France, Calvin converted to Protestantism and fled to Geneva, Switzerland. He spent most of the remainder of his life pastoring churches and authoring weighty volumes of the *Institutes of the Christian Religion*—essentially an educational manual in Protestant theology. Calvin believed that God created human beings to love truth and to seek it in all areas of life. Although he insisted on the necessity of spiritual conversion for Christians, Calvin also believed that God sprinkled his truth liberally throughout his creation, both in the workings of nature and in the minds of unbelievers. This notion of "common grace," that God has made insights about truth available to all persons, saved and unsaved, has been an important catalyst to Christian higher education over the centuries.[1]

Calvin thus placed a high value on Christian thinking. His mind roamed from Scripture to St. Augustine to the Roman pagan philosopher Seneca. He advocated learning in the home, and he founded the first Protestant university, the Geneva Academy, to which Protestants from all over Europe (some of them fleeing for their lives) came to receive a Christian education.

The Puritans were deeply influenced by Calvinism. Some Puritan leaders had studied at the Geneva Academy, and others were educated at Cambridge, one of the leading universities in England. As a whole the movement was imbued with a fire for Christian thinking. Thus, founding a college in the harsh New England wilderness was second nature to them. An early motto on the Harvard seal stated *Christo et Ecclesiae*—"for Christ and the Church"—and that truly was the guiding mission at Harvard College. Its primary purpose was to train pastors for Puritan churches, but the college also educated New England's political and social leaders. Harvard's course of study placed a heavy emphasis on Latin, the language of the classical writers and church fathers as well as the medium of scholarly discourse throughout the Middle Ages. Harvard students also devoted much time to studying Greek and Hebrew. Aside from languages, Harvard emphasized rhetoric (essentially public speaking and reasoning) and to a lesser extent theology, ethics, politics, mathematics, astronomy, botany, and history. Bible instruction was reserved for Sunday, when Harvard students would be expected to repeat to their tutors on Sunday evening the two lengthy sermons given in the meetinghouse that day.[2]

For much of the 1600s, Harvard was the only institution in colonial higher education. In the next century, however, several new Christian colleges were established in the Harvard mold. In 1701, Connecticut Puritans, fearing that Harvard was departing from Calvinism, established Yale College as an "orthodox" alternative to the Massachusetts institution. In the mid-1700s, a religious revival known as the Great Awakening swept through the English-speaking world. Church rolls expanded and new denominations—most notably Baptists—spread across the colonies. The new religious movements that the revival produced immediately set about founding colleges to train their own leaders. Thus were born many of today's Ivy League institutions such as Princeton (by Presbyterians), Brown (by Baptists), and Dartmouth (by Congregationalists). Indeed, virtually without exception, American colleges begun in the colonial era were created by Protestants with the explicit purpose of training Christian leaders in the church and society.

The Puritans were not a perfect Christian community. They were often ruthless in repressing those who dissented from their religious and social ideals. American Indian tribes who opposed them were harshly treated; Quaker missionaries who traveled to Massachusetts to convert them were hanged; even Baptists were whipped and placed in the stocks in New England village squares. Puritan education had its shortcomings as well. Educational methods were hardly inspiring. Class instruction typically employed "recitation," in which instructors quizzed students individually to see how well they had memorized the lesson for the day. At other times professors lectured by reading aloud from a textbook in Latin as the students took notes or followed along in their own text. Especially in the 1700s, when Harvard began attracting the sons of wealthy merchants, student disciplinary problems abounded.[3]

However, for all of their shortcomings, colonial colleges embodied an ideal that Christian colleges still pursue today: that Christian thinking should embrace not just biblical subjects but should range over all disciplines; that as God's image-bearers we are free—and indeed obligated—to pursue truth in all areas. As a modern

> As Henry Zylstra has put it in words that the Puritan founders would affirm, "In Christian education, nothing matters but the kingdom of Jesus Christ; but because of the kingdom, everything else matters."

educator, Henry Zylstra, has put it in words that the Puritan founders would affirm, "In Christian education, nothing matters but the kingdom of Jesus Christ; but because of the kingdom, everything else matters." In other words, the Puritans made no distinction between "secular" and "sacred" subjects—it was all God's world out there for his creatures to explore and enjoy.[4]

This ideal of the Christian intellectual life embracing all of nature and human culture was embodied by one of America's most influential thinkers, Jonathan Edwards, a New England pastor in the mid-1700s. As a teenager, Edwards composed a detailed description of the shape, design, and purpose of a spider's web. He even speculated as to the web's place in God's universal order: "The exuberant goodness of the Creator, hath not only provided for all the necessities, but also for the pleasure and recreation of all sorts of creatures, even the insects." Whether we agree with Edwards that the spider was spinning its web in order to have a good time, we can certainly follow Edwards's assumption, that studying nature is one way to commune with the Creator. Because God has created the natural world and us, his image-bearers, with minds to comprehend that world, all subjects of study were relevant for the Christian. Remarked Edwards, "All the arts and sciences, the more they are perfected, the more they issue in divinity, and coincide with it, and appear to be parts of it." Edwards intently studied the important ideas and thinkers of his day. His writings display an avid interest in the emerging fields of natural science, psychology, and Enlightenment philosophy, as well as a penetrating critique of the new ideas from a Christian perspective. Not surprisingly, Edwards was selected to lead Princeton College in 1758, only to die of a smallpox vaccination a few weeks into his presidency.[5]

By the late 1700s, the British colonies in North America had outgrown their subservience to the mother country, precipitating the crisis of the American Revolution that dominated the last quarter of the century. The Revolutionary Era posed some serious challenges to Christian higher education in America. For one thing, American society seemed to be growing more secular in the revolutionary decades of the late 1700s. Church membership declined to a paltry 10 percent of the population. Deism, a watered-down, non-supernatural version of religion that reduced Christianity to a set of moral principles, seemed to be the religious wave of the future. Politics, not religion, occupied the attention of America's cultural leaders. One historian has observed, "In 1740 America's leading intellectuals were clergymen and thought about theology; in 1790 they were statesmen and thought about politics."[6]

Faced with these challenges, Protestants mounted an effective response that resulted in a burst of Christian college-building in nineteenth-century America. An extended religious revival known as the Second Great Awakening resulted in a democratic, evangelical religious ethos that dominated American society until the Civil War.

Denominations that championed the "common man," such as the Methodists and Baptists, saw their membership rolls explode. By the 1850s, one-third of all Americans claimed affiliation with the Methodist Church. Other denominations were not far behind as new Protestant churches sprung up across the nation.

In the wake of the religious revival, American Protestants founded Christian colleges by the hundreds—over five hundred of them, to be exact, though only about two hundred survived into the twentieth century. For countless communities, establishing a Christian college was not so much a response to overwhelming demand for higher education (little of which actually existed) as it was a way to assert a town's significance and community spirit. The Presbyterians and Congregationalists—direct descendants of the Puritans—led the way, but they were soon surpassed (in quantity, at least) by the Methodists and Baptists. Even though these colleges were founded by particular denominations, because the denominational college drew its students from the surrounding community, a standardized Protestant ethos tended to pervade what became known as the "Old-Time College."[7]

College presidents were typically Christian ministers, and professors were expected to be generalists who could teach just about anything. The curriculum remained largely unchanged from earlier eras. Latin and the classics still served as the foundation of the curriculum. Christian educators believed that the intellect and conscience, like physical strength, could be developed through exercise. Thus, the goal of the college curriculum was not so much to impart particular knowledge as to develop a mature, balanced Christian young person who thought clearly and behaved morally. This was best done through a balanced assortment of courses in literature, science, and the arts. Mathematics, it was believed, was an especially useful form of mental exercise. Natural sciences were incorporated into the course of study primarily for their apologetic value. That is, students typically learned "evidences of Christianity" through observing the appearance of God's design in nature.[8]

The Old-Time College curriculum culminated in a course entitled "Moral Philosophy" typically taught to seniors by the college president. Drawing on subjects as diverse as psychology, political science, sociology, ethics, religion, and economics, this course sought to provide a unifying Christian capstone to the college career and a final exhortation concerning the kind of American citizenship good Christians were supposed to exercise. Our generation would call this course an exercise in the "integration of faith, learning, and living." While hampered by certain questionable assumptions of the day, the moral philosophy course did epitomize a quality of nineteenth-century higher education that was largely lost by the twentieth century: the desire to comprehend the interrelatedness of all knowledge as the product of a Creator.[9]

Nineteenth-century colleges were primarily residential. American educators followed the English model of building dormitories so that students lived on campus. The college thus operated *in loco parentis*—in the place of parents—by closely regulating the lives of its students. Colleges specified times for waking up, studying, attending classes, playing, and retiring. Strict rules governed student life; such "amusements" as Sabbath breaking, card-playing, alcohol, tobacco, foul language, and disorderly conduct were prohibited. Students attended college chapel daily and church twice on Sunday. Such strict supervision at times produced rebellions and violence. Student riots were not uncommon. One of Princeton's six rebellions between 1800 and 1830 left venerable Nassau Hall in ashes, and at least two college professors of the 1800s were murdered by students.[10]

As an antidote to student rebellion, and as testament to an age of revivalism, colleges promoted revivals to heighten the religious fervor of the student body. Yale College was especially known for the intensity of its campus revivals during the presidency of Timothy Dwight, a grandson of Jonathan Edwards. Throughout the 1800s Yale stood as the premier Christian college in the nation in both its academic quality and the spiritual fervor of its students. Its spiritually awakened graduates fanned out across the South and West founding and presiding over new Christian colleges, thus earning the reputation as the nineteenth century's "mother of colleges."[11]

Such religious characteristics were not limited to private colleges in nineteenth-century America. Even most public universities of the nineteenth century saw themselves as essentially Protestant colleges. University presidents were typically clergymen, and professorships were often rotated among members of the various Protestant denominations to ensure a fair representation of the main Protestant churches. Public universities maintained chapel and behavioral requirements that resembled those of the private Christian colleges. The University of Michigan, for example, operated as a Christian college by all of the conventional standards of measurement. Its student life was strictly regulated, all of the faculty professed belief in the Christian faith, and President Henry Tappan delivered annual lectures entitled "Evidences of the Christian Religion." In all, the colleges and universities of the day reflected the beliefs and values of America's most dominant cultural group, white, evangelical, middle-class Protestants.[12]

The colleges and universities of the day reflected the beliefs and values of America's most dominant cultural group, white, evangelical middle-class Protestants.

As America hurtled toward political schism and civil war in the 1850s, its Protestant leaders could take comfort in the notion that they had constructed a stable, vibrant, seemingly permanent system of Christian higher education rooted in a fusion of Christian morality and American democratic values. Little did they know that a few decades later, American academia would be almost completely secular and its Christian colleges relegated to the cultural backwaters of society.

The Decline and Revival of Christian Colleges, 1860 to 2000

To understand the swift collapse of the Old-Time College in the late nineteenth century, we must examine these institutions more closely. American Christian higher education in the 1800s seemed outwardly quite strong, but it contained serious internal weaknesses. First, these institutions were essentially havens for a small group of American white males. Except for innovative Oberlin College in Ohio, women and African Americans were largely excluded from nineteenth-century colleges. In fact, in 1870 only 1.7 percent of American young people aged 18-21 were enrolled in colleges and universities. The total college and university population in 1870 was just over 50,000, about the size of a single large state university today. College was essentially a four-year rite of passage for the nation's privileged class to endure before taking their positions in ministry, law, or medicine.[13]

College was essentially a four-year rite of passage for the nation's privileged class to endure before taking their positions in ministry, law, or medicine.

For anyone else in nineteenth-century America, college was largely perceived as impractical and irrelevant. Rather than combining a liberal arts core with practical courses in career fields, the nineteenth-century college maintained a rigid curriculum in which all students took the same classes throughout their four years of study. The system neglected educational interests of some of the wealthiest and most productive segments of society such as farmers, businessmen, and mechanics. Observed Francis Wayland, a college president who tried to reform the system, "We have produced an article for which the demand is diminishing." As a result, numerous colleges became extinct, and those that survived were forced to keep student costs artificially low in order to maintain enrollment. Those who often bore the brunt of the colleges' financial morass were the professors, whose paltry salaries kept them barely above the poverty level. Not that such professors were likely to command higher pay elsewhere.

Typically kindly old gentlemen, nineteenth-century college professors hardly commanded respect as an intellectual force in society. Remarked nineteenth-century Bostonian Henry Adams about the Harvard faculty in his day, "no one took Harvard College seriously."[14]

Adams's remark points to the most serious weakness of the nineteenth-century Christian college: its lack of deep, intentional, rigorous Christian thinking across a range of disciplines that had characterized people like Jonathan Edwards. The moral philosophy course purported to do that, but typically it devolved into comforting platitudes that science confirmed Christian truth and that American civilization represented the pinnacle of western historical development. In fact, the generic Christianity advanced by such courses differed little from the "religion of peace, reason, and morality" articulated by the deist Thomas Jefferson. As historian Mark Noll has noted, because Protestant educators' values fit so neatly with their society, they neglected to work out clear Christian reasoning or critique of their cultural situation. They neglected "to push thinking from the Scripture to modern situations and back again." Protestants created colleges that promoted warm-hearted evangelical piety and the formation of moral character but that hardly represented a mature, well-rounded Christian approach to higher education. When dramatic changes hit American society in the late 1800s, the Old-Time College found itself to be built on shifting sand.[15]

The first major development to affect higher education in America was a shift in the meaning and methods of science. Nineteenth-century Christians had believed that doing science was simply a matter of organizing one's observations of the natural world into general laws that revealed God's goodness and purpose in creation. By the mid-1800s, however, new views of science emanating from Europe questioned this notion. Science, European scholars were saying, should be guided by the assumption that all phenomena originated from natural, not supernatural, causes. The task of the scientist, therefore, was to trace events to their natural causes, thereby excluding any considerations of divine design and activity.[16]

Charles Darwin's theory of evolution, which was publicized in 1859, was both a product of and a catalyst for this new trend in science. Darwin argued that living things were not created by God but rather evolved through random changes over millions of years. Such a theory seemed to contradict Christians' belief in the literal truth of Genesis as well as the comforting notion that science confirmed Christian truth by revealing evidence of design in nature. The evolutionary system of brutal competition, survival of the fittest, and the occasional extinction of whole species seemed a far cry from the orderly, benevolent system of creation espoused by nineteenth-century American Christians. Christians who had proclaimed that science invariably promoted Christian belief could offer little by way of effective response now that science seemingly pointed in the opposite direction.

Another blow to the Old-Time College came from a highly acclaimed new model of higher education that emerged in Germany. In contrast to the English system of a four-year residential undergraduate college molding character through education in the classics, Germans had developed a system of higher education based on the graduate school seminar. In the German model, a small group of advanced students met with a trained expert in a particular field to conduct research and discuss the latest scholarly discoveries. By the late 1800s, a number of leading American educators had spent time in Germany and sought to import the more professional model to the United States.

Such reformers were aided by vast new sources of funding for American higher education that emerged after the Civil War. The Morrill Act of 1860 made government funds available for states to establish public universities that would advance agricultural and mechanical studies. Federal government support for higher education was joined by private donations. The new industrial society of the late-1800s produced fabulously wealthy men such as Ezra Cornell, Leland Stanford, and Cornelius Vanderbilt. These industrialists poured huge sums of money into universities which bore their names, both as a means of boosting their own stature and to generate the scientific discoveries and technological know-how needed by the new society.

Thus was born the modern secular research university in America, which overshadowed the pre-Civil War Christian college in size, money, and prestige. Where the Old-Time College counted its students in the hundreds (if not the dozens), the new universities educated thousands. In 1824, Princeton College was considered audacious when it sought to raise $100,000 from its alumni. A half-century later, Johns Hopkins, a banker and investor in the Baltimore & Ohio Railroad, personally donated $3.5 million to establish a German-style research university. Rather than employing retired, underpaid ministers to teach everything from geometry to ancient history, the modern university employed trained experts in particular fields. The Ph.D., not piety, became the most sought-after quality in professors. In 1870, Harvard president Charles Eliot discarded the college's traditional classical curriculum. In its place he introduced the elective system, whereby students chose their own course of study from a number of different subjects and departments. Eliot's innovation proved so successful in attracting students that other universities soon followed suit. By the end of the century the classical curriculum was rapidly disappearing in American higher education.

The large modern university displayed a more fragmented, secular character than the Christian college. The attempt to perceive a unified world of knowledge largely disappeared amid the specialized departments of the modern multi-university. Amid all the academic improvements in the modern university, the traditional Christian college concern for molding character—for linking head and heart—disappeared. The modern university was a secular enterprise designed to produce competency in a professional and technological society; religious perspectives that got in the way of progress and seemingly impeded scientific inquiry were excluded outright or pushed to the margins of university life.

The story of Christian higher education in the wake of these changes is a complicated one. To make some sense of it in a few pages we must generalize and simplify a complex process. Protestant Christians in higher education responded to these developments in two basic ways, neither of which was adequate. Many Christian colleges sought to keep up with the new universities by abandoning or obscuring their Christian identity. Rather than abandoning Christian belief outright, such colleges typically redefined Christianity as devotion to high moral ideals or service to humanity. Thus, a college that promoted academic inquiry and contributed to a technological society could be called "Christian" whether or not it still advanced any particular Christian beliefs. As Harvard professor Frederic Henry Hedge reassured alumni in 1866 who were concerned about the college's seeming secularization, "the cause of Christ and the Church is advanced by whatever liberalizes and enriches and enlarges the mind." By Hedge's criteria, whatever Harvard did was automatically Christian. Platitudes like Hedge's served temporarily to placate a college's religious supporters while Christian content quietly slipped out the back door. Eventually, even the Christian rhetoric disappeared as these institutions became miniature versions of the secular research university. Thus, college chapels and campus inscriptions such as Harvard's "For Christ and His Church" function largely as vestiges of a bygone era in American higher education.[17]

Of course, not all Americans abandoned Christian higher education in the late 1800s. Within the Protestant churches, a movement of conservative Christians (calling themselves "fundamentalists" because of their desire to defend the fundamental doctrines of Christianity) arose to combat liberal theology in the Protestant churches and secular trends in the culture. Fundamentalists were motivated partly by the fear that American higher education was destroying the Christian faith of young people. Conservative writer T. C. Horton exclaimed, "Christian schools were once the pride of our nation. Now, many are the progeny of Satan." Thus, fundamentalists transformed existing Christian institutions such as Wheaton College in Illinois and created "Bible colleges" such as the Moody Bible Institute to provide a Christian education that they believed had disappeared in the culture at large.[18]

Fundamentalist colleges admirably strove to provide a semblance of a Christian educational ideal in a secularizing age. However, as well-rounded Christian intellectual institutions they displayed serious shortcomings. A fervent piety often pervaded these institutions, and religious revivals among the students were common. However, this piety was often defined in elaborate lists of rules against "worldly amusements" that resembled the strict policies of the nineteenth-century colleges. Bible colleges sought to provide brief, practical training for young people who planned to become full-time Christian workers. This emphasis on "practical" Christian education (ironically paralleling the "practical" emphases emerging in the modern research universities) led such institutions to neglect a Christian interest in a wide range of subjects and academic disciplines. As historian Virginia Brereton has observed, "liberal or general education was considered an unwanted extravagance given the exigencies of the time." The Bible college's emphasis on "soul-winning" tended to crowd out a healthy Christian interest in all of God's creation that earlier Christian colleges had displayed.[19]

Furthermore, preoccupation with biblical prophecy—especially the belief in an imminent "rapture" of believers to heaven—led fundamentalists to de-emphasize attention to the concrete, often mundane affairs of the visible world. Why study politics or biology, they wondered, when the world is coming to an end anyway? The attempt to apply a Christian perspective to a wide variety of subjects, embodied however inadequately in the moral philosophy course of the nineteenth century, largely disappeared from the fundamentalist college. Secular learning came to be seen as either a set of false ideas to be refuted or as dangerous to the beliefs of Christian young people and thus best left alone. Subjects such as Bible, apologetics, and evangelism seemed safer and more practical. In general, fundamentalist colleges sought to produce soul-winning specialists, not well-rounded image-bearers of God. Thus, while Christian higher education continued in the first half of the twentieth century, it was merely a faint shadow of the robust vision articulated by Protestants such as Calvin and Edwards.[20]

While Christian higher education continued in the first half of the twentieth century, it was merely a faint shadow of the robust vision articulated by Protestants such as Calvin and Edwards.

Since the 1940s, however, Christian colleges have been gaining in strength. Part of their revival is due to the growing size and wealth of American conservative Protestantism in general. The growth of evangelical Christianity has meant that there are more students available to populate Christian colleges, and financially successful

Christians have more money to invest in them. Today the avowedly Christian colleges in America number about two hundred, in addition to eighty or so Bible colleges. Many of these colleges can now afford first-rate facilities and attract qualified professors that the financially strapped fundamentalist colleges of the early twentieth century could only dream about. Furthermore, the secularization of American higher education has produced among Christian colleges a greater awareness of their common identity and purpose, and thus greater cooperation. In 1976 thirty-eight leading Christian colleges formed an alliance known as the Christian College Coalition. That organization, now known as the Council for Christian Colleges and Universities (CCCU), currently enlists 105 member institutions.[21]

Among these colleges and universities, a revival of the Christian concern for breadth of learning has taken place in the past few decades. For many institutions, the catalyst for this recovery was the writings of Abraham Kuyper, a late-nineteenth-century Dutch theologian and politician. Kuyper urged Christians to engage their culture, and he articulated an approach to learning in which Christian truths were integrated into all academic disciplines. As Kuyper put it, "There is not a square inch on the whole plain of human existence over which Christ, who is Lord over all, does not proclaim, 'This is Mine!'" In Kuyper's plan, chemistry, psychology, history, and sociology had as much place in the Christian college curriculum as theology and philosophy. Moreover, the guiding methodology for Kuyper was the desire to integrate Christian faith with learning in a particular discipline.[22]

Of course, few American Christians bothered to read Dutch theologians. Kuyper indirectly impacted American Christianity through the vehicle of Calvin College, a Dutch Reformed school founded in 1876 in Grand Rapids, Michigan. Kuyper's educational approach became prominent at Calvin College in the mid-twentieth century. When the Christian College Coalition was formed, Calvin College exerted substantial intellectual influence on other institutions. By the end of the 1970s, Kuyper's "integration" model of faith and learning had become a mantra among Christian colleges—especially as articulated in Wheaton College philosopher Arthur Holmes's *The Idea of a Christian College*, which became standard reading at CCCU institutions—inspiring them to pursue broad academic excellence and a distinctively Christian approach to learning. In recent years, some Christian colleges in non-Reformed traditions such as Anabaptism and Wesleyanism have challenged the integration model and suggested other ways of relating Christian faith to learning. What they have agreed on, however, is the need for strong, vibrant Christian colleges and that Christian scholars have an important contribution to make to the academy.[23]

Thus, the Christian college in America today represents something different—and hopefully better—than simply a return to the Old-Time College of the 1800s. While not as socially dominant as the Harvards, Yales, and Princetons of the nineteenth century, the modern Christian college in some ways more closely approximates the historic Christian educational ideal. For example, the nineteenth-century model of the professor as a kindly old "jack of all trades" may have encouraged the development of Christian character, but it did not effectively prepare students for rigorous academic thinking. Christian college professors today are more likely to be mentors who care about the spiritual development of their students *and* qualified scholars in their particular disciplines. One important lesson of the past two centuries is that it was not too much thinking that led colleges to secularize; rather, it was a *lack* of clear, intentional, rigorous Christian thinking applied to the wide range of emerging academic disciplines that led institutions to see Christianity as basically irrelevant to their mission. Christian college professors who model spiritual commitment and academic excellence make secularization less likely. Furthermore, those who work with students outside of the classroom—whether that be in the residence halls, the athletic field, or the chapel—are likely to be trained professionals who combine a love for students with an understanding of the unique spiritual, emotional, and cultural challenges facing young people in modern society. Today's Christian colleges seek to weave together the curriculum and co-curriculum to transform students intellectually, emotionally, and spiritually.

It was not too much thinking that led colleges to secularize; rather, it was a *lack* of clear, intentional, rigorous Christian thinking applied to the wide range of academic disciplines that led institutions to see Christianity as basically irrelevant to their mission.

In educating young people to bear God's image throughout all of life, the modern Christian college thus seeks to instill a sense of curiosity and wonder at all of God's creation. It resembles that musty old wardrobe in C.S. Lewis' *Chronicles of Narnia*. Seen from the outside, the Christian college looks rather ordinary. Nothing would seem to distinguish its classrooms, dormitories, and professors from any other educational institution. On the inside, however, the Christian college opens up into new worlds, fresh perspectives, and unexpected possibilities for those who are willing to step in boldly.[24] Whether the Christian college achieves this ambitious goal depends on the ability of administrators to articulate the purpose of Christian higher education, professors and student development personnel to embody it, and students to seek it in every aspect of college life. In 1725, a young Jonathan Edwards, though not a zoologist, allowed his relationship with God to spur him to intense fascination with a spider web. He realized what every Christian needs to understand: that engagement with God's world makes us more human, more Christian, and better able to worship and serve our Creator.

Discussion Questions

1. Why did the Puritans place so much emphasis on higher education?
2. What strengths and weaknesses did colonial colleges display?
3. What explains the swift collapse of the "Old-Time College" in the late 1800s?
4. What traits characterized the "fundamentalist" colleges of the early 1900s? To what extent do these traits still characterize Christian colleges today?
5. Would you agree with the author's conclusion that today's Christian colleges are an improvement over the Old-Time College of the 1800s? Why or why not?

For Further Reading

Burtchaell, James. *The Dying of the Light.* Grand Rapids: Eerdmans, 1998.

Jacobsen, Douglas and Jacobsen, Rhonda Hustedt. *Scholarship and Christian Faith: Enlarging the Conversation*. New York: Oxford University Press, 2004.

Marsden, George. *The Soul of the American University.* New York: Oxford University Press, 1994.

Noll, Mark. *The Scandal of the Evangelical Mind.* Grand Rapids: Eerdmans, 1994.

Ringenberg, William. *The Christian College.* Grand Rapids: Baker Academic, 2006.

Rudolph, Fredrick. *The American College and University: A History.* New York: Vintage Books, 1962.

CHAPTER 3

INTEGRATION OF FAITH AND LEARNING

Stephen Beers and Jane Beers

Imagine two sisters, standing together, gazing onto the Atlantic Ocean with the sun rising over the horizon. The moment is engulfed in warm red, orange, and yellow beams that illuminate the crashing waves. Both women are moved into deep contemplation and awe. Unconsciously, these refractions of light initiate chemical transformations in receptor cells on the two women's retinas. These "images" are then "translated" by their individual brains in profoundly different ways. To one of the sisters, the image confirms created beauty, splendor and a Creator's handiwork. She whispers a grateful praise to God. Hearing this, her sister, impacted by the same shimmering light dancing with the waves, utters back, "I will not sacrifice even one goose bump to religion."[1] Each woman views similar scenery, yet influenced by her own "faith" ends up perceiving the world differently. What people "see" is shaped by their belief system or, put another way, their a priori lens.

One way to "see" this world is from a Judaic-Christian perspective. Here, the God of creation speaks through Scripture saying, "Let us make man in our image, in our likeness, and let them rule over . . . all the earth."[2] According to this Old Testament text, humans were created in the image of God and sent forth to be stewards of this earth. This statement begs the questions, "What does it mean to be made in the image of God?" "How might Christians be good stewards?" and then, "How does this call to stewardship impact the way Christian educators lead and teach future generations?"

The foundational distinctive of a Christian college education is the integration of faith and learning. As we saw in the previous chapter, American Christian higher education is currently focusing on the recovery of integrating a Christian worldview with "secular" discovery. The chapter concluded with a suggestion that the prevailing distinction between "sacred" and "secular" truth is being diminished or replaced with a holistic and integrated epistemology. Arthur Holmes's classic statement, "All truth is God's truth,"[3] provides a short but succinct phrase that encapsulates this way of thinking. This intentional re-integration of all truth ("sacred" and "secular") distinguishes the experiences of Christian college students. Ultimately, the process of integrating faith and learning must be done intentionally. To be intentional, one must understand it.

The formal training of most university educators, including Christian college educators, was completed at a secular university. At these institutions, a variety of worldviews (i.e., naturalism, secular humanism, atheistic existentialism, etc.) have more often than not replaced Christian theism as the guiding philosophy underlying the study of a particular discipline. In addition, the increased specialization within the academy has "bred fragmentation, rather than integration, of knowledge."[4] As George Marsden described, during the twentieth century Christianity was pushed to the outer boundaries of the academy as the progressive movement shifted the academy in a more broadly moral and less distinctively Christian direction.[5] Educational historian Douglas Sloan concluded that by the 1970s, the relationship between Christianity and higher education in America was sharply diminished and near collapse.[6] With this diminishment came the obvious loss of a primary source for the articulation and modeling of faith and learning integration. This chapter attempts to provide a simple starting point for both. Due to the book's scope, this chapter should be regarded as a primer on integrating faith and learning and not a comprehensive treatment.

Most university educators' formal training, even the Christian college educators' training, was completed at a secular university where a variety of worldviews (i.e., naturalism, secular humanism, pantheism, atheistic existentialism, etc.) have more often than not replaced Christian theism . . . .

The primary component of a predominant methodology for integrating faith and learning is the development of a Christian worldview. A worldview provides a discrete picture of reality based upon reasonable faith and observation. Much as a picture on the top of a puzzle box provides a framework for constructing the puzzle, a worldview provides a framework for interconnecting the diverse components of reality. It also provides direction for inquiry. The person who assembles the puzzle must skillfully and patiently navigate each piece into its proper place, but the large scale image is provided beforehand. This "picture" assists us in constructing knowledge and interpreting experience, and without it a person easily reaches false conclusions. Specifically, a Christian worldview is developed by organizing knowledge gathered from the world around us (general revelation) and knowledge from beyond our natural boundaries, such as the sacred Scriptures (special revelation). Ultimately, though, all philosophical presuppositions that construct any worldview are based upon faith.[7]

This chapter provides a basic description of faith and learning integration and defines commonly used terms. Additionally, we outline some of the various approaches to the faith-learning integration process, provide insight into integrating across the various disciplines, and highlight the importance of good interpretation of Scripture. We will then review several integrative strategies and conclude with suggestions for application, some of which may be more aptly utilized in the classroom and others in co-curricular settings. But first let's look at some common misconceptions about integration.

Common Misconceptions of Faith-Learning Integration

Chapel, student ministries, discipleship groups, and missionary fellowships are duplicated in different formats and fashions on virtually all Christian college campuses. So, one may naively assume that these high profile spiritual formation programs provide the primary basis for the Christian college integration distinctive. Less than one hundred years ago, the Christian worldview formed the academic foundation for much of American higher education, and these Christian co-curricular programs served as an outgrowth of the college community member's faith. But, as the prevailing worldview influencing American academia shifted, many Christian college leaders wrongly assumed that retaining these programs sufficed for its distinctive.[8] Infusing *spiritual formation programming within the curriculum and co-curriculum is not sufficient* as the Christian college distinctive. More than just programming, there must be a deeper integration at the core level of educating (both in and out of the classroom), specifically at the level of a discipline's subject matter.

Christian colleges are small in size when compared to most state institutions. This characteristic facilitates another misunderstanding of full integration. Integration is *not merely about encouraging personal relationships* between the educator and student. The smaller number of students in the classrooms and better faculty-student ratios, along with faculty and staff who are led by Christian principles of charity and kindness, may generate a university ethos that is pleasant and inviting. These factors have been suggested to provide a positive learning environment and may help with retention.[9] However, these factors do not necessarily entail the integration of faith and learning. Such relational opportunities can be reproduced in many non-Christian private colleges and in special programs on state school campuses like honors and athletics. Integration is more than positive educator-student relationships.

Some Christian educators facilitate prayer or other spiritual disciplines in the classroom. In so doing they may intentionally or unintentionally equate integration with praying before class. Interspersing the spiritual disciplines within a chosen teaching method may assist the student in grasping the material, but it falls well short of the full meaning of integration. By contrast, integration reaches down into the specific material being studied; it is *not an auxiliary or preparatory activity* to assist the student in retaining the material.

Christian colleges generally have a core curriculum that includes some biblical and theological coursework. In addition, most, if not all, have majors that prepare students for full-time Christian service. Integration of faith and learning is *not sufficiently satisfied at the curricular level*. It must go deeper than a set of additional courses on a graduate's transcript. These courses can serve to develop one's Christian worldview, but the real integrative distinctive is accomplished in how this worldview interfaces with each discipline.

Interspersing the spiritual disciplines within a chosen teaching method may assist the student in grasping the material, but it falls well short of the full meaning of integration.

Similar to this "insufficient curricular level integration" is the attempt to add biblical or Christian components to one's discipline. Full integration is not the addition of poetical sections of the Bible in a poetry class or utilizing Christian novels in a literature course. Though this may be helpful in understanding aspects of poetry or literature, it does not represent the full incorporation of the integration process on the body of knowledge within the discipline. Remember, *full integration is not an addition of biblical or Christian theological precepts as illustrative examples within any particular discipline*; rather, the discipline's integration must start at the epistemological level. It shapes how one sees all of the discipline at its core and should not be limited to an auxiliary role.

V. James Mannoia, in his book *Christian Liberal Arts: An Education that Goes Beyond*, outlines an alternative use of the term integration.[10] He argues that the American academy has drifted away from integrating knowledge between the various disciplines. For example, he suggests that the Christian college should be about integrating (or reintegrating) sociology and history, where one understands historical transitions from a sociological perspective. Instead of a cross-disciplinary understanding of the world, he believes that today's students' educational experience has become too specialized or truncated. The culprit here is that faculty focus has moved from teaching to research. He argues that Christian colleges have a special niche to fill—one where reintegrating the disciplines is the standard. He also challenges Christian college professors to conduct research that utilizes real world problems, thus putting their "faith into action."[11] Mannoia's challenge to reintegrate across the disciplines is an important discussion; however, it diverts us from our central theme: evaluating and shaping a discipline's body of knowledge from a Christian worldview.

All of the previously mentioned curricular and co-curricular components of today's Christian college are healthy outgrowths of the faculty and staff's commitment to follow Christ and facilitate developmental opportunities. These programs and activities are important for equipping the saints and challenging the seeker. But in themselves they fall short of the basic task of integrating faith and learning, which is the acquisition, organization, and presentation of knowledge informed by a Christian worldview.

Foundational Terms and Concepts of Integration

The central purpose of this chapter is to provide a primer on a method of integration, not an overview of a Christian worldview's salient themes. For a relevant description of a Christian worldview, we suggest reading Cornelius Plantinga's *Engaging God's World: A Christian Vision of Faith, Learning, and Living.*[12] The book outlines the central tenants of a Christian worldview: Creation (God created the world and man was created in the image of God), the Fall (all of creation suffers from the corruption of sin), and Redemption (the whole world can be re-created through God's grace).[13]

To help readers understand this process of integrating faith and learning, we provide definitions of some critical terms: faith, worldview, learning, and epistemology. *Faith,* in this context, is more than an emotional feeling or something "hoped for." Instead, it is a set of rational assumptions about life and truth embraced by personal trust. It encompasses more than a commitment to religious teaching and does not negate the need for normal forms of learning. Arthur Holmes says that faith "does not preclude thinking either about what we believe or about what we are unsure of, nor does it make it unnecessary to search for truth or to examine evidence and arguments. Faith does not cancel out created human activities; rather it motivates, purges, and guides them."[14] Faith is a rational, yet assumed, way of organizing all of the available knowledge. As a person organizes her faith-based assumptions about the world, she views her world in a particular way—much like the two sisters at the beginning of this chapter. This theoretical construct is her worldview.

A *worldview* is a set of assumptions that frame a person's understanding of reality. It provides one a discrete picture of reality and provides answers to the fundamental questions of life that form one's perspectives. Ultimately, these perspectives direct our behavior. The answers to the following questions expose one's worldview: "What is the nature of man?"; "Does God exist?"; "Can we know God personally?"; "What, if any, is the purpose of life?" These questions are usually answered prior to the academic inquiry, and the manner in which one answers them impacts what he studies, his methods of inquiry, and ultimately his interpretations. These assumptions bring clarity to his picture of the world, much like eyeglasses do. Nevertheless, any eyeglass prescription can be mildly or severely incorrect, which can impede the individual's ability to perceive, evaluate, and act correctly.

Faith, in this context, is more than an emotional feeling or something "hoped for." It is a set of rational assumptions about life and truth embraced by personal trust.

Learning, in connection with the integration of faith and learning, generally refers to acquiring and understanding knowledge gathered from educational pursuits. This includes knowledge from all disciplines and from various types of inquiry. Theologically speaking, academic knowledge is referred to as general revelation. In addition to general revelation, Christians believe God has also provided knowledge via special revelation (i.e. Scripture). Learning for the Christian includes the acquisition of general and special revelation secured from multiple sources.

We study, engage the world around us, and reflect on our experiences. What we eventually accept as knowledge and what we include as acceptable ways to obtain knowledge defines our *epistemology*. In his philosophy text, Donald Palmer defines epistemology as the "theory of the knowledge that answers questions such as: What is knowledge? What, if anything, can we know? What is the difference between opinion and knowledge?"[15] Prevalent Western epistemologies like rationalism (the predominance of reason to gain knowledge), naturalism (exclusion of all knowledge apart from empirical observation), and relativism (knowledge is subjective and socially created), all emerge from assumptions prior to engaging in research and study. These basic epistemological assumptions are all assumptions that require faith. Therefore, we must acknowledge that any author or researcher's theoretical premise will influence the shape and findings of the study.[16]

Core Issues Relating to Faith and Learning Integration

This section reviews a few core issues related to the integration process. Robert Harris, in his book *Integration of Faith and Learning: A Worldview Approach*, states, "The process of integration should not be seen, then, as a method of rejecting knowledge, but as an activity for clarifying, filtering, and correcting misinterpretations. Or better, integration provides a touchstone for testing the claims about knowledge."[17] While the integration of faith and learning is foundational to Christian higher education, there are a variety of approaches to integration. This section begins with a discussion of four prominent approaches. Second, the "visibility" or pervasiveness and the ease of the integrative process vary significantly between disciplines. Therefore, it will be helpful for the reader to understand where his discipline fits within this range. Last, because it is critical to understand how to interpret Scripture within the integrative processes, we will provide some direction to the reader for interpreting Scripture.

Four Approaches to the Integration of Faith and Learning

In his book *Foundations of Christian Thought: Faith, Learning, and the Christian Worldview*, Mark Cosgrove outlines four approaches to integration.[18] We summarize his approaches below because we find them useful in describing a range of views in Christian higher education on how one undertakes the process of integrating faith and learning.

Sole Authority Model: Faith against Learning

This model's foundational proposition is that the Bible is always trustworthy, and yet, because of its fallen nature, the human mind is not. This leads to the interpretation of Scripture being placed in a position that is always above or against "secular" learning. The *sole authority* approach tends to elevate Scripture in a triumphal manner to the sole source of wisdom for life and to relegate human learning to non-essential and misguided interpretations. This approach to integration tends towards anti-intellectualism, a general hostility toward academic pursuits, and indoctrination.[19]

The *sole authority* model is constructive in its recognition that frequently there are hidden anti-Christian assumptions to be found within human knowledge claims, and anti-theistic worldviews often produce biased research and interpretations. However, the triumphal attitude of this approach can be destructive to the learning process by preferentially upholding interpretations of special revelation, i.e., "God's word," to the extent of preventing students from engaging with general revelation, i.e., "God's works" as revealed in the world around us. Although it places an emphasis on the infallible word of God, it tends to forget that people lack infallibility in the interpretation.[20]

Separate Authorities Model: Faith and Learning

The *separate authority* or the *parallels* model views faith and learning as two separate entities existing side by side much like the parallel tracks of a train. Rather than being antagonistic to each other as in the *against* model, this model considers faith and learning to be two sources of truth that are complimentary but do not intersect. Therefore, truth about the world can be determined from the academic disciplines and the truth about God can be determined from Scripture.[21] A common academic arena for adherents of this model is the natural sciences. In addressing the question of whether there must necessarily be conflict between faith and science, Stephen Jay Gould, a preeminent Harvard scientist, stated that:

> . . . science covers the empirical: the composition of the universe ("fact") and the way it works ("theory"). Religion, on the other hand, examines questions of ultimate meaning and moral value. These two [realms] do not overlap, nor do they encompass all inquiry. Science gets the age of rocks, and religion the rock of ages; science studies how the heavens go, religion how we go to heaven.[22]

Adherents of this model of faith-learning integration would state that both areas are needed to live a God-honoring life; however, the two areas do not overlap.

The *separate authorities* or *parallel* model has the positive benefit of a jolt-free ride along the road of learning by not dealing with any potential conflict between the knowledge claims of the discipline and the Christian worldview. This approach works best when there seems to be little overlap between the subject area and Scripture, such as in the study of mathematics or chemistry. The shortcoming of the approach is that it lacks an evaluation of the discipline's baseline knowledge claims. [23] For example, the underlying worldview of many scholars in the natural sciences—scientific naturalism—has many tenets that oppose Christian theism.

Equal Authorities Model: Faith Plus Learning

The *equal authorities* or *integrate* model acknowledges the overlap between the subject matter of the Bible and that of the academic subject areas which leads to an interplay between faith and learning. In this model, Scripture and academic inquiry are equivalent sources of truth and when combined are more productive. Each source of truth, God's word (special revelation) and God's works (general revelation), contributes to our understanding of any particular topic, as in the study of human nature or ethics.[24]

The acceptance of both Scripture and human learning as equally valid sources of knowledge is a favorable aspect of this model. However, the quantity of information gathered among the vast array of academic writings tends to tilt the scales toward secular research. This unintentional secularization of a discipline's subject matter is of concern because the undisciplined student looks to the Bible only for details in certain subject areas. In areas that are not specifically addressed by Scripture, which is often the case with many academic subjects, non-integrated subject matter dominates the field. To address this concern, Cosgrove suggests that the student should consider that "the Bible contributes a different form of truth . . . a form excellent for building the Christian philosophical worldview from which the academic subject areas can be evaluated."[25]

Foundational Authority Model: Faith Supports Learning

"The *foundational authority*, or the *worldview*, model states that the major contribution of the Bible to our academic pursuits is that it gives us a worldview foundation from which to do our studies in science, social science, and the arts. This *worldview* approach acknowledges that beliefs do make a difference in academic pursuits. One's faith or worldview does matter when one engages in the learning process."[26] One's worldview affects the choice of subject areas to study, the methods of inquiry, and most importantly, the interpretation of the information discovered. "In other words, the learning process in school is never an academically unbiased process since one's learning is always affected by one's worldview beliefs."[27]

The *worldview* model recognizes that everyone has a worldview and that it has a profound impact on how one sees the particular tenants of an academic discipline. It is essential for students to be taught how to critically examine the worldviews underlying the various knowledge claims and to gain a thorough understanding of the rational basis of the Christian worldview. The worldview model is intellectually honest because it acknowledges and openly examines all worldviews including one's own and thus defuses anti-intellectualism. In this model, the Christian worldview becomes the cornerstone for integrating faith and learning. [28]

> It is essential for students to be taught how to critically examine the worldviews underlying various knowledge claims and to gain a thorough understanding of the rational basis of the Christian worldview.

One negative aspect of this model is that by utilizing a Christian worldview as the starting point of our academic pursuits, the researcher, scholar, or student may confuse the *worldview* model with the *sole authority* model and not allow general revelation to influence their interpretation of the biblical text. Our search for truth should be tempered with a heavy dose of humility and a strong understanding of our limitations.

Although this worldview integration model is currently the most prominent among evangelically oriented colleges, it is not without its critics. Jacobsen and Jacobsen state in their book, *Scholarship and Christian Faith: Enlarging the Conversation*:

> First, this [worldview] model contains the implicit claim that it is the only valid way to bring faith and learning together: it defines the singular path that all Christian scholars must follow regardless of their own particular understandings of faith or their specific fields of disciplinary expertise. The second limitation is its hyper-philosophical approach to Christian scholarship. In essence, the integration model requires that Christian scholars temporarily become philosophers (instead of being biologists, psychologists, engineers, artists, or whatever else they are), whenever they want to engage in the specific activity of doing Christian scholarship.[29]

They go on to state that, "Christian scholars will probably need to develop a range of new, less grandiose ways of relating faith and learning that are more attuned to contemporary scholarly practices."[30] Their text provides some new direction for integration that may be helpful for the Christian educator.

THE "VISIBILITY" OF INTEGRATION

Integration influences all disciplines because, as we have previously stated, our worldview establishes the framework for inquiry and interpretation. However, the ability to perceive this Christian worldview is more prevalent when the central topic of study is more closely associated with the nature, purpose, and daily living of human beings. Further examination exposes a continuum of how visible integration is among the academic disciplines. We will call this continuum the *Visibility Continuum.* This visibility continuum assists us in understanding why course materials of similar classes of Christian and secular schools look surprisingly similar or oddly diverse. At one end of the spectrum lie the hard sciences of math and natural science; on the opposite end are literature, philosophy, and theology.[31]

THE VISIBILITY CONTINUUM OF INTEGRATION

←――――――――――――――――――――――――――――――――――――→

Less Visible/Pervasive More Visible/Pervasive

Mathematics, Natural Science, Social Science, History, Art, Literature, Philosophy, Theology

The level to which the subject matter of any discipline's body of knowledge differs, when seen though different worldviews, is a matter of degree. Therefore, the disciplines that focus more on the physical matter, such as mathematics, chemistry, and physics, tend to have a similar worldview perspective on the essence and nature of matter (less pervasive). So, even though the underlying assumptions about the purpose and genesis of life may differ, or the acceptability of certain research methods may differ, there are shared premises of the discipline's inner workings. Therefore, we might have a difficult time distinguishing between a day in an algebra course taught at a state university and a similar one taught at a Christian college. To be sure, there would be some introductory comments that reframe the subject in a Christian or naturalistic worldview, but the general class material will look surprisingly similar.

However, visiting the same two institution's courses in psychology or theology may have noticeable even striking differences. In this scenario, the general academic body of knowledge may be similar (i.e. how the synapses in the brain work), but the interpretation and explanation of the particular activity may differ greatly (i.e. If man has a soul, how does it interact with the brain? or, How does one define deviant behavior?). Here in the social sciences the conflict of worldviews permeates and differentiates even more of the discipline's subject matter. Due to the nature of the academic discipline's knowledge, the pervasiveness of a Christian worldview or the integration of faith and learning is more observable. Questions concerning the presence of a person's soul and the underlying assumptions about the goodness of human beings saturate the more pervasive discipline and the assumed answers to these questions alter the discipline's accepted forms of inquiry and knowledge.

The Importance of Interpretation: Hermeneutics

The words of the creator God found in special revelation (Scripture) should influence all disciplines of study. But clearly, Scripture is not a comprehensive text for any academic disciplines (i.e. earth science, psychology, kinesiology, philosophy, astrophysics, etc.), thus the methodology of interpreting Scripture, also known by the term *hermeneutics*, becomes critical. The scope of this chapter does not lead to a full discussion of hermeneutics, but every Christian should use caution and wisdom when interpreting Scripture as it applies to an academic discipline, especially when the text was not intended to provide definitive knowledge on issues peripheral to the objective of the text. In *How Christian Faith Can Sustain the Life of the Mind*, Richard Hughes states, "... if I confess the sovereignty of God and the finitude of humankind, I confess as well that my reason is inevitably impaired and that my knowledge is always incomplete."[32]

The Christian educator engages both general and special revelation. She observes and interacts with nature and reason (general revelation), and she reads and studies the sacred texts (special revelation). She reads with a finite perspective and this incomplete, finite perspective limits her judgment of events and even the texts being studied. Hermeneutics attempts to answers the question, "What is the text really saying?" or, "What does God have to say about this?" So, as a Christian interprets special revelation in relation to her discipline, the wise and prudential use of appropriate hermeneutical skill is critical. Some passages may be appropriate to interpret at face value, and others will need intensive study and wisdom. It is also prudent to remember that the Bible was written in Hebrew and Greek over two thousand years ago within a particular culture and time, though the words are relevant for every generation.[33]

A two-way street illustrates the interaction between general revelation and special revelation in the worldview model. Here the information gained from inquiry and reason informs, clarifies, and directs one's understanding and interpretation of special revelation. The same is true going the other direction: an interpretation of special revelation informs, clarifies, and directs how one works with and utilizes general revelation. When one limits Scripture's impact on a particular discipline or allows Scripture to "trump" a particular set of observations without carefully applying appropriate study of the biblical text, she has failed to utilize appropriate hermeneutical methodology. Like a two-way street, information from general and specific revelation travels both directions.

The problem with a two-way street, though, is that it creates opportunity for conflict. When such conflicts arise we have four response options: side with special revelation, side with general revelation, suspend judgment until further review, or "live in the midst of paradox." The first two responses we will call the "revelation coup." In the first situation, the person attempting to integrate her faith and learning devalues general revelation and trumps any "conflict" with her interpretation of Scripture. The second situation is similar in that when reviewing the conflicting data, she lays aside her understanding of the text and allows general revelation to trump Scripture. The third option may at times be most prudent. When perceived conflict arises, the need to pass final judgment may be suspended until further study. Remember, although Scripture is the final authority for Christians, interpretation of specific Scripture passages may be erroneous and, therefore, the "revelation coup" should be avoided when possible. The fourth option calls us to invite diversity, embrace ambiguity, and welcome creative conflict.[34]

In an article on the difficulties surrounding integration Roger Ebertz concludes with a call for Christians to approach scholarship with an attitude of humility.

> Genuine understanding begins with intellectual humility and openness. As finite, historical beings, we must be aware that we are not God. We rejoice

that God has chosen to reveal himself to us through prophets and apostles, in the person of Jesus Christ and in the Scriptures, but we should be careful not to identify our finite understanding with the Truth that surpasses understanding. We must stand before the world and before God with the recognition that our perspectives are by necessity incomplete and limited. This humility, in turn, should lead us to be genuinely open to others. In the case of the Christian scholar I believe this openness faces several directions. The Christian scholar is open to Scripture. She is open towards the subject matter of her field. And she is open to applying concepts like "love" and "compassion" to the intellectual activity of scholarship. I am inclined to think they apply. Genuine openness to another is only possible when we care about what the other has to say.[35]

Application

This section presents three strategies for integration, as well as some practical integrative tools for use in and out of the classroom.

Three Integrative Strategies

Cosgrove's four models presented in the earlier section (Sole Authority, Separate Authorities, Equal Authorities, and Foundational Authority) provided a general framework for understanding a range of approaches to faith-learning integration. This section draws upon the work of William Hasker who proposed three integrative strategies that present a framework for faith-learning integration with a specific discipline.These three strategies ". . . differ in their assessment of the existing relationships between the disciplines and the Christian faith, and therefore also in their understanding of what must be done in order for a Christian scholar to pursue the discipline with integrity."[36] These strategies were first proposed by David L. Wolfe[37] and Ronald R. Nelson[38] and then further expounded upon by Robert Harris.[39]

The Compatibilist Strategy

As implied by its name, the *compatibilist* strategy for integration seeks to emphasize areas of harmony or compatibility between knowledge from special revelation and academic inquiry. This strategy seeks to highlight areas of common ground in basic assumptions, methods of inquiry, knowledge claims, and interpretations. A compatibilist may also utilize a Christian worldview as a supplement to fill in the perceived "truth voids" in the academic discipline, but he focuses on the unity between the discipline and Christian faith and does not see the need to challenge the underlying assumptions of his discipline. Integration strategies involve the identification, connection, and elaboration of any points of compatibility that are discovered.[40] For example, a biologist using the compatiblist strategy to teach about DNA would relate its structure to its function as an information molecule but would avoid discussing the origins of the DNA molecule itself.

A positive aspect of compatibilism is that by focusing on the compatible aspects, it has a tendency to defuse anti-intellectualism in students who may fear academic engagement because of perceived inherent conflicts.[41] The drawback to this approach is that by failing to address real points of epistemological and ontological conflict between the academic discipline and a Christian worldview, students may fail to grasp that conflicts even exist. Another potentially negative aspect of the compatibilist strategy is that there is often no systematic approach to the areas of harmony. Compatible pieces from both the discipline and the Christian faith are picked up and pieced together with the resulting integration often resembling a patchwork quilt.

Harris suggests the following as examples of this strategy[42]:

- Seeking common ground between faith and scholarly discipline (basic assumptions about reason, truth, evidence)
- Using Christian and biblical examples to show the application of disciplinary concepts
- Showing that Christianity is relevant to learning in that the Bible has much to say about knowledge (human nature, beauty, history, etc)

The Transformationist Strategy

A scholar who pursues the transformationist strategy assumes that there are areas of commonality between the discipline and a Christian worldview, but recognizes areas in which the discipline is seriously lacking in the validity of knowledge claims and worldview assumptions and interpretations.[43] A transformationist critically examines the discipline by testing its claims against a Christian worldview and desires to "remake or transform the discipline into one with a Christian orientation."[44] The transformationist does not deny the commonality between the discipline and the Christian faith but sees the need for a transformation of the discipline to correct what he perceives as serious defects in its assumptions and knowledge claims.

The benefit of this strategy is that it recognizes that most academic disciplines develop their knowledge claims from non-theistic worldviews, which leads to skewed disciplinary interpretations and theories. It also recognizes that ideologies often play a powerful but hidden role in many disciplines, and it seeks to address them.[45] The transformationist strategy can be challenging in that the scholar must venture below the surface to expose the assumptions and ideologies of the discipline, develop the modes of transformation, and then implement them. For example, students in a science course could be challenged to keep the following questions in mind as they come across some of the theories presented in their textbook: Can this data be backed up by repeated experimentation? Are there any alternative interpretations to the same piece of data? What is the researcher's presuppositional framework and could this have affected his/her interpretation of the data? Utilizing these types of questions can help prevent students from simply swallowing information presented in textbooks as facts and teaches them to be on the lookout for underlying assumptions that may significantly affect the interpretation of data.

The transformationist strategy recognizes that ideologies often play a powerful but hidden role in many disciplines, and it seeks to address them.

The development and implementation of critical thinking skills are essential to the transformationist strategy of integration. Harris again provides some examples of the utilization of this strategy of integration[46]:

- Asking integrative questions that require a connection between biblical knowledge and disciplinary knowledge
- Advocating the existence of truth, reason, meaning, and interpretative standards against postmodern rejection
- Upholding biblical authority in the world of knowledge
- Using Christian knowledge to test and correct claims made by the discipline

The Reconstructionist Strategy

Scholars who pursue this strategy have found that the tension between the fundamental assumptions of the discipline and a Christian worldview are severe enough to warrant a rejection of the foundation of the discipline, which means that the scholar must then engage in a "radical *reconstruction* of the discipline on . . . fully biblical foundations."[47] This is often due to a deep permeation of the discipline by anti-theistic assumptions, such as relativism. For example, philosophical naturalism, a pervading worldview in the natural sciences, which by definition excludes anything but natural causes for all that exists, must be exposed and challenged by those who believe in a supernatural agency whose presence is a far superior explanation for the natural cause and effect processes that we regularly observe in the universe.

Examples of this strategy from Harris include[48]:

- Employing the Christian worldview as the organizing principle that informs and interprets the subject area and all knowledge
- Replacing assumptions underlying the discipline (e.g. replacing philosophical materialism with theistic assumptions)
- Identifying alternative interpretive schema for the analysis of data and evidence

Which Strategy to Utilize?

Although these strategies differ in their assumptions, it is not necessary for a Christian scholar to compartmentalize them in their practical applications as though they are exclusive from one another. Hasker encouraged scholars to utilize the three strategies as an integrative framework and suggested that the strategies "... may better be viewed as three points on a continuum, than as three mutually exclusive alternatives."[49] Harris explains:

> At this point it is crucial to remember that the goal is not simply to connect faith and learning or to overlay learning with a "faith perspective." The concept of integration refers to a process that will produce a unified, coherent system, an interrelationship, a holistic understanding, a seamless landscape of truth where the physical realm, spiritual, and rational all combine into one realm. ... The answer to "which approach?" will become clear if you think for a minute that (1) disciplines vary widely in their content, philosophy, and methods, (2) most disciplines have more than one school of thought, and (3) even within schools of thought controversy, change, adaptation, and development are common. For these reasons, a combination of the [three approaches] will likely be the most useful depending on the circumstances. The goal is to integrate faith and learning, to develop and apply the Christian worldview, to welcome worthy knowledge, to avoid being taken in by false knowledge—not to apply mechanically some mental formula. Integration is a complex and lifelong practice and will require a number of methods and approaches.[50]

One of the biggest challenges for Christian scholars in the process of faith-learning integration is in the determination of how to integrate biblical truth into our disciplines. The following list of questions may provide a starting point in analyzing the intersections between the content of our faith and our disciplines[51]:

a. *What does my field say about what is and is not real, about what is true and what is false, and how do I understand that as a Christian?*

b. *What does my field say about the nature and limits of knowledge?*

c. *What methodology for gathering data does my field require before someone is able to assert their view about something?*

d. *How can what I know and teach in my field point to God's existence and presence in everyday life and nurture a hunger to understand and know him?*

e. *What are the ethical issues involved in my field of learning, and how do they relate to my ethical beliefs as a Christian? How does my faith promote principles of justice, charity, and concern for others within my field?*

f. *Is Christian scholarship in my particular field vocational, implicit, explicit, or a combination of the three? Vocational means the scholarship may not appear uniquely Christian, but it is done with excellence and contributes to the development of new knowledge. Implicit means your work touches on concerns common both to Christians and everyone else. Explicit means your work is directly and obviously Christian and has value for apologetics as well as daily living.*

Practical Tools for Integration of Faith and Learning within the Classroom

With some models and strategies outlined, one may now be asking the question, "What are some practical tools that can be utilized to accomplish the integration of faith and learning in the classroom?" Due to the space limitations of this chapter, we do not have the liberty to discuss the myriad of discipline-specific particulars of faith-learning integration. In his text, *Faith and Learning on the Edge: A Bold New Look at Religion in Higher Education*, David Claerbaut addresses specific faith and learning issues across a broad spectrum of disciplines.[52] A cumulative bibliography for faculty on the topic of designing integrative assignments for academic courses is available on the CCCU Resource Center's Web site.[53] This section overviews two broad examples of putting integration into practice in the classroom: reflective action and the integrative question.

Reflective Action

One can engage students in the process of integration through a three-level hierarchy of reflective actions throughout their course of studies. This hierarchy can be applied to a single issue, an entire course, or even to an academic discipline. It is important for Christian educators to recognize that students enter the classroom with presuppositions of their own, and the process of encouraging students to identify, acknowledge, and discuss them can be challenging. The goal in these types of reflective classroom activities is not to provide students with all the answers, but to help them ask the right questions. As students are taught to progress through these three levels, their reflections guide them through an effective process of integration.[54]

First level: THE WHAT—the investigation

Hermeneutic reflection— understanding and investigation into what is going on

On this first level, one should reflect on knowledge claims within a particular issue, course, or academic discipline. At this level students are taught how to 1) distinguish verifiable facts from value claims and also relevant from irrelevant information, claims or reasons, 2) determine the factual accuracy of a statement, including the credibility of a source, and 3) identify unstated assumptions, logical fallacies, etc. The key on this level is using critical thinking skills to investigate the information presented.

The following types of questions are appropriate at this level:

- What are the foundational assumptions that are stated or presupposed as the basis of this issue, course, or discipline?
- How do I know that this knowledge claim is true?
- What alternative ideas oppose that idea? What has been omitted or ignored?
- Is there an agenda or ideology behind this conclusion?
- What is the worldview behind or implied by the claim?

Second level: SO WHAT?—the interpretation

Normative Reflection—defined as when to say "yes" and when to say "no"

On this level, students deal with the interpretation of the facts. Students should struggle with whether they should reject or affirm different approaches, theories, or concepts as Christians.

The following types of questions are appropriate at this level:

- How does the claim or conclusion fit in with the Christian faith?
- How does my Christian faith/worldview affect my learning in this subject? How could my worldview act as a filter to evaluate this subject?
- What created goodness is present? What fallen aspects are here?
- What ethical questions does the knowledge/expertise in this subject raise?
- What does this subject tell us about God's creation? About God?
- Does this subject look different to a Christian than to an atheist? A Muslim? Why?

Third Level: NOW WHAT?—the application

Strategic reflection—what can be done with the "yes" and the "no"

On this level, students should reflect on the role of the redemptive process on this issue, course, or discipline. Application is the key on this level.

The following types of questions are appropriate at this level:

- Where is the hope here?
- How might we reclaim this area for the glory of God?
- How could the restoration of this issue be a signpost for the kingdom of God?
- How could learning in this subject affect my faith development?

The Integrative Question

Harold Heie has developed an integration application strategy that he calls the integrative question, which he defines as "a question that cannot be addressed adequately without drawing from both biblical and theological understanding and knowledge in the academic disciplines."[55] He has found that the pedagogical strategy of posing integrative questions to students and helping them address such question has been an effective way to initiate students into their own quest for the integration of knowledge. This is a sample listing of Heie's integrative questions[56]:

English: *What are the similarities and differences in interpreting the biblical text and interpreting other literature texts?*

Political Science: *What is the role of forgiveness in international relations?*

Fine Arts: *What are the limits, if any, on the freedom for human creative expression?*

History: *How do alternative views on the "direction of history" (e.g., linear, cyclical, teleological) fit or not fit with the Christian narrative?*

Economics: *What is the relationship between the quest for profitability and the Christian call for compassion and justice?*

Education: *What is the relationship between subject-centered and student-centered teaching pedagogies in light of a Christian perspective on personhood?*

Physics: *What are the similarities and differences between the use of models in scientific inquiry and the use of models in theological inquiry?*

In general, asking students to process disciplinary, ethical questions can be a powerful integrative tool for use in a wide variety of classroom setting.

ENGAGEMENT IN THE INTEGRATION OF FAITH AND LEARNING OUTSIDE THE CLASSROOM

As stated earlier in the chapter, integrating faith and learning in the classroom is the distinctive of a Christian college. When we take seriously the holistic nature of our institutions' educational missions, the student development staff and their programs become a unique and primary educational tool for integration. *The critical ingredient is staff members who are intentional about the integration process.* The integration process for the student development staff member builds upon the process outlined above. The reflective hierarchy questions, "What? So What? and Now What?" form a powerful formula for the integration process that can be utilized in all aspects of educational programming. This application section will address the integration issues related to the different role the student development staff member plays within the college experience.

> "When we asked students to think of a specific, critical incident or moment that had changed them profoundly, four-fifths of them chose a situation or event outside of the classroom."

Christian college student development programs have a critical role in integrating faith and learning. The student development staff utilizes formal (e.g. presentation), non-formal (e.g. interactive programs), informal (e.g. athletics), and serendipitous (e.g. day-to-day life experiences in the residence hall) learning experiences. As an educator, imagine teaching on social justice or racial reconciliation with opportunities for lecture and reflection on real life experiences being played out in the residence hall living environment. The student development programs have the ability to capture real life—real time—situations and use them in the learning process. The power of the "outside the classroom learning experience" is chronicled in Richard Light's book *Making the Most of College.* He states, "Learning outside of classes, especially in residential settings and extracurricular activities such as the arts, is vital. When we asked students to think of a specific, critical incident or moment that had changed them profoundly, four-fifths of them chose a situation or event outside of the classroom."[57]

Integrating faith and learning in student development programs means organizing programs in ways that highlight a Christian worldview. The best programs are organized in ways that take advantage of the student's experience or that can be facilitated by students (i.e. what does Scripture say about conflict resolution, racial reconciliation, stewardship, and leadership). The list of organized learning opportunities facilitated by student development staff include residential hall programming, spiritual disciplines training, club involvement, mission trips, chapel services, service learning, leadership training, vocational calling development, mentoring, small group involvement, sports and wellness activities. Although many of these activities are duplicated on other college campuses, the integrative faith and learning distinctive is facilitated by embedding a Christian worldview within the program's specific purpose. Integrating faith and learning at the foundational level in student development programs is similar to the way professors integrate in the classroom.

Arthur Chickering's developmental theory outlined in his original 1969 text, *Education and Identity* and then revised in his second edition, provides an initial framework for many student developmental programs. He suggests that college students develop in seven vectors: Developing Competence, Managing Emotions, Moving Through Autonomy Towards Interdependence, Developing Mature Interpersonal Relationships, Establishing Identity, Developing Purpose, and Developing Integrity.[58] However, Chickering neglects a basic construct of a Christian worldview; namely, that our identity is ultimately found in Christ. Chickering's work is seminal for understanding the college student's journey through normal developmental stages, but without integrating a Christian worldview, any program based solely upon his theory is insufficient to provide an opportunity for the student to mature fully into a disciple of Christ. *The Christian student development staff member must have a baseline understanding of how to live out biblical truth in real life situations.* She must be a disciple of Christ and a conduit for speaking truth into unique and diverse experiences.

Beyond the unique educational methodologies, the student development staff member has another and possibly more powerful opportunity for communicating an integrative message—an authentic relationship within the context of real life situations. These educational modalities are enriched with a relationship between the student and staff member. The hall director living among the residence hall students or the activities director partnering with the student activity council member to facilitate campus activities provides rich opportunities to meet students where they are. It also provides opportunities for staff members to be available at the teachable moments. This means that the student development staff must be ready to provide wise Christian council when helping students work through roommate conflicts, leadership challenges, and other developmental issues. *Within these "discipleship" relationships, staff members may find their most significant and challenging opportunity for integration.*

CONCLUSION

As Christians we are called by God to be stewards of the earth. As Christian scholars and educators, teaching our students how to think Christianly about all of life is a primary means of responding to this call. Arthur Holmes states, "The challenge of worldview thinking now is to reintegrate biblically based theology and values with the humanities and sciences and apply them to contemporary society and culture. This involves both critical and creative thinking: critical of non-theistic assumptions and their influence, but creative in exploring more consistent alternatives."[59] Faith-learning integration is indeed a central challenge before us.

Mark Noll, in *The Scandal of the Evangelical Mind*, reminds us that for far too long Christians have abdicated their responsibility to pursue truth and knowledge in all areas of life. He believes we have accepted the fallacy that anti-intellectualism is more spiritual.[60] General revelation and special revelation are partners, both with significant roles, in helping us understand who we are as created beings and how we are to interact with this world. The integration of faith and learning in the academy is the foundational step towards assisting all learners in obtaining a fuller understanding of the Creator and his creation. These Christian truths not only shape our knowledge, but they also give direction for the pursuit of further knowledge.

The Apostle Paul states, "Do not conform any longer to the pattern of this world, but be transformed by the renewing of your mind. Then you will be able to test and approve what God's will is—his good, pleasing and perfect will" (Rom. 12:2a). As both followers of Christ and educational scholars, faith-learning integration is a task to which we are called. This integration must sink into the foundational assumptions and epistemology of our academic pursuits. We must avoid simply tacking on a spiritual discipline to our classrooms or our campus programs, thinking this constitutes integration. All we have accomplished is to produce more or less an integrative veneer that strengthens the misperception that our faith and learning do not mix. Let us take seriously the real work of integration.

Discussion Questions

1. Discuss any surprises you had when reading the list of common misconceptions of the meaning of faith-learning integration. How might you continue to use your current methods of sharing your faith experience with students in combination with a deeper understanding of faith-learning integration?

2. Discuss which of the four integration models from Cosgrove best describes your current approach to integration. Is there one that you believe should predominate in Christian higher education?

3. Do you agree or not agree with the authors' premise that integration is more easily observed in some disciplines than in others? Describe your discipline in the context of the visibility continuum.

4. Discuss how the interpretation of Scripture affects faith-learning integration (revelation coup).

5. Discuss an integrative strategy or practical tool that you could use in your educational setting (classroom, residence hall, etc.).

6. Practice writing an integrative question for your own discipline.

For Further Reading

Cosgrove, Mark. *Foundations of Christian Thought: Faith, Learning, and the Christian Worldview.* Grand Rapids, Mich.: Kregel Publications, 2006.

Harris, Robert. *Integration of Faith and Learning: A Worldview Approach.* Eugene, Ore.: Cascade Books, 2004.

Holmes, Arthur. *The Idea of a Christian College.* Revised Edition. Grand Rapids, Mich.: Eerdmans, 1987.

Hughes, Richard T. *How Christian Faith Can Sustain the Life of the Mind.* Grand Rapids, Mich.: Eerdmans, 2001.

Jacobsen, Douglas and Rhonda Hustedt Jacobsen, *Scholarship and Christian Faith: Enlarging the Conversation.* Oxford: Oxford University Press, 2004.

Plantinga Jr., Cornelius. *Engaging God's World: A Christian Vision of Faith, Learning, and Living.* Grand Rapids, Mich.: Eerdmans, 2002.

Poe, Harry Lee. *Christianity in the Academy: Teaching at the Intersection of Faith and Learning.* Grand Rapids, Mich.: Baker Academic, 2004.

Chapter 4

Relevant Pedagogy for a New Generation

Tim Herrmann

The idea of good teaching is an appealingly simple proposition. If one clearly articulates a set of facts or concepts to a receptive audience, learning ought to occur. How hard can it be? Consider Robin Williams's masterful teaching in *Dead Poets Society*—and he never had a moment of formal preparation. Simple though it may seem, anyone who has ever taught at any level can attest to the fact that this apparent simplicity is a cruel ruse. I once succumbed to this deception and made the nearly fatal blunder of agreeing to teach a seventh-grade boys' Sunday school class. While I emerged from this experience physically unscathed, the emotional and psychic wounds may never fully heal. Although the course material was straightforward and I was (at least at the beginning) reasonably coherent, the outcome was anything but successful. Lest it be lost, the point of this chapter is to establish that the teaching and learning process is complex and must be treated as such for success to be achieved.

Like a good sermon or milking stool, this treatise on pedagogy will rest on three reasonably stable supports. These supports come in the form of a set of fairly straightforward propositions, namely: that facilitating the acquisition of knowledge is a pretty tricky proposition; that the development of good pedagogy takes a lot of good old-fashioned hard work; and that, despite the difficulties involved, the potential benefits of what a teacher does are important enough that it is worth all the effort to try to figure out how to do it right. And why do so many believe that it is, in fact, worth the investment of so much effort? It is the almost universal belief in the transforming power of learning. The conviction that knowledge changes things, fuels the arts (*My Fair Lady, Dead Poets Society, The Miracle Worker*), polarizes politics (No Child Left

Behind, school vouchers, sex education), and inspires heroic human sacrifice (The Jesuit Society, Saint Paul's missionary journeys, Wycliffe).

Although learning is universally endorsed as a powerful vehicle for driving social, economic, political, and personal change, the failure of higher education to deliver on this potential has been the focus of an extraordinary amount of attention in recent years. Only a few examples are needed to illustrate this point. *Greater Expectations: A New Vision for Learning as a Nation goes to College*, the report of a powerful panel representing the Association of American Colleges and Universities, insists that higher education institutions must step up to the plate and fulfill their collective responsibility by delivering education that is "personally empowering, intellectually challenging, beneficial to civic society, and eminently useful."[1] Ernest Boyer, in his landmark work *Scholarship Reconsidered: Priorities of the Professoriate,* is pointed in his criticisms of collegiate conditions, particularly those that work at cross-purposes with effective teaching.

Although learning is universally endorsed as a powerful vehicle for driving social, economic, political, and personal change, the failure of higher education to deliver on this potential has been the focus of an extraordinary amount of attention in recent years.

> In the current climate, students all too often are the losers. Today, undergraduates are aggressively recruited. In glossy brochures, they're assured that teaching is important, that a spirit of community pervades the campus, and that general education is the core of the undergraduate experience. But the reality is that, on far too many campuses, teaching is not well rewarded, and faculty who spend too much time counseling and advising students may diminish their prospects for tenure and promotion.[2]

Almost seventeen years later, the Madison Avenue-like emphasis on image, marketing, reputation, and revenue causes one to wonder whether or not these conditions may have deteriorated even more.

In a recent article, Derek Bok, former president and current interim president at Harvard University, laments the flawed pedagogy and lack of attention to the development of critical thinking skills, writing skills, moral character and preparation for citizenship that characterize contemporary higher education.[3]

In the news recently, Peter Ewell suggested that, while higher education can be applauded for modest improvements in attempting to measure learning progress, the resulting data indicates that the abilities of America's college graduates have declined in recent years.[4] Lately educators have been troubled by the Spellings Commission on the Future of Higher Education report that characterizes America's colleges as "self-satisfied" and "risk averse."[5]

Given these gloomy assessments, one considering career options might be tempted to think there are more attractive alternatives than those presented by American higher education. Indeed, the challenges are great, but for many the potential rewards are even greater. Despite these negative commentaries regarding the collective performance of the nation's colleges and universities, it remains true that learning, especially learning rooted in the knowledge that God is the creator of all good things, holds immeasurable potential to stimulate both individual and societal change. Many of us resonate with the words of James Freedman, president emeritus of Dartmouth College and the University of Iowa, who, reflecting on his own college experience, recalled, "I was indelibly marked by teachers and writers who changed me utterly and forever. They were models of the life of the mind in action."[6] Is it any wonder that he chose to invest his own life in facilitating for the next generation the kinds of experiences that had so deeply touched him? It is likely that most who have chosen academic careers have been motivated similarly by those who taught them.

Whether instructor or administrator, you bear the title of "educator"—one who teaches. With this title comes a tremendous stewardship responsibility—essentially, the responsibility to do all in your power to motivate and enable student learning. And, like the servants in the parable of the talents found in Matthew 25:23, we are accountable for the return on investment, not the size of the original deposit. What is it that separates the teachers who change students "utterly and forever" from those who simply certify academic credit? Or, worse yet, those who convince would-be learners that school is just not their cup of tea? Actually, the answer is simple, even if accomplishing it is not: teachers who change students are so convinced of the strategic significance of their work that they are compelled to find ways to help students connect hearts and minds in the joy of learning. I once had a friend, a minister, who told me with great earnestness and emotion of the sense of both honor and duty that he felt at being addressed as "pastor." Teachers who stir their students have a similar sense of the significance of their calling. What believing instructor has not been given pause when confronted with the scriptural caution from James 3:1 that "not many of you should presume to

Teachers who change students are so convinced of the strategic significance of their work that they are compelled to find ways to help students connect hearts and minds in the joy of learning.

be teachers, my brothers, because you know that we who teach will be judged more strictly"? Surely these words speak to the potential—both good and bad—that exists within the teaching process.

We must acknowledge that students also have a great deal to do with what occurs in this process. In child development we talk about the concept of "reciprocal socialization"—the idea that while, of course, parents influence their children, children also influence their parents and their parenting behaviors. For example, a compliant child and a difficult child from the same family are likely to have very different experiences of being parented. The compliant child is more likely to get the best their parents have to offer, while the difficult child is more likely to receive parenting influenced by frustration and even exasperation. The point is that receptive children and receptive students are more likely to experience good parenting and good teaching, respectively. I am quick to remind my students that even if I am a bad teacher they, by their hard work, can still learn a great deal. However, no matter how good a teacher I am, I cannot make an impact on a student who will not try. The student has tremendous responsibility in the learning process, even, perhaps, more influence on the outcome than the teacher. However, with this point conceded, let us invoke the metaphor of the teacher as a locksmith. When we need the help of one to gain access, the most important issue is getting the door opened, not figuring out whose fault it is that it is locked.

Let us invoke the metaphor of the teacher as a locksmith. When we need the help of one to gain access, the most important issue is getting the door opened, not figuring out whose fault it is that it is locked.

Recently, after viewing an incredibly dynamic presentation on future world challenges, a colleague remarked with great disdain that he had been warning his students of these same concerns for the past thirty years, but because they were soft, self-absorbed, closed-minded, and lazy, they had never valued or heeded his cautions. Since the student qualities he notes are all characteristics of fallen humankind, his observations may well be true. However, no matter how well founded his observation may have been, the point he makes is simply irrelevant. His comments beg the stewardship admonition that we are responsible not for what we are given but for what we do with what we are given. The paradigm that underlies his evaluation understands the teacher as simply a purveyor of information—good students (apparently none of which have ever taken his courses) get it while bad students do not. While his equation is attractive in its simplicity, it fails to understand the role of the teacher as a problem solver or "locksmith," sometimes unlocking difficult material and other times unlocking difficult people. Thus, as we proceed, our focus will be on pedagogical trends, with the assumption that good practice will improve the knowledge and understanding of bright, highly motivated students and also provide the greatest likelihood of opening locked doors and waking sleepers—both literally and figuratively.

It's Not Your Father's Higher Education Anymore . . . Maybe!

Things are changing: during the past twenty years, there has been an unmistakable shift in higher education. External and internal critics have impacted our understanding of teaching and learning. In a bellwether article published in *Change*, Barr and Tagg alerted us to a "paradigm shift" in education that was moving attention from teaching to learning.

> In its briefest form, the paradigm that has governed our colleges is this: A college is an institution that exists to provide instruction. . . . Now, however, we are beginning to recognize that our dominant paradigm mistakes a means for an end. It takes the means or method—called "instruction" or "teaching"—and makes it the college's end or purpose. To say that the purpose of colleges is to provide instruction is like saying that General Motors' business is to operate assembly lines or that the purpose of medical care is to fill hospital beds. We see now that our mission is not instruction, but rather that of producing learning with every student by whatever means works best.[7]

In the years since this article appeared, this theme has become quite familiar. The spotlight on learning has been so bright that it has become a prime driver of change in the academy. The learning movement has given energy to a number of significant collegiate trends including the reemphasis on teaching versus research, the assessment movement, the ubiquitous presence of first-year programs, and the explosion in the application of instructional technology, to name just a few. Perhaps the clearest sign that things have changed is that both instructors and institutions are increasingly expected to provide evidence of student learning. Whereas in the past it was enough to document educational processes (for example, the number of hours spent in class or volumes in the library), teachers and colleges are now expected to articulate expected and achieved learning outcomes.

If the paradigm is changing, what are the implications for practice? Before considering the consequences for instructional strategies and techniques, we must give at least brief attention to the question: "What is good teaching?" However, consideration of this question leads one quickly to the conclusion that effective teaching and learning are neither simple nor singular propositions. Thus, reviewing several understandings or conceptions may be helpful. A fairly classic perspective offered by John Gregory in *The Seven Laws of Teaching* (first printed in 1884) defines teaching as "arousing and using the pupil's mind to grasp the desired thought or to master the desired art" and learning as "thinking into one's own understanding a new idea or truth, or working into habit a new art or skill."[8] Although the language is dated, his proposed "test" of successful teaching is so contemporary that the modern assessment movement could claim him as a patron saint! In his words, "the test and proof of teaching done—the finishing and fastening process—must be a reviewing, rethinking, reknowing, reproducing, and applying of the material that has been taught, the knowledge and ideals and arts that have been communicated."[9] Stated more directly, until learning has been evidenced, teaching has not been accomplished. The measure of teaching is not the performance of the instructor, but rather its observable impact on students.

Larry Spence offers a critical assessment of the current state of teaching, along with recommendations for reform. In discussing the American academy he says that "its assumptions are that teaching is telling, learning is absorbing, and knowledge is subject-matter content. . . . Physical and institutional arrangements are teacher-focused and stimulus-deprived." He predicts that "we won't meet the needs for more and better higher education until professors become designers of learning experiences and not teachers."[10] This picture and corrective aids our understanding of "what is" and what many believe "is coming." And his assessment is consistent with the thinking that is driving current educational reform efforts.

Many of us have participated in one of those activities in which we are asked to think about the best teacher we have ever had and catalog the qualities that made him or her so good. I suspect for many even the brief seconds it took to read the preceding sentence were enough to conjure up the memory of a person or two who vie for this title in your life. And, if we follow through on the task and complete the inventory of the traits that made them unique, perhaps even beloved to us, as teachers, it is likely that there is a high level of correspondence between their behaviors and the recommendations encouraged by the literature on best classroom practices.

Chickering and Gamson provided one of the first attempts to review the literature with the purpose of identifying effective undergraduate practices. Their straightforward "Seven Principles for Good Practice in Undergraduate Education" is still among the most commonly cited and studied guides to effective teaching. Why? Because it focuses on uncomplicated student and teacher behaviors that are easily incorporated into any learning environment. Certainly those who value whole-person conceptions of the educational process must take satisfaction in the holistic focus implicit in their guidelines. Their principles of good practice recommend strategies that:

- Encourage contact between students and faculty
- Develop reciprocity and cooperation among students
- Use active learning techniques
- Provide prompt feedback
- Emphasize time on task
- Communicate high expectations
- Respect diverse talents and ways of learning[11]

Although extended discussion of these elements is not among the goals of this chapter, it is vital that all educators—those serving both in and outside of the traditional classroom—grasp the persuasive weight of the evidence indicating that the environments most conducive to effective learning are relational, responsive, active, purposeful, dynamic, challenging, and diverse.

With this compelling confirmation of what seems to be a reasonable prescription for educating students, it is fair to ask how we are doing. Though few would argue with Gregory, Spence, or Chickering and Gamson in theory, there is a tendency for teachers to deviate significantly in practice. In a study of changes occurring as a result of the "teaching and learning revolution," Lazerson, Wagener, and Shumanis found that "efforts to improve teaching and learning have been supported only in part by faculty and institutions as a whole, with results that were neither significant nor pervasive."[12] There is often a difference between the real and the ideal when it comes to teaching practices. These differences are fairly well evidenced in data from the 2004 Higher Education Research Institute Faculty Survey (Table 1). When asked to indicate methods used in "most" or "all" of the courses they taught, faculty from four-year private colleges (*n*=15,144) named class discussion, essay/mid-term/final exams, cooperative learning initiatives, student presentations, and extensive lecturing as the five most common methodologies. Only three of these five reflect substantially the principles

The persuasive weight of the evidence indicates that the environments most conducive to effective learning are relational, responsive, active, purposeful, dynamic, challenging, and diverse.

of effective undergraduate education cited by Chickering and Gamson, and the use of even these three was limited to about half of the faculty surveyed.

Table 1. Most Commonly Used Instructional Methods	
Method	**Percentage indicating use in most or all courses taught**
Class discussion	84.2
Essay, mid-term and/or final exams	61.9
Cooperative learning (small groups)	51.9
Student presentations	51.6
Extensive lecturing	48.0

The least used methods reported by the same group indicate that two very promising approaches—service learning and student critiquing of other's work—were used in a relative handful of courses (Table 2). While it would be a mistake to conclude too much from these results, it is safe to presume that a great deal of opportunity remains for transforming the educational experience of America's undergraduates.

Table 2. Least Commonly Used Instructional Methods	
Method	**Percentage indicating use in most or all courses taught**
Teaching assistants	6.0
Community service as part of coursework	7.6
Online instruction	10.6
Student-selected topics for course content	15.4
Student evaluations of each other's work	17.1

Changes in Perspective and Practice

Although changes in teaching practices are occurring more slowly than the generally acknowledged need for them, nonetheless changes are in the air. Just what are these changes and how might they be leveraged to improve the experience of college students? A review of the literature related to trends in educational practice reveals a pattern of changes that fall into five categories. While several are quite broad and are not, technically, "teaching techniques," each is linked to issues of applied and strategic significance that will yield practical (as well as theological and philosophical) relevance to both academic and student affairs practitioners. While a variety of perspectives are related to the importance of each trend, no effort is made here to qualify their significance. Rather, each will be reviewed briefly and considered for its potential application in Christian higher education.

The five trends are:

1. A focus on teaching versus research
2. The use of active learning strategies
3. Accommodation of diverse learning styles
4. A focus on holistic education
5. Emphasis on assessment

Focus on Teaching Versus Research

Much of the criticism noted earlier results from the widespread belief that the academy has abandoned the teaching of students in order to pursue a more prestigious, lucrative, and self-serving research agenda. Although research initiatives can and in many cases do support and improve student learning, this is not always the case. It is not hard to find evidence to support this contention, particularly in large, flagship institutions that depend upon research contracts for both revenue and reputation. However, what might be somewhat more surprising is that the research agenda also made inroads into much smaller, traditionally teaching-centered colleges and universities. Naylor and Willimon argue that "there are too many small universities whose quest for university status has distracted them from the task of undergraduate education."[13] They go on to assert that American students have not been well served by the growth in size of colleges and universities or by the promotion of the graduate-research agenda. Incidentally, most of those reading this chapter can count among their blessings that they work in the type of institutions that Naylor and Willimon describe as ideal.

The point here is not to denigrate the value of research—quite the contrary as there can be great value in its appropriate promotion. One of the most exciting developments in undergraduate education is the promotion of research opportunities in which students are mentored while working side-by-side with faculty guides. The winter 2003 issue of the Association of American Colleges and Universities publication *Peer Review* was devoted entirely to undergraduate research as a path to engagement, achievement, and integration. Clearly, there is no effort here to portray research and good teaching as mutually exclusive interests. Rather, the thrust of this discussion is to underscore the notion that undergraduate learning must be the central focus of any baccalaureate program.

Boyer was among the first to raise the concern that this was not the case. He offered this straightforward assessment: "Even institutions that enroll primarily undergraduates—and have few, if any, resources for research—seek to imitate ranking research centers. In the process, their mission becomes blurred, standards of research are compromised, and the quality of teaching and learning is disturbingly diminished."[14] While this issue has not been entirely resolved, progress has been significant. For instance, results from the 2004-2005 HERI Faculty Survey indicate that 98 percent of faculty across all institution types believe that it is "very important" or "essential" to be a good teacher.

Perhaps the outcome of Boyer's work that had the most direct influence on changing the status quo was the establishment of the credibility of the "scholarship of teaching." He called for research on the improvement of teaching and learning and proclaimed it one of the four foundational research foci (along with discovery, integration, and application) of the professoriate. The Carnegie Academy for the Scholarship of Teaching and Learning, which exists to promote the scholarship of teaching and learning by "[fostering] significant, long-lasting learning for all students; [enhancing] the practice and profession of teaching, and; [bringing] to faculty members' work as teachers the recognition and reward afforded to other forms of scholarly work," is but one example of the attention now being given to this critical priority.[15]

This first trend represents a change in priorities rather than in pedagogy. It might be argued that this change was necessary in order to pave the way for the remaining four developments. However, because this first trend is more about issues of institutional mission and values than about classroom instruction, it cannot be said to have direct instructional applications. This being said, there are very direct implications for the expenditure of institutional resources. If institutions value teaching, then budgetary allocations, as well as reward structures such as promotion, tenure, salary, and award policies and processes, will reflect that value.

If institutions value teaching, then budgetary allocations, as well as reward structures . . . will reflect that value.

Finally, we must again underscore the message that excellent, learner-centered teaching is not incompatible with a research agenda. Furthermore, some outstanding learning outcomes are achieved when teachers collaborate with advanced students in cooperative research projects.

An Emphasis on Engagement

The remaining four trends are linked by a common emphasis on student engagement or involvement. In other words, each represents some significant effort to more fully engage students in meaningful learning activities. Involvement, a very simple concept, has had an unmistakable impact on higher educational practice both in and outside of the classroom over the past twenty-five years. Thus it may be helpful to discuss briefly this influential idea.

Alexander Astin's theory of involvement provides the conceptual framework for understanding this phenomenon. His highly regarded theory, first proposed in 1984, has been influential because it has helped educators more fully understand the connection between students' experiences and their growth both in and out of the classroom. Involvement theory is refreshingly straightforward. In essence it asserts that the way a student invests his or her time and energy determines what that student will ultimately gain from the college experience. Astin proposes that the best way to evaluate the educational efficacy of any "policy or practice" is to consider the degree to which it enhances student involvement.[16]

One significant result of the student involvement focus has been the attempt to use experience measures to evaluate instructional and institutional practices. Such efforts have gained widespread prominence in higher education and have led to the creation of more meaningful standards for assessing institutional quality. In other words, institutions are being encouraged to evaluate themselves by discerning the degree to which students engage in educationally beneficial practices. The most prominent of these efforts is the well-known National Survey of Student Engagement (NSSE). NSSE collects self-report data from students regarding their college experiences with the intent of measuring their level of involvement in educationally meaningful activities. This assessment is based on the involvement theory premise that "the more students put into using the resources and opportunities an institution provides for their learning and development, the more they benefit."[17] Kuh makes the focus of NSSE very clear in the following explanation.

> The engagement premise is deceptively simple, even self-evident: The more students study a subject, the more they learn about it. Likewise, the more students practice and get feedback on their writing, analyzing, or problem solving, the more adept they become. The very act of being engaged also adds to the foundation of skills and dispositions that is essential to living a productive, satisfying life after college. That is, students who are involved in educationally productive activities in college are developing habits of the

> mind and heart that enlarge their capacity for continuous learning and personal development.[18]

NSSE findings have added an important element to the quest to better understand the relationship between students' experiences and their learning, and it is having an impact on the way we think about higher education. Now let us return to our consideration of the remaining four pedagogical trends.

Use of Active Learning Strategies

Talk of active learning is really not new. For years educators have understood that there were benefits in facilitating deeper student interaction with material that was being presented. The Socratic Method, probably the most revered and longstanding form of instruction known, is an active approach to learning that uses questions to "teach students to reason general principles from specific cases."[19] Despite this, it does not require a great deal of investigation to discern that the actual use of active learning strategies is far less prevalent than the discussion of them. According to Gardiner: "The research on college classes is consistent: Faculty can strongly influence the amount of students' active involvement and the cognitive level of the classroom. Nevertheless, faculty overwhelmingly lecture, primarily transmitting facts requiring low cognitive levels to students who function as passive listeners."[20]

The actual use of active learning strategies is far less prevalent than the discussion of them.

Active instructional strategies involve students in the subject matter in ways that require high levels of attention, involvement, application, and manipulation of the material being dealt with. Lecturing allows even well-prepared and highly motivated students to simply process material at a surface level. Worse yet, unmotivated, underprepared students may not process the material at all, but rather sit passively while the teacher's words go over their heads. While the appropriate, selective use of traditional lecture methods has value, its singular use cannot accomplish the desired end of deep learning. Lecture simply does not promote the kind of intense subject matter interaction necessary for optimal learning. Cognitive science clearly indicates that the deeper and more intricate the level of interaction with the material, the greater the level of learning that occurs.[21]

The National Research Council cites two key benefits of employing active learning strategies. First, such approaches aid students in generalizing their learning to new or novel situations. This active involvement helps students unlearn previously understood but inaccurate representations. Strong evidence indicates that bad or inaccurate knowledge is highly persistent. Active learning approaches help to "unseat" such information because it not only replaces bad information with good information but goes on to reinforce the good information (often self-discovered) with experience and testing. Second, active strategies allow students to move beyond simple factual understanding to more complex understandings, allowing for and lending to greater use and application of knowledge.[22]

If these benefits were not enough, active learning is highly complementary to the kind of whole-person education valued and promoted by Christian institutions. Gardiner asserts that "using abstract symbols, epistemology, and principled, ethical reasoning—as well as the ability to work cooperatively in teams with people different from oneself—require for their development that students be actively involved in learning." He goes on to say that "because many students are not yet formal operational [thinkers], they have difficulty learning abstractions from lectures. These students require active methods to grasp important concepts. The superiority of actively involving students has been well established."[23]

While most educators acknowledge and embrace the benefits discussed above, there is still a persistent inclination to rely on lecture as the primary teaching tool. Why is this? There are two likely explanations: first, because active approaches are perceived as less efficient; and second, almost certainly because they are more complicated to perform. While there is some legitimacy to both of these concerns, the potential of deepening students' understandings, enabling them to apply their knowledge to new situations, and helping them become independent, self-directed learners clearly outweigh these perceived drawbacks. The efficiency argument is most often promoted by those who hold the fallacious assumption that "because I have said it they have learned it." Although it is tempting to embrace this assumption when pinched for class time, we do it to our own and our students' detriment as it is without scientific or rational support.

The efficiency argument is most often promoted by those who hold the fallacious assumption that "because I have said it they have learned it."

Recognition and Accommodation of Diverse Learning Styles

As access to higher education has increased, so has our understanding that not all students learn in the same manner. We are now much more aware that students once thought incapable of performing the higher-order intellectual tasks required for collegiate success may just learn differently, not less effectively, than others. Perhaps one of the most significant benefits of the learning movement has been the realization that communication of content and the design of learning activities must accommodate a variety of learning styles. Pascarella and Terenzini declare that individualized instruction "constitute[s] the single most dramatic shift in college teaching over the last two decades."[24]

How People Learn: Bridging Research and Practice, an incredibly comprehensive treatise on the elements critical to fostering learning, reflects upon the need for teachers to design environments that give attention to students' knowledge and abilities, cultural understandings and progress. The authors also cite the importance of challenging students with "just manageable difficulties,"[25] a concept very similar to Vygotsky's Zone of Proximal Development. In other words, learners make the greatest progress when they are confronted with tasks and problems difficult enough to challenge them but not so difficult as to render their efforts inconsequential.

Undoubtedly, all believing educators sense their duty to help all students realize the potential and express the giftedness that God has placed in them.

In *Student Success in College: Creating Conditions that Matter,* George Kuh and his colleagues give a fascinating report on Project DEEP institutions. These institutions have been recognized for creating conditions that have resulted in exceptional student success. In the excerpt below a student from one of these institutions speaks powerfully about the life changing difference that the emphasis on accommodating diverse learning styles has made:

> My family was just amazed. I had never received good grades. I always struggled with tests. People thought I was not smart. No one expected me to go to college. But I got in here. The environment here has allowed me to demonstrate the knowledge I was acquiring, which had never happened before. I always thought I was not smart, but I soon realized that I just didn't perform well on standardized tests. I brought my report card home and my parents could not believe it was mine. I have been very successful here and I appreciate that this environment allowed me to realize I was smart and could learn after all.[26]

Certainly there are economic and social benefits in increasing the workforce and broadening the talent base, but perhaps a more compelling argument in favor of accommodating and embracing diverse learning styles is that this idea meshes so well with the biblical conception of the different "giftedness" of the body of Christ.

Although 1 Corinthians 12 is speaking specifically of the diversity of spiritual gifts necessary for the church to function as intended, surely the recognition in verse 22 that "those parts of the body that seem weaker are indispensable" is a concept dear to the hearts of all dedicated teachers. Undoubtedly, all believing educators sense their duty to help all students to realize the potential and express the giftedness that God has placed in them.

Some actually argue that the emphasis on multiple learning styles is just another sign of the encroachment of relativism into the American educational scene—that this focus is simply an attempt to further weaken or water down standards and expectations. Although certain aspects of modern American education give reason to be concerned about such things, the focus on diverse learning styles is more likely part of the cure than part of the problem. The accommodation of diverse learning styles is not about watered-down standards and diminished expectations. Rather, this approach is more likely to lead toward meaningful academic engagement and away from lower-order intellectual activities associated with rote memorization and multiple choice test performance.

As a teacher I am continually amazed at the diversity of student's academic performances who have similar backgrounds. While some students excel in virtually every type of instructional activity, most have definite areas of strength and weakness. Many strong test takers are weak writers, and many of those who struggle with traditional objective exams that place a premium on memorization are able to write well-conceived, clearly articulated essays. Though admittedly simple, this example helps illustrate the importance of structuring courses and learning environments in a manner that allows students who are equally bright but who possess different ways of approaching information, problems, and tasks to demonstrate and further their knowledge. Most importantly, this example should serve as motivation for all teachers to understand the critical responsibility they have to help their students unlock existing and discover new, more effective learning strategies.

> The educator who is not energized by helping even difficult, less obviously gifted students to learn is perhaps laboring in the wrong field.

The educator who is not energized by helping even difficult, less obviously gifted students to learn may be laboring in the wrong field. Kuh reminds us that "academic excellence is not a strain of educational Darwinism" and that teachers and leaders in excellent institutions "tirelessly advocate on behalf of responsive, learner-centered support services, such as peer tutoring, special labs for writing and mathematics, and—if necessary and appropriate, given the audiences—intrusive academic advising."[27]

Understanding and applying the appropriate balance of challenge and support is important both individually and institutionally. Teachers as well as academic and student affairs administrators must artfully adjust classroom and institutional practices to create the best possible learning environments and facilitate optimal learning for all students.

Holistic Understandings of the Educational Process

One would be hard-pressed to find a college in America that does not embrace, at least in word, the concept of whole-person education. Even generically faith-based colleges and universities, by the very label, communicate a commitment to focus on more than *just* the intellect. Specifically, Christ-centered institutions are further compelled to promote holistic education by virtue of the great commandment. This New Testament command found in Luke 10:27, instructs believers to "love the Lord your God with all your heart and with all your soul and with all your mind" and to "love your neighbor as yourself." This mandate provides a wonderful synopsis of the complex, dynamic nature of a life of discipleship with all of its internal, external, horizontal, and vertical aspects.

Clearly, a utilitarian educational philosophy focused simply on imparting information necessary for future vocational or educational pursuits does not stand a chance of helping students achieve the type of lofty ideals communicated in Christ's mandate. Furthermore, such an approach sacrifices a tremendous amount of the motivational power essential to the learning process. Compare the motivational influence of encouraging a student to value education so that they can get a better job versus helping them to see education as a vital element in the process of knowing and serving the Creator of all that is good. Some significant evidence indicates that Christian college students are motivated more by issues of meaning and purpose than they are by the potential of increasing their opportunity to achieve material success.

Consider the results (Table 3) of the 2004 Higher Education Research Institute freshmen survey. This survey of incoming freshmen included 11,432 students from the CCCU, 34,625 from all religious four-year colleges, and 289,452 from all four-year colleges and universities. Even a cursory review of the data evidences two things, neither of which is surprising: first, an important reason that students choose CCCU institutions is that they believe they are entering an environment that will help them grow spiritually; and second, their spiritual orientation (belief system) strongly influences the values and goals they hold.

Table 3. Freshman Activities, Values, Goals

Item	CCCU	All Religious 4-Year Colleges	All 4-Year Colleges & Universities
During the past year frequently discussed religion/spirituality with friends	58.0	36.1	26.7
During the past year typically spent 3 or more hours per week in prayer/meditation	33.5	18.7	10.6
Attending college to find purpose in life	58.0	53.2	51.8
Chose this college because of its religious affiliation/orientation	71.7	28.0	6.7
Becoming very well off financially is an essential or very important objective	42.4	62.7	73.6
Helping others in difficulty is an essential or very important objective	74.7	66.2	62.4
Developing a meaningful philosophy of life is an essential or very important objective	46.2	42.1	42.1
Integrating spirituality into my life is an essential or very important objective	88.0	56.5	39.5
Student estimates chances are very good that he/she will strengthen religious beliefs/convictions during college	80.8	43.6	24.8

While much more could be said about Christian college students and the results of this particular study, the basic point is that if we disconnect students' learning from other aspects of their experience, including their spiritual formation, we will have missed an incredible opportunity to motivate them intellectually and to help them deepen their understanding of the interconnectedness of all aspects of life. *Powerful Partnerships: A Shared Responsibility for Learning* cites a series of learning principles, the first of which claims that "learning is fundamentally about making and maintaining connections: biologically through neural networks; mentally among concepts, ideas, and meanings; and experientially through interaction between the mind and the environment, self and other, generality and context, deliberation and action."[28]

Despite general acknowledgement of the importance of holistic approaches to learning, sometimes in reality there is a gulf between the curricular and co-curricular aspects of students' experiences. Many institutions and faculty members make little effort to promote, accentuate or integrate the non-classroom experience of students.

Conversely, many of those responsible for the out-of-class aspects of the student experience do not grasp the importance of their roles as teachers and educators and do very little to help students "make and maintain connections."[29]

Kuh has coined the phrase "seamless learning environments" to describe institutions that achieve a holistic educational vision.

> The word "seamless" suggests that what was once believed to be separate, distinct parts are now of one piece, bound together so as to appear whole or continuous. In seamless learning environments, students are encouraged to take advantage of learning resources that exist both inside and outside the classroom; faculty and staff use effective instructional practices; and students are asked to use their life experiences to make meaning of material introduced in classes, laboratories, and studios, and to apply what they are learning in class to their lives outside of the classroom.[30]

An easy test of whether or not an institution genuinely values, understands and promotes out-of-class learning is simply to evaluate the curriculum that guides such experiences. If no such curriculum exists, it is unlikely that an institution views the co-curriculum as an integral element of its students' education. Imagine for a moment a college that possessed no formalized general education curriculum. Besides the fact that such an institution would be unable to gain accreditation, it would be impossible for its students to experience the benefits of a well-conceived, cohesive educational experience. Consider carefully the co-curricular goals of your institution and whether or not they provide a clear articulation of educational goals and expectations.

The Broad Use of Assessment to Guide Educational Practices

Peter Ewell, in his *Brief History of Assessment*, identifies the birth of the assessment movement as the First National Conference on Assessment in Higher Education in 1985.[31] For such a recent development, the impact on the academy and those served by it has been enormous. And, much to the dismay of those who are waiting for the passing of what they see as one more higher educational "flavor of the day," the news is not good—assessment is not going to go away.

The difference between the assessment movement and the many vaporous trends that have been witnessed by veteran higher education practitioners is that a powerful coalition of stakeholders, including the state and federal government, business and industry, and students and their parents, are demanding accountability and evidence of learning. These demands have found their way into the conversation in a manner that is changing the way colleges and universities must do business. The government is increasingly suggesting a No Child Left Behind approach, including high-stakes testing, as the way to assure accountability for America's colleges and universities. The Council for Higher Education Accreditation (CHEA), under pressure from the Department of Education to increase the quality of higher education, is passing that pressure on to the regional accreditors. Finally, the cost of a college education in a competitive environment that now includes "for-profit" institutions as well as a number of "not-for-profits" that act like them, has led consumers of education to become a much more sophisticated lot. For a fascinating discussion, invite your director of admissions to talk about the educational marketplace. It is not unusual for prospective parents and their students to shop for a college much the way they shop for a car: "Here is what I want—now what will you give it to me for?" Simply put, for a multitude of reasons, assessment is here to stay.

If the preceding paragraph depresses you a bit, welcome to the club. Most of us in Christian higher education have chosen this path because we feel a sense of calling. We want to do a good job, not because someone is looking over our shoulders, but because we believe deeply in the importance of what we are doing and we truly care about our students. If this is your orientation, take heart. Two years ago at the annual meeting of the Higher Learning Commission, Executive Director and keynote speaker Steven Crow urged his listeners to move from "compliance to commitment" as they worked to improve the state of their particular institutions and higher education in general. This challenge should be close to the hearts of those who feel called to this work and who try to do it "as unto the Lord." Former Taylor University President Milo Rediger used to declare that "love prompts more than the law demands." Certainly this spirit ought to pervade all that we do in our work as educators. Thus, the chief motivation for assessment efforts should not be to satisfy external stakeholders or to comply with governmental or accreditation standards and, certainly, not to "sell our product" to more consumers; rather, our motivation should be stewardship. Assessment is simply a means for making sure we are accomplishing what we are attempting in the best possible manner. Surely we agree that meaningful evaluation and evidence will help us to do better the things that we feel called to do? If we act on this belief, "we will shine like the stars in the sky" in a "universe" that has a reputation for being notoriously reticent to subject itself to external scrutiny.

One of the greatest obstacles to effective assessment is making the mistake of overcomplicating the process and measures.

Many excellent resources are devoted to assisting individuals and institutions to conduct effective assessment. Because assessment is so multifaceted, a detailed discussion here would not be particularly advantageous. However, several items warrant cursory coverage before we finish this section. The table below provides a simple model for assessment planning (Table 4).[32] The purpose of this model is not to offer a final template for assessment planning, but rather to provide a sketch of the kinds of elements that an assessment plan should include and the types of questions that should be addressed. Avoid giving significant attention to the particular labels and language used here, as the particular terms are unimportant. For instance, the words mission, outcomes, objectives, etc. often hold very different meanings from one campus to another. While a universal language related to these matters is not necessary, it is important that institutions clearly define the way that they intend terms to be used, and then that they use them in that manner consistently. One of the greatest obstacles to effective assessment is overcomplicating the process and measures. The most pressing purposes of assessment would be fulfilled if colleges, programs and professors could provide simple, concrete answers and evidence to the question: "What can a student expect to gain from this experience?"

Table 4. Assessment Planning Model

Model Elements	Institution	Major/ Department	Course	Program
Mission	What is the big purpose for which this institution exists?	Why does this major exist? How does it uniquely serve the larger mission of the institution?	Why does this course exist? How does it help to fulfill the departmental mission?	Why does this program exist? How does it uniquely serve the larger mission of the institution?
Objectives	What are the objectives of the institution?	What are the objectives of this major?	What are the objectives of this course?	What are the objectives of this program?
Outcomes	What knowledge, skills, values should a student possess as a result of their graduation from this institution?	What knowledge, skills, values should a student possess as a result of their completion of this major?	What knowledge, skills, values should a student possess as a result of their completion of this course?	What knowledge, skills, values should a student possess as a result of their participation in this program?

Measures	What measures should be used to determine that the intended outcomes have been achieved?	What measures should be used to determine that the intended outcomes have been achieved?	What measures should be used to determine that the intended outcomes have been achieved?	What measures should be used to determine that the intended outcomes have been achieved?
Bench-marking	How do these results compare to those from other excellent institutions?	How do these results compare to those from other similar majors at other excellent institutions?	How do these results compare to those from other similar courses in other excellent institutions?	How do these results compare to those from other similar programs at other excellent institutions?
Feedback	How can resulting information be used to clarify the institutional mission, objectives, outcomes, measures, and benchmarks?	How can resulting information be used to clarify the major mission, objectives, outcomes, measures, and benchmarks?	How can resulting information be used to clarify the course mission, objectives, outcomes, measures, and benchmarks?	How can resulting information be used to clarify the program mission, objectives, outcomes, measures, and benchmarks?
Improve-ment	How can all resulting information be used to improve the institution?	How can all resulting information be used to improve the major/department?	How can all resulting information be used to improve the course?	How can all resulting information be used to improve the program?

One of the perceived problems in assessment is that many of the ideals we aspire to accomplish are difficult to quantify. While this concern exists for all institutions, it is especially problematic for Christian institutions with their unique focus on nurturing the spiritual formation of their students. While this difficulty must be acknowledged, it is also important to remember that even a rough measurement is generally better than no measurement at all. Furthermore, while we would all agree that it is impossible to evaluate the heart, it is oftentimes possible to find evidence that can reliably serve as a proxy for more direct measures. For instance, if we measured student involvement in volunteer service we would expect Christian students who are taking their faith seriously to be more involved in service to others than those who do not. To be sure, there are many such measures that can help us better understand student progress in nonacademic realms. For instance, the HERI freshman and senior data indicates that Christian college students are in fact participating in activities that we would associate with Christian discipleship (prayer, meditation, volunteer activities, etc.) at much higher levels than students from other institutional categories.

One of the biggest hindrances to effective assessment is being unwilling to accept less-than-perfect measures. Therefore, when dealing with assessment at the course, program or institutional level, one should use the standard of reasonable evidence rather than absolute proof. Simply put, perfection is not necessary for improvement to occur.

FINAL THOUGHTS

A central proposition of this essay is that although connections to students do not assure that meaningful learning will occur (this is the ultimate goal of employing relevant pedagogies), without them it will surely not! Therefore, let us put aside any notions that relegate relevant pedagogies to the arid realms of the ancient sage or the out-of-touch academic and understand them as methods that allow teachers to help their students to bring life to learning and learning to life.

Consider the teaching-learning pictures provided by Scripture. Biblical examples add strong support to the proposition that the most meaningful learning occurs within the context of a relationship. But let us be careful not to fall to the temptation of understanding such relationships purely in light of our modern sensitivities, particularly our tendency to worship at the altar of tolerance. The teacher-pupil connections illustrated in Christian Scripture are robust, challenging, confrontational, insightful, and caring. Consider just one example—has any teacher ever been more loving, more direct, or more confrontational with their students than Jesus was with Peter? I suspect not.

Biblical examples add strong support to the proposition that the most meaningful learning occurs within the context of a relationship.

Let those of us called "teacher" consider more thoughtfully how we might "feed his sheep," especially those sheep that come to us in "student's clothing." C. S. Lewis advises us in *The Abolition of Man* that "the task of the modern educator is not to cut down jungles but to irrigate deserts."[33] Many years later, Neil Postman's book, *The End of Education,* made a powerful case for the influence of guiding metaphors.[34] If there is any merit to his thoughts then there is tremendous significance to which of Lewis' metaphors—"cutting down jungles" or "irrigating deserts"—one chooses to employ. If one of the ways we care for our students—God's sheep—is to make sure they are well-fed, or in Lewis' terms well-watered, then I want to do what I can to provide what they need to sustain life—both the life of the Spirit and the life of the mind. And, when correction is in order, I want to better follow the example that God has shown me by his gentle action in my own life—to prune as a loving gardener trying to cultivate life rather than hack like one trying to eliminate it.

Several years ago, I attended an educational conference where a prominent keynote speaker, nearing the end of his talk, began sharing the Christian worldview that undergirded his work. Given the secular setting, his words were quite unexpected; however, he spoke in a respectful and winsome manner. The audience of five hundred or so sat in a silence that could almost be felt. The only way that I can describe it is to say that there was a sense of a holy presence. While discussing the audience response with two friends afterward, we agreed that something very unusual had taken place. One of these friends commented that perhaps this was the "sound of people having their souls spoken to." Well, after much reflection I have concluded that he was right. Even though most in the audience surely disagreed with this man's understanding of life and God, something deep within their hearts had been stirred. While I have no idea how many of these people may have responded to God that day, I have no doubt they encountered him and that he was honored. In some similar manner, I want to call each of us to feed our students by speaking to their souls at the same time we attempt to nurture their minds. And, if we can accomplish this challenge, it will surely constitute relevant pedagogy.

Discussion Questions

1. What are the characteristics of millennial students and what are the educational implications of these characteristics?

2. What are some practical measures you have employed to enhance the involvement/engagement of your students?

3. What are some possible ways that you might evaluate the level of engagement/involvement of your students?

4. What do you do to build rapport with students?

5. How might your institution better promote engagement?

6. What are the key challenges to employing more active learning strategies in your classes/work with students?

7. What is the co-curriculum of your institution? What should it be?

For Further Reading

Donovan, Suzanne, John Bransford, and James W. Pellegrino. *How People Learn: Bridging Research and Practice.* Washington, D.C.: National Academy Press, 1999.

Garber, Steven. *The Fabric of Faithfulness: Weaving Together Belief and Behavior during the University Year.* Downers Grove, Ill.: InterVarsity Press, 1996.

Gardiner, L. F. *Redesigning Higher Education: Producing Dramatic Gains in Student Learning.* ASHE-ERIC Higher Education Report, 23, 7 Washington, D.C. The George Washington University, Graduate School of Education and Human Development.

Kuh, George D. *Student Success in College: Creating Conditions that Matter.* San Francisco: Jossey-Bass, 2005.

McKeachie, Wilbert James, and Graham Gibbs. *McKeachie's Teaching Tips: Strategies, Research, and Theory for College and University Teachers.* Boston: Houghton Mifflin Co., 1999.

Palmer, Parker. *To Know as We Are Known: A Spirituality of Education.* San Francisco: Harper & Row, 1983.

Chapter 5

Managing Professional Interdependence

A Model for Christian Scholarship

Tom Jones and Skip Trudeau

A call to teaching in higher education has long been associated with a life of scholarship. In the traditional sense of the American professoriate this has included engaging in scholarly activities, usually but not limited to research, as a means to professional development and advancement in academic rank and tenure. While these activities are present in Christian colleges and universities, it is our intention to encourage Christian scholars to engage in an ongoing life of scholarly activities as a part of their Christian calling.

The focus of this chapter is twofold. The first is to establish the need to engage in a steady program of scholarly and professional growth for those who have entered into Christian higher education. The second is to provide a working model for how academic and student affairs educators alike can pursue this growth within the context of the Christian academy.

The Need for Scholarship in Christian Higher Education

A call to scholarship in the Christian college setting stems from the biblical admonition to "offer our bodies as living sacrifices" as part of our "lives of spiritual worship" via the "transformation by the renewing of our minds" (Romans 12:1-3). In our setting this calls for a combination of spiritual commitment and scholarly rigor. Consider the many examples of Jesus' interaction with the disciples. He continually challenged them to think of familiar teaching in new ways. He used the everyday, routine events as well as the extraordinary situations that came along to underscore new perspectives on old themes such as forgiveness and love for one's neighbors. Clearly Jesus did not view knowledge or understanding as gifts that can be developed primarily or exclusively within the context of a classroom or a good lecture given on a mountainside. He taught as a teacher who understood that discovery and integration take place best in a community that links the soul and the mind.[1]

What is the primary purpose for the Christian liberal arts university? What makes an undergraduate education from a Christian liberal arts university worth the cost? Richard Hughes of Messiah College envisions the Christian college campus as a special place where faculty and students are given an opportunity to pose the most important questions of life and pursue answers with the expectation that God will guide them in the search for truth.

> Christian scholars must search diligently for truth and affirm with conviction and affirmation those things that can be affirmed. But they must also allow the wonders and mysteries of the Christian faith to inspire doubt and, at certain levels, even skepticism. For skepticism and doubt breed questions, and without the questions, there can be no life of the mind.[2]

Michael L. Peterson writes that Christian scholars' "love of truth is an expression of our love of God, and our complete love of God will overflow into love of the world he created."[3] Peterson urges Christian scholars to think of education as a process through which we "develop our divinely created abilities to think logically and to evaluate matters wisely."[4] The authors of this chapter believe that Christian liberal arts universities must place greater emphasis on activities that challenge academic and student affairs educators to think more deeply and work more collaboratively.

> The most effective learning communities are those in which classrooms, residence halls, campus leadership activities, and travel at home and internationally give students a wide variety of opportunities to apply newly acquired knowledge and skills.

We have approached this chapter with three fundamental assumptions regarding the mission of Christian liberal arts universities. The first is the vital role of honest, open Christian scholarship in "sustain[ing] the life of the mind." The second is that academic and student affairs educators must both be scholars if the twenty-first century Christian liberal arts university is to succeed in its mission of providing activities that enable students to pursue truth as "an expression of our love for God."[5] And the third is that the most effective learning communities are those in which classrooms, residence halls, campus leadership activities, and travel at home and internationally give students a wide variety of opportunities to apply newly acquired knowledge and skills.

The task is too great for academic and student affairs educators to accomplish within their separate spheres of campus influence. However, there is little or no preservice preparation that prepares student and academic affairs faculty to work collaboratively. Academic affairs faculty arriving as newly minted Ph.D.s on the Christian liberal arts university campus are highly motivated to (a) make their mark in their particular discipline within the academy and (b) participate in campus discussions and leadership narrowly focused in their areas of professional specialization. Student affairs educators arrive on the job as highly motivated professionals who have been hired to manage residence halls, plan and coordinate student leadership programs, and administer a myriad of programs designed to attract bright, successful students to campus and to retain them through graduation. Neither faculty group has been prepared to plan and participate in collaborative programming that combines the best of both program areas in ways that promote student learning on a deep level. Universities that wish to promote such collaboration must, therefore, create their own training activities that equip their academic and student affairs educators to approach the development of learner outcomes and assessment of outcomes more holistically.

Duane Litfin reminds us that "we are salt, meant to permeate culture."[6] We believe that one of the best ways to prepare students to permeate world cultures is through an intentional collaboration between academic and student affairs. Through this collaboration, students witness a community of scholars who take their mission seriously and seek ways to model how their Christian faith impacts the search and application of truth.

There are at least four reasons to engage in this pursuit. They are (1) to help keep Christ at the center of the educational enterprise; (2) to sustain the life of the mind of the Christian scholar; (3) to nurture the heart of the Christian scholar; and (4) to extend the Christian scholar's influence beyond the traditional classroom.

In his book, *Conceiving the Christian College*, Litfin devotes an entire chapter to developing the argument for keeping Jesus Christ at the center focus of all that occurs on the Christian campus.

> To speak of Christ-*centered* liberal arts education is to make the claim that Jesus is the centerpiece of all human knowledge, the reference point for all our experience. It directs our attention to the only One who can serve as the centerpiece of an entire curriculum, the One to whom we must relate everything and without whom no fact, no theory, no subject matter can be fully

> appreciated. It is the claim that every field of study, every discipline, every course, requires Jesus Christ to be understood aright."[7]

Litfin goes on to ask whether we who are engaged in this Christ-centered approach really mean what we say. If our answer is "Yes," then we must actively engage in ongoing activities that will advance our discipline's knowledge base in ways that incorporate a Christian worldview.

But in this pursuit, as Richard Hughes points out, Christian scholars inevitably face a dilemma. Hughes captures the dilemma in the three questions that follow: "How can we teach from a Christian perspective while honoring, at the same time, the values and integrity of the academy? How can we embrace these two commitments simultaneously? How can we live between the two poles of this dialectical frame of reference?" The process of answering these questions forces Christian scholars who are intellectually and spiritually honest to develop a deeper appreciation for faith that "is built on a paradoxical framework at every crucial turn."[8] He suggests that Christian scholars can refuse to accept such a paradox and "seek to reduce the Christian religion to a set of simple, linear statements that have no paradoxical qualities about them whatsoever." However, Hughes believes that doing so risks the peril of robbing "the Christian faith of its power to sustain the life of the mind."[9]

Nurturing the heart of the scholar is a third rationale for engaging in the pursuit of scholarship in Christian higher education. Parker Palmer, in his seminal work *The Courage to Teach: Exploring the Inner Landscape of a Teacher's Life*, gives a vivid description of the heart of a teacher:

> Small wonder, then, that teaching tugs at the heart, opens the heart, even breaks the heart—and the more one loves teaching, the more heartbreaking it can be. The courage to teach is the courage to keep one's heart open in those very moments when the heart is asked to hold more than it is able so that teacher and students and subjects can be woven into the fabric of community that learning, and living requires.[10]

This "heart" that facilitates the positive transformation in students is worth nurturing. This process is like growing a garden: the teacher's heart is the seed which, with the proper combination of nutrients, water, and sun, become the blossoming plant—a transformed student. Engaging in Christian scholarship provides a rich environment, full of nutrients, ample water and sunlight, perfect for the developing seed. Scholarship keeps the teachers' hearts strong, enabling them to continue transforming the lives of their students.

To extend the Christian scholar's influence beyond the traditional classroom, Boyer recognized the importance of moving education beyond the traditional classroom, extending the scholar's influence through engagement in community projects that imply a new cooperation between faculty in academic and student affairs.[11] Describing the "New American College," he writes that it "would organize cross-disciplinary institutes around pressing social issues" and that students would participate in field projects, relating ideas to real life through course-related projects carried out in "health clinics, youth centers, schools, and government offices."[12] The scope of this engagement appears to require a new paradigm of collaboration between academic affairs and student affairs faculty who are committed to community projects that "enrich the campus, renew communities, and give new dignity and status to the scholarship of service."[13]

Boyer's ideal "New American College," with its deep ties to the community beyond the campus, is contained in the Christian liberal arts university mission. For example, one Christian university statement of mission and purpose includes the following bullet: "To offer liberal arts, professional and lifelong education based upon the conviction that all truth has its source in God, and that being biblically anchored, the Christian faith should permeate all learning leading to a consistent life of worship, servant leadership, stewardship, and world outreach."[14] The assumption underlying this statement is that Christian scholars (faculty and students) have a responsibility to apply their knowledge and skills in ways that lead to the betterment of the world beyond the university's classrooms, residence halls, and other public spaces.

Christian scholars (faculty and students) have a responsibility to apply their knowledge and skills in ways that lead to the betterment of the world beyond the university's classrooms, residence halls, and other public spaces.

A Christian College Model of Scholarship

We now come to the question of how one sustains a commitment to scholarly and professional growth within the Christian college context. In the traditional professoriate model these activities would fall under the categories of teaching, research, and service. This is a model that has permeated American higher education for the better part of the last century and is still used in varying forms by many institutions of higher education as the litmus test for scholarly activity and as the basis for granting promotional rank and tenure. On the student affairs side there has been a lack of a systematic approach across the academy for the monitoring of professional growth; attempts to fill this void have largely called for the employment of business models that have not adequately taken into account the educational nature of student affairs work. In 1990 Ernest Boyer proposed some new ways of thinking about the traditional roles associated with the professoriate. He proposed that the traditional model of teaching, research, and service be reshaped into four new categories: the scholarship of *discovery,* the scholarship of *integration,* the scholarship of *application,* and the scholarship of *teaching*. We propose an adaptation of the Boyer model with the addition of a fifth category: the scholarship of *collaboration*. We will provide descriptions of these five categories and insights as to how both academic and student affairs can engage in meaningful activities within each category.

To facilitate this discussion we are adopting Boyer's language of referring to professors as scholars, since we feel this is an appropriate reminder to those who are called to this task. We are also applying this descriptor to those engaged in student affairs. We believe they too should take part in scholarly activities that address a holistic model of Christian higher education.

The Scholarship of Discovery

As described by Boyer, this category refers to what the traditional model spoke of as research. Boyers's unique contribution to this area was a call to expand the concept of research beyond the notion of contributions to human knowledge and include the processes and passions associated with research endeavors. Boyer explained: "The *scholarship of discovery,* at its best, contributes not only to the stock of human knowledge but also to the intellectual climate of a college or university; not just the outcomes, but the process, and especially the passion, give meaning to the effort."[15]

Boyer saw the need to engage in discovery as a necessary ingredient to sustain the academic enterprise. He believed that this discipline would keep those on campus exhilarated and renewed and would in turn contribute to the needs of society.

In the Christian college context this passionate pursuit finds additional meaning in the belief that all truth is God's truth, and this exploration leads ultimately to greater and deeper knowledge of the divine. In our venue the quest for knowledge (research) is a natural outpouring of our vocational calling to Christian higher education.

An Academic Affairs Perspective on the Scholarship of Discovery

Most Christian liberal arts universities make references in their catalog to learning as a lifelong process. Boyer saw the scholarship of discovery as something that should be at the core of how we think, plan, and deliver undergraduate education. There is a temptation in the university system to assign discrete boxes (e.g., courses, co-curricular residence hall wings, etc.) where professors and students engage in activities that lead to discovery. Christian liberal arts universities have fought this temptation and have made a commitment to engage in this holistic scholarship of discovery.

A dynamic that should characterize the learner focus of a Christian liberal arts experience is the removal of the walls that separate all of the individuals who engage in the scholarship of discovery. For example, international travel that includes study and research in which educators collaborate with students to fulfill academic and service learning objectives may help educators from both academic and student affairs to think and act more holistically. Christian liberal arts universities begin with the declaration that all truth is from God and is to be pursued with all diligence so that it can be learned and applied in transformational ways beyond the classroom or even the campus.

This principle lies at the heart of Boyer's vision of an undergraduate education: "And to sustain the vitality of higher education in our time, a new vision of scholarship is required, one dedicated not only to the renewal of the academy but, ultimately, to the renewal of society itself."[16] He called on all who are part of the higher education community to re-think the purpose of an undergraduate education with a new type of scholar, those "who not only skillfully explore the frontiers of knowledge, but also integrate ideas, connect thought to action, and inspire students."[17] We believe that the renewal he sought is most achievable on the Christian liberal arts campus. It is on such campuses that a clear focus on knowledge and its application are emphasized as part of learning, living, and serving.

While Boyer's vision may involve a level of campus integration not possible in most large secular institutions, it plays to an area of strength that should be at the heart of what Christian liberal arts universities are doing. In particular, the inclusion of service learning projects and global engagement bridging academic affairs and student affairs programs provides new and innovative ways for scholars from both areas to collaborate. This new level of collaboration will encourage students to approach their studies with a greater sense of purpose and a larger view of how their academic study connects to a broader world.

A Student Affairs Perspective on the Scholarship of Discovery

This area of scholarship may seem a daunting task for student affairs educators. It could be argued that, as a field, this area lacks a theoretical foundation provided by traditional academics. There are many venues for research and advancement of knowledge within the field of student affairs, and this is especially true for those who would apply the lenses of Christian thought and practice to their discovery.

A number of journals focus on scholarship pertaining to student affairs. Examples include the National Association of Student Personnel Administrators's *NASPA Journal*, the *Journal of College Student Development*, and the *Journal of College Student Housing*. In addition, several journals have a broader focus that includes materials submitted by student affairs scholars. Examples here include *About Campus, ASHE Eric Higher Education Report, College Student Values, Change, Chronicle of Higher Education, Educational Record,* and *Research in Higher Education*. There are also several venues for student affairs related scholarship publication in periodicals with a primary Christian higher education focus. These include *Christian Scholar's Review, Growth,* and *Research in Higher Education*. All of these journals also publish materials submitted by academicians as well.

Publication is not the only avenue for student affairs scholars to be involved in the scholarship of discovery. Three other options deserve mention here. First, staying current in the literature of the field and applying theoretical concepts from the reading in practical settings is one valuable way to demonstrate scholarship. Second, presentations at regional and national conferences are another venue for the student affairs scholar to contribute to the body of knowledge in the field. Finally, informing academic affairs and other colleagues within your own institution concerning student affairs practices at your school and within the broader field is another way to contribute to the scholarship of discovery.

The Scholarship of Integration

Boyer's concept of integration calls for scholars from differing areas of expertise to find areas of connection across discipline specific boundaries. In addition, he recommends that they work in multidisciplinary climates to produce scholarship that has broader impact and applicability. He defines this scholarship as follows: "By integration, we mean making connections across the disciplines, placing the specialties in larger context, illuminating the data in a revealing way, often educating non-specialists too."[18] In the Boyer model this cross pollenization would provide for broader applicability of knowledge from differing disciplines and thus make higher education more effective in serving societal needs.

In the Christian college, this pursuit is enriched by the concept of all truth being authored by God. This concept has been a mantra for Christian higher education for several decades,[19] but in the context of the Boyer model it takes on additional meaning due to his emphasis on academic interdisciplinary work.

An Academic Affairs Perspective on the Scholarship of Integration

One of the major challenges for the Christian liberal arts university in the increasingly job-focused curricular environment for the last twenty or more years is that of convincing parents and students to think of an undergraduate degree as being something more than a ticket to a steady, high paying job.

Every student ought to reasonably expect that her/his undergraduate education will, indeed, include knowledge and skills essential for landing a good job or winning admission to the best graduate and professional schools. However, students enrolled in a Christian college should expect more than an education that leads to a good job. Boyer also recognized the dual purpose of the college experience:

Students enrolled in a Christian college should expect more than an education that leads to a good job.

> We more comfortably embrace the notion that the aim of the undergraduate experience is not only to prepare the young for productive careers, but also to enable them to live lives of dignity and purpose; not only to generate new knowledge, but to channel that knowledge to humane ends; not merely to study government, but to help shape a citizenry that can promote the public good.[20]

The dual purpose that Boyer identified cannot be accomplished through academic or student affairs programs that are focused exclusively on their separate areas of responsibility or on narrow segments of a specific academic discipline.

W. James Mannoia Jr. explores the question, "How Can a College Pursue Integration?" in his book, *Christian Liberal Arts: An Education That Goes Beyond*. Like Boyer, he concludes that one of the primary goals of a college must be "to produce graduates who are able to tackle real-world problems."[21] One of the ways in which integration is achieved on campus is through ongoing conversation and debate among scholars who share a common set of core values and "are deliberately committed to finding common interests."[22] This type of idea exchange among scholars with common interests and values ought to involve faculty from both academic and student affairs and students in a variety of settings that range from the classroom to the residence hall, from the chapel to the student union.

Accepting controversy as a necessary ingredient to achieve integration may, as Mannoia writes, "seem contrary to community."[23] In an effort to ensure that the common focus is not lost or blurred, some in academic affairs or student affairs leadership may do everything possible to avoid dissonance. Mannoia counsels that they do so at the peril of weakening the university as a learning community:

> If there is not first a diversity to be brought together, there can be no integration and no community, only sameness. Students and faculty alike will find it very easy to lose sight of problems in the community that is too homogenous. Controversy as a deliberate strategy means to bring real-world problems into the environment and apply integrative approaches. The lack of controversy makes any college, and particularly Christian colleges, anemic.

However, integration involves more than spirited conversations and mission focused controversy. Integration requires that the Christian scholar research, teach, and engage in all of her/his work with conviction that "the highest levels of scholarship and teaching" are achieved "because of [his/her] commitment to the Christian faith, not in spite of that commitment."[24] Christian scholars should begin with belief that the search for truth—if done honestly—involves relationships with a world that is larger than a single academic discipline.

Christian scholars should begin with belief that the search for truth—if done honestly—involves relationships with a world that is larger than a single academic discipline.

A Student Affairs Perspective on the Scholarship of Integration

For the student affairs scholar the scholarship of integration should be a natural endeavor owing to the fact that the undergirding theoretical models for the field have roots in a variety of academic fields such as psychology, sociology, business management, and theology. By its very nature student affairs is an integrative discipline, so working with those from other areas should be achievable.

How might a scholarship of integration venture look? Here is one example. Student affairs has historically utilized theoretical models from other areas, such as Chickering's Student Development Theory[25] with roots in psychology, Astin's Involvement Theory[26] with roots in sociology and psychology, and Fowler's Faith Development Theory[27] with roots in psychology and theology. All of these models have attempted to describe the progression in important developmental tasks as students proceed through college. The scholarship of integration can occur as the student affairs scholar works with representatives of these other areas to develop a developmental model that incorporates aspects from all the represented disciplines into a practically applicable model for the Christian college.

The Scholarship of Application

This area is an adaptation of the traditional model's call for service. In Boyer's model this area is responsible to answer these three questions, "How can knowledge be responsibly applied to consequential problems? How can it be helpful to individuals as well as institutions? And further, can social problems themselves define an agenda for scholarly investigation?"[28] The Boyer model was a call to higher education to return to this notion of applying knowledge gained both on and off campus toward the goal of bettering society.

In the Christian college context this scholarship of application can easily be seen embedded in the nature of Christian service. As we serve Christ we are able to apply our professional training into the furthering of his kingdom, and we have both the privilege and obligation to include students in this pursuit. We must take this area of scholarship seriously if we are to be "salt and light in the world" that desperately needs God's salt and light.

An Academic Affairs Perspective on the Scholarship of Application

Traditional doctoral programs tend to prepare myopic professors. They have learned their craft at the feet of mentors committed to the traditional model of scholarship that emphasizes research, publication, and extended dialogue with one's peers in her/his part of the academy as the pathway to promotion and tenure. However, Boyer—while recognizing the significance of intellectual questioning that leads to original research—championed a new vision in which more scholars are engaged in research that matters in the everyday world. In other words, Boyer was challenging scholars to think more deeply about pursuing the scholarship of application.

Loeb writes about "an ethic of connection" that leads to the development of an identity that "is discovered and realized only within the context of community."[29] The community about which Loeb and Boyer write is one where there is a level of engagement that "builds a sense of loyalty to others similarly struggling for a better world."[30] The kind of community that effects change is best achieved when academic and student affairs scholars share in planning and implementing university programs involving community groups.

But there is danger when the emphasis on application overshadows reflection. Jim Wallis warns that "without the space for self-examination and the capacity for rejuvenation, the danger of exhaustion and despair is too great." He counsels that time spent in focused reflection will help the scholar avoid the tendency to "become barren and even bitter."[31]

A Student Affairs Perspective on the Scholarship of Application

It would be a mistake to think that this area of scholarship doesn't apply to the student affairs scholar due to the service orientation of the field. Student affairs scholars needs to be involved in the scholarship of application both internally on their own campuses and externally in off campus settings as well.

On their own campuses, the student affairs scholar needs to be involved in the committee and governance structures that monitor the curricular and co-curricular program of the institution. As experts on student behavior and student learning, student affairs persons can provide valuable insight across a wide span of curricular and co-curricular aspects of the college experience. We advocate that when the credentials and experience of the student affairs scholar match institutional expectations for faculty members that they be included in the same arenas as the academic affairs faculty.

The student affairs scholar also needs to be involved in application scholarship in off campus settings. Two avenues are especially attractive for this service. A first avenue is service learning, which has emerged as an effective pedagogical method to increase student learning. Here, student affairs educators are a valuable resource to provide opportunities to enhance specific classroom learning outcomes and transformative, serendipitous learning experiences. A second avenue for the scholarship of application is involvement with professional organizations and other groups that work to promote the field in broader contexts. These two avenues provide the student affairs scholar with opportunities to engage in the scholarship of application, traditionally known as service, to their local and professional communities.

THE SCHOLARSHIP OF TEACHING

This of course is a direct holdover from the traditional model, and here again the Boyer model served as a reminder for all higher education to take this role more seriously regardless of whether the school is a large research university or a small liberal arts college. In the context of this model, Boyer claims that as "scholarship, teaching both educates and entices future scholars." He also describes teaching as a dynamic process that goes beyond transmitting knowledge to "transforming and extending it as well."[32]

For most Christian colleges, teaching remains a central focus of the academic enterprise. The university's mission is transmitted through professors who believe that truth will transform students and ultimately the world. Transformational learning is the goal that most Christian colleges pursue. It is a goal that is impossible to achieve without professors who love their disciplines and have a genuine desire to present ideas in ways that lead to greater understanding of the world and inspire students to apply their knowledge as informed and responsible citizens. Students are attracted to colleges where, as an expression of their faith, professors are inspired by their love for truth.

Students are attracted to colleges where, as an expression of their faith, professors are inspired by their love for truth.

Peterson provides a descriptive insight concerning Christian colleges that continue to have strong appeal. He suggests that where there is a genuine love for truth, both professors and students are encouraged to learn. He continues by stating that this love for truth is "an expression of our love for God," and where the pursuit of truth is a means of redeeming the world this gives students and professors a vision that has meaning.[33]

An Academic Affairs Perspective on Teaching

Lent has stated it simply: "Universities are characterized by more (but not less) than great teaching. A university is about learning and it is in the nature of a university that faculty are great learners as well as teachers."[34] The mission statement of one university's center dedicated to teaching and learning excellence begins with a similar recognition of the integral role of teaching:

> Believing that faculty are the central motivating force in the achievement of the university mission, the Center for Teaching & Learning Excellence has been established to equip professors with skills, knowledge, and a common vision. The primary goal of the CTLE is to create and sustain an academic community in which faith and learning are effectively and creatively integrated in curricular, co-curricular, and extra-curricular programs. The CTLE is focused on the encouragement of faculty in research and discussion promoting the scholarship of teaching and learning within the context of a Christian liberal arts university in which faculty and students are committed to lifelong learning and ministering the redemptive love of Jesus Christ to a world in need.[35]

Good teachers know their discipline and are committed to creating and sustaining classrooms that become part of a larger learning community. Their classrooms "stimulate our students to exercise their God-given imagination and creativity and free them to wonder, to search, and explore."[36] And for those who teach in Christian liberal arts universities there is another part of the classroom equation: the classroom becomes a place where students learn to deal with the paradoxes upon which Christian faith is constructed.

This implies that Christian scholars view their classrooms, not as places to engage in propagandizing, but as learning spaces where life's most important questions are researched, analyzed, and discussed. Hughes has captured this critical aspect of what good teachers in Christian liberal arts universities do:

> While I avoid propagandizing in the classroom, I am quick to let my students know that I am a Christian. I neither dwell on that fact nor make an issue of it. But once I have made that point, many of my students are quick to discern why I wish to explore with them the questions of fate and death, or emptiness and meaninglessness, or guilt and condemnation. And they are equally quick to discern why I encourage them to take seriously the marginalized and dispossessed. Once the students know who I am and where my deepest commitments lie, they have a context for understanding everything that goes on in my classroom.[37]

Whatever the Christian scholar's academic discipline, it is imperative that she/he creates a classroom climate in which students develop a growing awareness of their professor's faith and are invited to participate with the professor in reaching for "the highest levels of scholarship and teaching" that result from their mutual "commitment to the Christian faith, not in spite of that commitment."[38]

A Student Affairs Perspective on Teaching

It might be easy to assume that this scholarship area is reserved for the academic affairs scholar and that those involved in student affairs need not be concerned about engagement here. We believe this is a faulty conclusion and urge student affairs scholars to see their role as inclusive of this area of scholarship, indeed as paramount to their role as educators. Student affairs scholars must see themselves being engaged in the scholarship of teaching not as ancillary to their roles but as primary.

For the student affairs scholar, the call to be involved with teaching is a call to utilize all of the teachable moments. He or she needs to capitalize on these experiences to provide a seamless whole-person education that enhances classroom instruction. This "teaching" takes place in numerous venues—residence halls, co-curricular programming, formal and informal counseling, and engagement of student affairs scholars in more traditional teaching experiences.

THE SCHOLARSHIP OF COLLABORATION

Higher education has seen a paradigm shift from a teacher-centered approach to a student- or learner-centered approach. This pedagogical shift includes a shift from reliance on the traditional lecture, "sage on the stage" format to a more eclectic approach that uses multiple pedagogies designed to incorporate the total experiences, both in and out of the classroom, of students in a seamless learning environment.[39] This seamless approach focuses on learning outcomes and seeks to measure what students have learned and how they are able to apply it rather than the amount of information they are presented. For this to occur the scholarship of collaboration must be engaged.

The Christian college context provides an ideal environment for the scholarship of collaboration. The institution's production of graduates who can apply this transformation into their post graduation activities creates a critical need for institution wide collaboration. In fact, for these goals to be achieved collaboration appears to be a necessary factor.

An Academic Affairs Perspective on Collaboration

We believe that learning involves the active, ongoing engagement of professors and students in activities leading to the acquisition of knowledge and skills that enable both to live "a life of moral and intellectual excellence and spiritual commitment."[40] We believe that academic and student affairs faculty are best able to inspire the highest moral development in students when they work collaboratively, resisting the temptation to work in separate silos. Their best hope for creating a learning community that successfully integrates their own areas of specialization into the world beyond campus is to work on the alignment of program objectives and activities that connect the classroom with the rest of the campus.

We believe that academic and student affairs faculty are best able to inspire the highest moral development in students when they work collaboratively, resisting the temptation to work in separate silos.

Holmes writes that the development of moral responsibility and character "is really a lifetime process," with the college years representing a particularly formative period for students:

> Subsequent changes, of course, do occur, not only for the better but also sometimes for the worse. But college can establish goals and set a direction, and it can build bridges into the future by means of ongoing friendships that are established, institutional loyalties that persist, and the exemplars in various fields who continue to influence the graduates. Commencement,

> like landmark celebrations in other communities, should mark the beginning of a new stage of life in a lifelong process of developing character that grows increasingly responsible, increasingly virtuous, and that loves God with heart and mind and strength—a single minded Christian moral identity that is . . . solid all the way through.[41]

Students who are part of a community in which student and academic affairs faculty model what it means to teach and live collaboratively experience "the language of a community of moral discourse" that "affirms who we are as a people, the people of God."[42]

A Student Affairs Perspective on Collaboration

The scholarship of collaboration implies several things for student affairs scholars. First, they must become experts on student behavior. In much the same way as academic scholars are experts in their chosen field, student affairs scholars choose students and their behavior as their field of study. This positions them to be able to educate their colleagues from academic affairs thus helping bridge the gap between institutional expectations and student performance. In other words, this focus on student behavior can help all scholars better focus on student learning.

Second, student affairs scholars must pay attention to professionalism, including the areas of prior academic preparation and ongoing development. For true collaboration to be possible, student affairs scholars must demonstrate their willingness and ability to engage in the vibrant academic life of the institution. In short, they must work against the nostalgic image of the "house mother" or "hand holder" which results in a bifurcated system where student affairs work is relegated to the periphery while academic affairs engages in the real work of educating students. To do this student affairs scholars must be credentialed with advanced degrees in higher education or related fields and pay particular attention to ongoing engagement in the scholarships of teaching, discovery, integration, application, and collaboration.

Third, student affairs scholars and their departments must align with the academic mission of the institution. For true collaboration to occur, both academic and student affairs must be on the same page and avoid the temptation to compete with each other. This competition can be in the form of constrained resources, which is a very real issue for nearly ever sector of higher education including Christian institutions, and in more political areas such as who should have the most clout in institutional decision making. Student affairs scholars must examine themselves and their programs to ensure that they are truly pursuing the mission of the institution.

Finally, reward structures, including salary and advancement, need to reflect the scholarship of collaboration for student affairs scholars much the same way as they do for academic scholars. Collaboration needs to become more mandatory and common rather than optional and rare. It is incumbent upon student affairs and academic affairs scholars alike to seek opportunities for this to occur.

Summary

The purpose of this chapter has been to call those engaged in academic affairs and student affairs in Christian colleges to a life of scholarship. We have provided both a rationale for engaging in Christian scholarship and a model for it. We have discussed four reasons for engaging in scholarship: (1) to help keep Christ at the center of the educational enterprise; (2) to sustain the life of the mind of the Christian scholar; (3) to nurture the heart of the Christian scholar; and (4) to extend the Christian scholar's influence beyond the traditional classroom.

The model for Christian scholarship is built on the premise that all truth is God's truth, and therefore the pursuit of this truth expresses both the Christian scholar's spiritual life and his or her professional progress. Within this context we have discussed five areas of scholarship that contribute to this pursuit: the scholarship of discovery, of integration, of application, of teaching, and of collaboration.

Scholarship as we have envisioned it should become the *modus operandi* or business as usual for both the academic and student affairs scholar as they fulfill the calling to Christian higher education. Engaging in the scholarships of discovery, integration, application, teaching, and collaboration based on the claim that all truth is God's truth will help both those in academic and student affairs to renew their hearts and minds as they minister in Christian higher education.

Discussion Questions

1. What does it mean for the Christian scholar to pursue Richard Hughes's vision of a diligent search for truth and affirmation of affirmable things? What will it take to accomplish this on the Christian college campus? What changes will be necessary, what collaborations will be required, and what roadblocks will inhibit this search?

2. How wide a spectrum of viewpoints should the Christian college embrace? If all truth is God's truth, then what voices should be heard?

3. Why is it important for the Christian scholar to be active in the broader academy?

4. Do academic affairs and student affairs scholars have "blinders" that will inhibit them to pursue collaborative scholarship and integration?

5. What is there about scholarship that enables the scholar to maintain the Parker Palmer notion of the "heart of the teacher" that is necessary for the healthy maintenance of a community of learning?

6. What would cross-pollination or collaborative scholarship between academic affairs and student affairs look like? What structural, leadership, policy, and strategy changes would it take to make this work?

7. Where is the balance between sharing our faith with students via scholarly and other work and the potential impact this may have and the developmental task of students developing a sense of their own belief systems?

8. How is the paradigm shift from the teacher-centered to a learner-centered educational approach impacting engagement with students and how does this impact the engagement between academic and student affairs?

For Further Reading

Boyer, Ernest L. *Scholarship Reconsidered: Priorities for the Professoriate.* Princeton, N.J.: Carnegie Foundation for the Advancement of Teaching, 1990.

Hughes, Richard T. *The Vocation of a Christian Scholar: How Christian Faith Can Sustain the Life of the Mind.* Grand Rapids, Mich.: Eerdmans, 2005.

Litfin, Duane. *Conceiving the Christian College.* Grand Rapids, Mich.: Eerdmans, 2004.

Mannoi, W. James. *Christian Liberal Arts: An Education that Goes Beyond.* Lanhan, Mass.: Rowman & Littlefield, 2000.

Marsden, George. *The Outrageous Idea of Christian Scholarship.* New York: Oxford University Press, 1997.

Parker, M. L. *With All Your Mind: A Christian Philosophy of Education.* Notre Dame, Ind.: University of Notre Dame Press, 2001.

Palmer, Parker. *The Courage to Teach: Exploring the Inner Landscape of a Teacher's Life.* San Francisco: Jossey-Bass, 1998.

Chapter 6

Collaboration

To Labor Together

Norris Friesen and Wendy Soderquist Togami

In Noah benShea's international best selling and timeless book, *Jacob the Baker,* he tells the story of a professor who takes his student deep into the woods. At the darkest point, the professor extinguishes the torch and continues to walk. The fearful student asks if he is going to be left alone in the woods without any light. The professor replies saying, "No," he is leaving the student *to search* for the light.[1] This inspirational story summarizes the intent and purpose of Christian higher education—to teach students how to search for truth, and to provide the environment that best supports that search.

For decades a prominent student development challenge and support theory has provided a fundamental understanding of how we seek to help students "search for the light."[2] One of the most important aspects to be considered is maintaining a suitable balance between challenge and support. When students are challenged beyond their means, they report feeling overwhelmed, immobilized, and abandoned. However, well-intentioned support can be suffocating if offered incorrectly. So, as partners in the educational enterprise, it is important for *both* the academic and student development professions to provide challenge *and* support to students in order to maximize success.

A powerful way to invigorate Christian student learning on college campuses is to promote collaboration among student development and academic affairs in new and creative ways that capitalize on each profession's strengths. There has never been a better time to elevate the conversations across our campuses than in today's changing educational arena. Patricia King, in her 1999 article, "Putting Together the Puzzle of Student Learning," surmises that "college students get more out of their educational experiences when the collegiate purposes are *clear and consistently communicated* across the campus."[3] She states further that the cognitive, interpersonal, and intrapersonal developments of students are *equally* important.

This chapter is designed to promote new conversations between the academic and student development communities that will, in their end, promote meaningful learning for our students. As the Apostle Paul states in Philippians, "If you have any encouragement from being united with Christ, if any comfort from his love, if any fellowship with the Spirit, if any tenderness and compassion, then make my joy complete by being like-minded, having the same love, being one in spirit and purpose."[4]

Collaboration Defined

At its core collaboration allows people to achieve work that could not otherwise be accomplished. It includes "the process defined by the recursive interaction of knowledge and mutual learning between two or more people working together toward a common goal typically creative in nature."[5] According to the National Network for Collaboration, it is "a process of participation through which people, groups, and organizations work together to achieve desired results. Starting or sustaining a collaborative journey is exciting, sometimes stressful, and even new for many."[6] Inherent in each of these definitions is the truth that collaboration takes work toward a specific goal, is a two-way street, and does not come naturally to us. This accurately reflects the academic community within the last twenty years.

Where Are We?

Historically there has been a division between academic affairs and student development. The distinction between the roles has been divided by classroom versus out-of-the-classroom, formal versus informal, curricular versus co-curricular. The formal classroom has been relegated to academic affairs and co-curricular activities assigned to student development. In recent years academicians and student development professionals have taken great strides toward viewing both aspects as integral to the educational mission of the institution. Student development has assumed a greater role as educator, and academic affairs have begun to promote the out-of-the-classroom experience as a rich learning environment.

The shift in student development from psychosocial and developmental theory (Chickering, Kohlberg, Perry) to increased focus on student learning is evident in the last several years. Documents like the *The Student Learning Imperative*[7] and *Powerful Partnerships*[8] have helped to shape much of the discussion. *The Student Learning Imperative* identifies principles that assist student development professionals to "intentionally create the conditions that enhance student learning and personal development."[9] *The Student Learning Imperative* discusses how collaboration and partnerships are essential to a "seamless learning environment." The document identifies the characteristics of a liberally educated individual, which includes such things as "reflection and critical thinking,"[10] application of knowledge to problem solving, and diversity. A major emphasis of *The Student Learning Imperative* is to identify the outcomes of a learning-centered institution. One of the more significant items is collaboration as a necessary ingredient of student learning. Of particular interest is the dismantling of "functional silos" that have hindered collaboration in the past.

> "What we have to learn to do, we learn by doing."
> —Aristotle

> The learning-oriented student affairs division recognizes that students benefit from many and varied experiences during college and that learning and personal development are cumulative, mutually shaping processes that occur over an extended period of time in many different settings. The more students are involved in a variety of activities inside and outside the classroom, the more they gain.[11]

The idea that learning is, in fact, comprehensive and all encompassing should give each of us reason to intentionally seek avenues for partnership with one another in ways that are worth the extra time and effort associated with collaborative work.

Potter expands *The Student Learning Imperative* by emphasizing the practical outcomes of learning.[12] Many different facets influence learning. Of particular interest to this discussion are the principles related to relationships, community, ethos, and environments that are "informal and incidental." Learning is enhanced by the interaction of students, faculty, and staff in meaningful ways in a climate that stresses challenge and support. A learning community that exhibits respect and acceptance and provides opportunities for expression and exchange of ideas is one in which students will have opportunity to experience growth. A learning ethos seeks to create a distinctive culture where informal interactions are encouraged and spontaneous.

The obvious function of higher education is to graduate knowledgeable, well-informed students, but it begs these questions: "What does knowledgeable and well-informed look like? How do we know that is what we are doing? Does classroom evaluation give us the sum total of a student's learning? En route to getting a degree, students receive more than knowledge, and in the Christian college students begin to understand how their faith influences their learning and living. Both documents mentioned previously emphasize that students are responsible for their own learning and that the institution can provide many out-of-the-classroom experiences that can enhance learning.

Bourassa and Kruger identified several initiatives that have been implemented in colleges and universities to enhance student learning. In their review of 42 programs, they noted the following recurring features: faculty-in-residence programs, first-year programs, learning communities, student life programs, the college student programs, and academic-student affairs planning teams.[13]

Several of the initiatives stress the importance of faculty and student interaction. For example, college student programs utilize the expertise of student development professionals to explain and identify trends of student populations and how to work effectively with these students, e.g., the millennial student, generation X, etc. Academic-student affairs planning teams are ongoing committees to address specific needs of the campus. For example, a committee including an English professor, a biology professor, a residence hall director, and the dean of students assigned to assess both formal and informal student learning would bring a holistic perspective to the discussion. Potential for all parties to learn about student motivation would be greatly enhanced.

A Collaborative Look at Faith and Learning

Collaboration of student and academic affairs in Christian higher education has enriched an additional and vital part of the Christian experience. Learning has not only been emphasized, but the integration of faith and learning has been a major agenda for Christian institutions. It is not only the integration of faith and learning in the classroom, but also of faith and learning in co-curricular programs. Faculty members seek to weave their faith into the fabric of their respective academic disciplines. By looking at the discipline through the lens of faith, one is able to determine how faith in Christ illuminates truth and how the subject matter might inform one's faith. In addition, faculty join with student development professionals in assisting students in applying their faith. The Council for Christian Colleges and Universities (CCCU) provides seminars and resources on faith and integration, and many universities provide seminars on their campuses to help faculty learn how to

> "The ultimate goal of the educational system is to shift to the individual the burden of pursuing his own education. This will not be a widely shared pursuit until we get over our odd conviction that education is what goes on in school buildings and nowhere else."
> —John Gardner

integrate faith and learning. It continues to be a major focus in Christian institutions and, although difficult to do, remains the hallmark of Christian higher education.

The integration of faith and learning in student development has been less formalized, but is incorporated in all efforts to impact students. Through mentoring, discipleship programs, residence life seminars, and talk back sessions, student development professionals can assist students in identifying how their faith influences their daily lives.

In the authors' experience, it takes significant intention for leaders in the academic community as a whole to make the informal, yet all-important connections with students inside and outside the classroom. By the nature of his work, a leader, whether an academic dean, division chair, or student development vice president, is juggling the urgent and often complex issues of each day, along with the important relationship building activities so vital to the community. In the authors' experience, when leaders take the time for such activities as campus lunch meetings with a handful of students, book discussion groups, service projects, and travel experiences with students, they find themselves connected in healthy, dynamic, learning relationships which transcend any conversation of curricular vs. co-curricular.

Another area that provides unparalleled opportunities for integration of faith and learning is the process of discipline both inside and outside the classroom. If handled well and if dealing with willing hearts on all sides of the issue, these situations can have a profound impact on individual students both for their academic pursuits as well as their spiritual lives.

The writer of Hebrews reminds us that God disciplines those he loves and that those who are willing to be trained by the discipline will reap a life of harmony and uprightness. To help students understand that the purpose of discipline is training is an important challenge, one that should not be relegated to one segment of the academic community as a whole.

Examples of Healthy Collaboration

Faculty support of student development and student development's support of the faculty is crucial. We work in partnership with students, and we must find ways to collaborate when there is no obvious way to do so. Healthy examples of collaboration are orientation, first-year programs, faculty-in-residence programs, learning communities and centers, planning teams, counseling, and career development. Faculty are excellent resources and are often willing to participate on panel discussions or talk on areas of interest outside the classroom. Student development professionals are excellent subject matter experts to invite to classroom settings.

Huntington University (Indiana) has invited faculty to discuss films or topics of discussion in the residence halls. One particular program is called "Test Everything," based on 1 Thessalonians 5:21, which states, "Test everything. Hold on to the good." The residence hall director worked with his RA staff to identify several films and then invited students in his hall to watch the movie and participate in a discussion of the film. Students invited different faculty to take part in the discussion. Often these discussions went late into the night, and there was a free exchange of ideas and, sometimes, heated debate.

Another good example is co-hosting a campus discussion. Westmont College (California) organizes a Focus Week each semester. A team of faculty, student development staff, and campus ministry leaders plan a week in which chapel speakers focus on an assigned topic, and discussions are organized for students and faculty to participate. The theme of the week is also discussed in classes, which often leads to additional conversations outside of class. Azusa Pacific University (California) organizes a chapel series called "Last Lecture." Various faculty are invited to share with students what they would say if this was their last lecture. These lectures also provide good opportunities for discussion.

Many colleges and universities have worked together on first-year experiences. Gordon College (Massachusetts) coordinates its new student orientation with a core class that is required of all new students. The class is entitled "Christianity, Culture, and Character" and is organized by the faculty. Azusa Pacific University offers a four-day wilderness course for student leaders. The course includes a solo wilderness experience in which students are on their own for 24 hours. At the conclusion of the experience, students meet with faculty and student development staff to debrief the event.

"No discipline seems pleasant at the time, but painful. Later on, however, it produces a harvest of righteousness and peace for those who have been trained by it."
—Hebrews 12:11

Several campuses have worked together to address controversial issues. At Wheaton College (Illinois) the provost and vice president for student development worked together on a response to homosexuality, which involved many student development staff and faculty. Student development staff at Wheaton also participated in a shared faculty workshop prior to the beginning of the fall semester by helping to plan the workshop and by providing seminars.

Larger colleges have implemented learning communities in which the same students are enrolled in the same set of classes. This could be connected to an orientation group so that the students overlap with each other in several common classes. Some have even added a living element to this concept. That is, the students are clustered on the same floor. The purpose is to provide continuity with several aspects of the first-year experience. Students develop a strong bond with the students in their classes and with the faculty member who has responsibility for the orientation class.

Learning centers are another good example of collaboration. Students who struggle academically often have more than one issue that is complicating the situation. Having learning center staff that understand developmental theory and can challenge students to organize and prioritize their time commitments is critical. Academic probation students at Huntington University must put together a learning contract with the director of the learning center. Students must include their extracurricular activities as well as their academic obligations. Together with the director they seek to work out a plan that will help the student be successful in and out of the classroom. The learning center at Huntington also provides a seminar on study skills and matches peer tutors with students who are struggling in specific courses. Here the peer tutors gain a better understanding of the material by teaching it, while the struggling student finds the peer tutor to be less threatening than a faculty member.

Obstacles to Effective Collaboration

Collaboration can be a big challenge. It can be time consuming, frustrating, and seem redundant at times. It takes a high level of commitment to the particular collaborative endeavor to achieve success.

Important questions need to be asked. Has student development unwittingly removed itself from major discussions where indeed they have a vested interest? Have narrowly focused academic disciplines disregarded the importance of their counterparts in student development? Are stereotypes reinforced and used as limitations? Identifying potential conflicts can assist us as we seek to overcome them.

The differences in career paths of academic affairs and student development can work against natural collaboration. Faculty tend to have terminal degrees and pursue positions with long term intent, while student development professionals tend not to possess terminal degrees and change positions every two to three years, particularly early in their careers. Due to the high intensity of their work, student development professionals have a much higher attrition rate within the first five years of their careers than their counterparts in the classroom. Academic faculty tend to view their counterparts' young age and lack of experience and/or graduate degrees, for example, as making them less qualified to impact student learning. It is imperative that student development view these positions as professional and avoid a self-fulfilling prophecy by downplaying the positions. Martin and Samels state that career mobility of student development professionals is a hindrance to the profession.[14]

The administrative structure itself can be a hindrance to collaboration. It is not uncommon for student development and academic affairs to report through their respective senior administrators (e.g., dean or vice president), who in turn report to the president. Ideally, the two positions are on par and should encourage collaboration, but often they compete for limited resources, which often results in animosity between the two offices. Universities like Taylor University (Indiana) and Bethel University (Minnesota) have resolved this issue by having the chief student development officer and chief academic officer report to a provost. This structure reinforces the partnership and seeks to create a synergetic milieu for academics and student development. Key positions in student development and campus ministries are also granted faculty status in this structure, which encourages collaborative activities.

Funding is also a concern. Faculty view teaching as the major activity of the college, and student development needs often require additional resources. Students are coming to college expecting more and more services, and when these are not available, they must seek other alternatives or leave the institution. Students today also have more emotional needs than previously. So, the demand for counseling, wellness, and health services has dramatically increased and can be very costly. Students have come to expect assistance with internships, career planning, and placement as well. These are all services that come with a price. As a result, academic and student affairs compete for the same limited resources, which can create a competitive environment rather than one which encourages and fosters collaboration. The human body is used in Scripture to describe the larger body of Christ. Every facet is important and when one part hurts, the entire body hurts. Unfortunately, in Christian higher education, this isn't always the case, and even though there are many reasons to collaborate, competition and jealousy rule the day and can cause division and undermine the mission of the institution.

In addition to these obstacles, Adrianna Kezar indicated that "faculty disciplinary ties, faculty resistance, and lack of established goals" also hindered collaboration.[15] Kezar noted in her research of partnerships between academic and student affairs that, even though there are many obstacles, these are not insurmountable and with senior administrative support can be overcome.[16]

Elizabeth Blake looked at the difference between the personality attributes of faculty members and student development staff. The differences exhibited by both sides offer unique challenges to the collaboration process. Each side is distinct and yet complimentary, and it is important for those involved in the collaboration effort to be aware of the differences and to know how to utilize the strengths of the individuals involved. While these observations could be considered overgeneralizations, Blake has identified several potential conflicts that might hinder collaboration from the start.[17]

Student development staff members, for example, tend to be more extroverted; they are energized by people and find group work rewarding. They often have a high tolerance for ambiguity and can empathize easily with others. They are more spontaneous and are likely to plan on the run, and they can shift from one project to another without much hesitation. They facilitate groups easily and can speak with ease in front of groups. They struggle with writing projects and projects that require extensive planning.

> "We must always change, renew, rejuvenate ourselves; otherwise we harden."
> —Goethe

Faculty members, in contrast, are drawn to the world of ideas and reflection. They like to work alone and are likely to structure their time by planning and preparing. Faculty solve issues or problems with logic and tend to distrust feelings or emotions. Faculty members like to put ideas and thoughts in writing and analyze data to reach conclusions. In light of this, student development might unknowingly create the kind of environment that many faculty members would prefer to avoid.

Because faculty value autonomy, students are encouraged to develop ideas that must be supported by research and analysis. This push for research can promote individualism over a commitment to the larger community. Student development, however, values harmony and seeks to build communities that are supportive and cooperative. Whereas faculty encourage independent thinking, student development fosters a climate of accountability where guidelines are followed.

The differences are noteworthy, but should not be detrimental. Each division compliments the other, and when they work together students benefit from the best possible educational environment.[18]

Additional Benefits of Collaboration

In spite of these concerns, the university benefits when the entire campus collaborates. Bourassa and Kruger noted that student development mission statements have begun to reflect the academic mission of the institution, thus creating more "seamless learning environments."[19] Specifically, the core or general education requirements and the philosophy of education can provide opportunities for the integration of mission statements. The core requirements outline institutional values. Christian liberal arts universities, for example, have a Bible requirement and a liberal arts foundation. The Bible requirement can range from 9-12 hours which each student takes in addition to his or her major. Biblical literacy is a concern, and providing students a good understanding of Scripture is very important. Other areas of emphasis include the arts, natural and social sciences, literature, and history. But the core also seeks to help students understand and appreciate different cultures, enhance interpersonal skills, develop an interest in lifelong learning, and establish a commitment to lifelong wellness. These other skills are consistent with student development goals. Student development can help reinforce these values in residence halls and campus organizations by fostering leadership development and providing opportunities for students to put into practice what they are learning in the classroom. Student development should seek to participate in discussions on general education and on the assessment of the core. The more faculty perceive that student development has a vested interest in the general education requirement, the more they will value the input student development can bring to the discussion.

Teams that include both faculty and student development staff members, such as task force work or other planning committees, benefit from new perspectives. For example, student development views the residence hall environment as more than a place to sleep. Students on a residential campus spend a significant amount of their time outside of class and much of that time in the residence halls. Residence halls might be the most important retention strategy a college can invest in. Providing opportunities for learning and socializing in a residence hall makes a lot of sense, and including faculty in the planning process makes even more sense. Helping faculty understand that residence halls have a learning component could provide further opportunities for collaboration. Another example is to have faculty appointed to the judicial process or the committee that has responsibility for determining student life policy. Again, the purpose is to expand the circle of influence and to invite faculty to help shape the environment.

Students tend to live compartmentalized lives. What happens in one part of the student's life has little influence in another. We know this is not ideal, and by focusing on student learning, we create the kind of environment that is more seamless and less rigid thus making learning a more exciting and challenging activity.

Where Do We Go from Here?

If we value collaboration, then what principles can help promote or enhance existing efforts? First, experience supports the claim that collaboration will not happen by default. Institutions of higher learning must be intentional in creating and supporting collaborative efforts. Banta and Kuh state that senior leadership must model the importance of collaboration.[20] That is, the more emphasis senior administrators place on modeling, offering direction, and extending incentives, the more likely other faculty colleagues are to embrace the need for collaboration. Appointing student development *and* faculty to key decision-making committees communicates the need to collaborate. Seldom is a decision made at that level that does not have an effect, positive or negative, on multiple areas of an institution.

Second, Fuller and Haugabrook note that "much of the actual work of collaboration boils down to team building and attending to the individual relationships behind the larger partnerships."[21] Christian institutions that value relationships will embrace true collaboration when they commit to this core principle. Intentionally building relationships across disciplines and administrative areas affords multiple opportunities to connect and reinforce the value of collaboration. Having a resident director team teach a class with a faculty member or having resident directors audit courses can open doors that otherwise might be difficult to open. Attending campus seminars led by faculty or developing small group studies around a shared interest can have a significant impact on building relationships, and informal relationships can build opportunities for collaboration over time.[22]

> "The body is a unit, though made up of many parts, and though all its parts are many, they form one body."
>
> —Apostle Paul

Third, both the academic affairs and the student development educators have a unique perspective that needs to be shared in order to paint the entire picture of the student experience. It may be too obvious to state, but a Christian institution must intentionally seek input from the different departments on campus in order to operate at its optimal level.

Lastly, the emphasis on learning assessment has raised the bar for academia across the nation. Developing learning outcomes for the academic and student development areas provide a common understanding of what learning means inside and outside the classroom.

Discussion Questions

1. How can the university work together to make student learning the major focus of the university?

2. How does learning occur on the campus? What do we know about learning, and how can it be enhanced by both student and academic affairs?

3. What should guide our efforts to make student learning a major agenda item for the university?

4. How can we move beyond our respective visions to nurture a shared vision for student learning? What is the best way for this to happen?

5. How can the activities inside and outside of the classroom be used more effectively to enhance student learning?

For Further Reading

Association of American Colleges and Universities. *Greater Expectations: A New Vision for Learning as a Nation Goes to College*. Washington, D.C.: Association of American Colleges and Universities, 2002.

Astin, Alexander. *What Matters in College? Four Critical Years Revisited.* San Francisco, Calif.: Jossey-Bass, 1993.

Boyer, Ernest. *College: The Undergraduate Experience in America.* Princeton, NJ: Carnegie Foundation for the Advancement of Teaching, 1987.

Kezar, Adrianna, Deborah Hirsch, and Cathy Burack. *Understanding the Role of Academic and Student Affairs Collaboration in Creating a Successful Learning Environment.* The Jossey-Bass Higher and Adult Education Series. San Francisco, Calif.: Jossey-Bass, 2002.

Kuh, George, J. H. Schuh, E. J. Whitt, & Associates. *Involving Colleges: Encouraging Student Learning and Personal Development Through Out-of-Class Experiences.* San Francisco, Calif.: Jossey-Bass, 1991.

Light, Richard. *Making the Most of College: Students Speak Their Minds.* Cambridge, Mass.: Harvard University Press, 2001.

Nathan, Rebekah. *My Freshman Year: What a Professor Learned by Becoming a Student.* Ithaca, N.Y.: Cornell University Press, 2005.

Chapter 7

Finding and Sustaining Joy in Your New Role

Kina S. Mallard and Mark Sargent

William Henry Devereaux Jr.—a middle-aged professor and the protagonist of Richard Russo's novel *Straight Man*—is in trouble. Plagued by his father's towering scholarly shadow and his own family's quarrels, he finds himself by a strange twist of fortune crawling through the heating ducts above the ceiling tiles of the humanities building, navigating the dust, candy wrappers, mouse droppings, and suffocating humidity, only to overhear his department in the room below voting in his absence whether or not to oust him as chair. There, as he hovers overhead, he has something of a disembodied vision of his own academic life. How many more books could he have read or written if he had not given so many hours to "brain-scalding" meetings like this one? Is this pathetic solitude in a ventilating system the reason he devoted his youthful career to the study of critical theory? Russo's send-up of the American professoriate is a droll hyperbole, but it is all the funnier because it does hit a nerve: so much of academic life can indeed be overcome by doubt, fear, petty rivalries, and inertia.

The Christian college, we hope, offers an alternative vision, but it would be foolish not to realize that some of the same anxieties of Russo's protagonist can infiltrate any academic community. All of us, whether newcomers or veterans, need to remind ourselves often that we should avoid huddling in the usual academic silos and resist the scholarly cynicism that too often dampens our best natures. We have the privilege of working at institutions that can be defined by a transforming vision of Christian community—a society of students and scholars characterized not only by the quest for truth, but also by charity, trust, and grace. David McKenna, former president of Seattle Pacific University and Asbury Theological Seminary, used to say that the distinguishing mark of a Christian college or university should be "joy." That joyfulness stems from deep gratitude for Christ's redemptive work in our lives. It stems from a sense of wonder that we have been granted the minds and the freedom to explore God's creation. But, with all of our busyness and the cross-currents of academic change and decision-making, we can find that being joyful takes work and will.

For educators new to an institution, sustaining joy does require some benevolence, foresight, and discernment. In this chapter we offer a few perspectives on staying joyful throughout your academic journey. First, one begins finding joy in the richest ore of the institution's heritage—those aspects of its culture and history that represent its best promise, its vision for Christian thought and service. One also finds joy in working in community, tackling the mundane, daily duties that steal some of our time but provide occasions to strengthen collaboration and collegiality. To stay joyful does require some maneuvering over institutional roads that have a few potholes; each college does have some idiosyncrasies in practice and policies that can cause the unvigilant to stumble. Finally, joy is found in oneself, in the stretching and exercising of the mental muscle it takes to create the work life you desire, one that is positive, fulfilling, and rooted solely in the service of Christ and others.

Finding Joy in Your Institution's Heritage

Just before the turn of the millennium, when everyone seemed to be turning prophetic, President Bill Clinton told his State of the Union audience that he wanted to build a "bridge to the twenty-first century"—a vision for education full of new technology and experimental zeal. Soon afterwards Paul Willis, a poet, fiction writer, and chair of the English department at Westmont College, was asked about his own vision for his department. With his usual dry wit, he admitted that he was eager to help students build a "bridge to the nineteenth century." Indeed, for literature professors, the nineteenth century is full of wonders: a few hours with Dostoyevsky, Tolstoy, Austen or Dickens promises riches quite different from those of Google. But Willis's remark is more than just an endorsement of Romantic and Victorian classics; it was an appeal to some of the boldest and most innovative edges of nineteenth-century evangelicalism. Christian colleges have taproots in this nineteenth-century evangelical ethos. Whether they began as Bible institutes or denominational seminaries in the late 1800s or were started as liberal arts colleges near the time of the first World War, many modern Christian colleges took inspiration from the spirit of moral reform, social activism, global outreach, educational piety, and biblical study that defined American evangelicalism after the Second Great Awakening of the nineteenth century. Our own institution—Gordon College—began in 1889 as an experimental missionary training institute in the basement of Reverend A. J. Gordon's Baptist Church in Boston. For many new educators at Christian colleges, the nineteenth-century history is a distant shadow. But part of the joy of belonging to a Christian college community is understanding and interpreting that history, not only for oneself but also for one's colleagues and students. To look forward clearly, it is often helpful to look back.

Our culture does not always prompt us to look back. In an era when the half-life of each new technology is defined by months rather than years, and when scholarly knowledge within a discipline nearly doubles in a decade, there is enormous emphasis on staying current in one's field. Compared to the Ivy League schools and the grand roster of elite American colleges, most Christian institutions are relatively young and still in a state of rapid development in scope and quality, and it is easy for new educators to enter an institution with a mandate to help the institution improve and make rapid progress. And, admittedly, as with any era, there are mixed aspects to the record of nineteenth-century evangelicalism (as alluded to in chapter 2). Sometimes Christian colleges would rather let much of its past rest in silence. But in the midst of the motley record of any institution there are powerful stories worth telling, many about veteran colleagues still at the institution. Your enjoyment of your institution and, perhaps more importantly, your ability to build a bridge to its future can depend largely on how well you serve as the custodian of the best of its heritage.

Your enjoyment of your institution and, perhaps more importantly, your ability to build a bridge to its future can depend largely on how well you serve as the custodian of the best of its heritage.

Here's why. In previous centuries, as we have often heard, faculty did it all: they lectured and graded, counseled and preached, managed dorms and discipline, and, from time to time, even did their stint as the college dean or president. The enormous changes in higher education over the past hundred years—more fundraising, public relations, and government lobbying, more academic specialization, more knowledge about the psychology and social needs of young persons, for instance—have led to the professionalization of the separate components of the college. Student development and spiritual formation are now staffed with professionals with master's and doctoral degrees. Most college administrators are not academics. Faculty are divided into schools with their own budgets and increasing autonomy. New scholars often have greater loyalty to their guilds than to their institutions. For the past couple of decades, Christian institutions have exerted considerable efforts to restore a collaborative, holistic vision for college life and learning. There is more focus on communities of educators, rather than just on a curricular faculty with a co-curricular support programs.

Yet despite this new emphasis on holistic education, Christian colleges continue to be diverse in their mission, purpose, quality of students, denominational affiliation, expectations of faculty, staff, and students, behavioral codes, and philosophies of learning. Sometimes these differences have long historic roots, such as the denominational sponsorship of the institution. But many of the changes are more recent, as colleges adapt to reach adult learners, start more applied programs, or loosen some sectarian ties. Faculty and staff are often surprised by the sometimes vast differences of institutions that proclaim a common faith and are, for the most part, focused on undergraduate education.

It is not uncommon for new hires to experience confusion about the purpose of Christian colleges. Each new hire has committed to work at a specific college for a variety of reasons. Some see Christian colleges as a nice place to work where one can depend on everyone holding the same Christian values. Others believe the purpose of Christian colleges is to serve as protectors of the faith or to provide a place to acquire a good education with some Bible courses peppered throughout the curriculum. For others Christian colleges establish a place for people entering church-related vocations or provide a nurturing environment to practice personal piety while earning a degree. Often the decision to accept a job at a Christian college is driven simply by location, cost of living and simply the number of openings during a given search year.

Because faculty and staff hired today become the defenders of the institution's mission in the future, it is critical that they spend time learning as much as possible about their institutions. In his *The Dying of the Light*, James Burtchaell warns about the importance of campus educators holding onto mission:

> College and university histories are in large part given their bearings by official policy documents. But academic kind cannot bear very much reality, and their public declarations are often poorly indicative of what is really under way. Whatever presidents and trustees do, whatever the market forces imposed by those who pay (students and benefactors), the inertial force of these institutions is in their faculties [and staff].[1]

When educators do not fully understand their institutional history, purpose, and mission when hired, they are less likely to own and protect them when challenged by constituents or pressured by low enrollments, tight budget years, social advocacy groups, government policy discussions and the like. (Chapter 9 provides an additional discussion concerning the importance of understanding the "context of place.")

Consider one associate professor at a Christian college. Dr. Johnson came from a solid private liberal arts undergraduate experience. When he was hired, the catalogue referred to the college as a "liberal arts" institution, although it did have a couple of master's degree programs. Professor Johnson was excited to be joining a campus environment similar, he thought, to the college where he graduated. Once on campus he listened closely to the president's convocation address and noticed the phrase "liberal arts-*based* university" used several times. He began to sense that he had joined an institution in rapid change. During his first year two additional graduate programs were approved by the curriculum committee. Economics and physics were dropped as majors; marketing and physical therapy were added. Professor Johnson began to feel he might have made a mistake and began to express anxiety and concern to others about his decision and the institution. Colleges and universities do change over time, highlighting even more the need for clear understanding on the front end and the ability to adapt if needed to institutional changes. Not fully understanding and/or choosing not to embrace the institution's purpose and mission can lead to frustration and disappointment.

The value of studying the institution the first six months on the job cannot be overestimated. Educators who take the initiative to ask questions and seek information about organizational thought and practice concerning mission and process quickly earn the respect of their colleagues and the administration. Questions that can help begin the conversation include:

- What is the history of the college?
- What is the history of the department?
- Who are the college's heroes? The department's heroes?
- What documents are used to drive decision making?
- Is there a strategic plan?
- What measures/surveys are used to assess the department? The college?
- Where are the results of national survey data on teaching, student satisfaction, etc., found?
- What are the demographics of the students?
- Where do I find student profiles?
- What are the unwritten expectations?

For new professionals who are eager to flourish within the institution's mission, we offer the following advice. Ask questions. Learn the stories. Learn about colleagues and alums. Learn about programs, thriving or abandoned. Some of the stories may seem a little dusty, like the old Bible camp photos that may adorn a library wall. But the challenge is to see those stories, even with all of their antiquated features, as harbingers of an institutional future that remains full of promise. And a shared sense of the past—drawn from either nineteenth- or twentieth-century wells—holds special promise for the collaboration between faculty members and co-curricular leaders. It holds promise for the task for integration, for the full-orbed, holistic vision of education.

FINDING JOY IN OTHERS

Faculty and staff workload studies vary, but it's safe to estimate that the average educator at small, Christian colleges spends approximately 20 percent of his or her time in committee meetings. Some educators bloom in these settings while others burn. Those who see committee work as a chore will relate to the words of humorist Richard Armour:

> At meetings of clubs, by a gesture of will
> I always conspire to keep perfectly still;
> For it takes but a word of annoyance or pity
> And, wham, there I am on another committee.

Committee life, indeed, does inspire plenty of groans. Everyone has been saddled with meetings they did not want to endure. And committees do absorb time that could otherwise be devoted to teaching, scholarship, relationships with students, and creating new programs. Some educators, you will notice, actually become good at finding their way onto the committees that seem to meet only every other leap year. But if committee life is ripe for satire, it can also represent some of the academy's highest ideals—the principles of shared governance and democratic decision-making. The intellectual ethos of an institution is often best defined by the vitality and relevance of its committees and can be a place to find joy and fulfillment.

If committee life is ripe for satire, it can also represent some of the academy's highest ideals—the principles of shared governance and democratic decision-making.

It has become increasingly commonplace for new hires to request an exemption from committee service during their first year at the institution. There are some good reasons for this, including both a need to focus on launching one's teaching, program development, and scholarship and a need to learn more about the institutional culture. But committee work is something that can be embraced with earnestness and joy, even in a first year. It is a way of learning institutional history, assessing the culture of decision-making, and establishing interpersonal relationships early.

So how does one flourish in committee life? First, enjoy the social. One of the most valuable aspects of committee life is connecting to colleagues from other disciplines, often individuals with whom you would not, by discipline or disposition, immediately choose to know. All committees have tasks, of course, but the purpose of the committee is not simply its tasks—it is about the communities that are formed when educators simply get together to share their lives and their hopes.

Also, remember that committee conversations, even if they focus on the simple and pragmatic, are almost inevitably a way that educators sort out the "first principles" that direct its ambitions and priorities. When Mark came to Spring Arbor College in rural Michigan as the academic vice president, the institution had just been through some restructuring to accommodate its rapid growth, and in defending the restructuring some professors cited the fact that two full faculty meetings during the previous academic year were devoted to the debate about the dates for spring break. That seemed, at least to some, to be the poster event for institutional inefficiency. And, coming as he did from a larger university in Los Angeles, Mark was certain that he had a few operational and structural suggestions that could help. So, on a public occasion or two, he indicated that some restructuring could help break through the quagmires on such minor issues and insure that faculty did not abdicate their opportunities to engage more vital questions during faculty meetings. Soon, though, he was approached by a few faculty who took some justifiable exception to his critique. The debate about spring break, they claimed, was indeed about something vital. It was about whether the college was going to make every endeavor to align its spring break with the local schools, thereby insuring the ability of faculty and staff to share their break with their families. What Mark presumed to be the experience and sophistication of a larger institution was, in fact, a threat to a cherished value—the will of the college, with all of its competing schedules and pressures, to put a premium on family life. What struck him at first as an obsession with a minor quarrel was, from another view, a bold counter-cultural resistance to the forces that absorb and fragment our lives. By all reports, faculty could laugh at themselves for letting the debate get lead-footed for a while, but the incident was a reminder that even in the debates about some small things there are high principles at stake.

In a bittersweet essay about "Going Home" to rural Fresno as an adult child, Joan Didion describes her urban husband's frustration with her family's tireless discussions about real estate maneuvers in the foothills of the Sierras, only to admit that what her husband never realized is that "when we talk about sales-leasebacks and right-of-way condemnations we are talking in code about the things we like best, the yellow fields and the cottonwoods and the rivers rising and falling and the mountain roads closing when the heavy snow comes in."[2] Committee conversations about some of the minutiae of academic life can, at times, become a code for the things we like best: the sense of freedom and wonder in students, the traditional hymn at the Christmas musical, and the legacy of an esteemed colleague.

Even if we occasionally find poetry and first principles in those long discussions, the inefficiencies of committee life can be exasperating. But there are ways for educators, even in their early years, to help revitalize committee life. The reasons committees stumble are generally obvious: agendas are not clear, little gets done between meetings, and too much time is spent advocating or obstructing one member's ideas. What the best committee members generally have is a synthesizing spirit—an ability to listen well, discern the common ground, anticipate objections, and project a possible solution. Many committee members have done extraordinary work by volunteering to draft the next rendition of a committee's proposal. After a meeting he or she endeavors to capture the heart of the discussion and frame it into a possible solution. Far more often than not, committees are grateful for members who undertake to write the next draft synthesizing its discussions. New educator members often demonstrate their leadership potential by developing that draft and then listening, non-defensively, to the perspectives that will inform a revision.

Harold Heie, former director of the Center for Christian Studies at Gordon College and, quite frankly, one of the best committee members we have known, taught us two important practices for committee work. First, he always came to a meeting with a draft on paper, something to which the members could respond. Second, he reminded faculty about the value of shaping the committee conversation by having others debate his draft. He modeled a practice that garners gratitude from other members for having written a draft, wins trust of colleagues by listening to their advice and critiques, and advances one's own vision by synthesizing the possibilities into a proposal or program that the educators can endorse. Good leaders listen, synthesize, and give vision to the future. Committees provide you an opportunity to shape that vision.

Good leaders listen, synthesize and give vision to the future. Committees provide you an opportunity to shape that vision.

Committees are also places to observe the influence of those in power. Because many decisions are formed at the committee level, the influence of those chosen to "sit" on a committee cannot be underestimated. As Christians we often recoil at the idea of power. The abuse of power in government, church, educational and civic leadership leaves a bitter taste in our mouths and clouds our thinking about how organizations work. Unfortunately, some institutions of higher learning have become political palaces of power where the needs of the students fall low on the list of priorities behind competition for resources, navigation of mega-egos, discussion of unethical practices, and downright stubbornness. When Woodrow Wilson was asked why he was running for governor of New Jersey, the then-Princeton president responded that he wanted out of politics! Despite our feelings about power, it exists. Every organization has people with formal and/or informal power who influence the decisions and direction of the organization. Formal power is given by virtue of title and rank. Those with formal power land on the organizational chart; however, in reality, those with formal power may have little influence but hold a seat at the table where important decisions are made because of their positions in the institutions.

By contrast, employees with informal power are often those with real influence in the organization. Some employees build influence by having strong interpersonal and relational skills or contributing valuable input to critical conversations. It is often hard to pinpoint how they have acquired their informal influence, but knowing where these folks are in an institution and treating them well aids success. Others earn influence by election to key committees, recognition as scholars in their guilds, and sometimes just because they work with or for someone with formal power. For example, one of the key positions for possessing informal power is the administrative assistant who has access to those with influence and can make an off-handed, informal comment that affects major decisions. Much power resides with those on the front line: support staff, RAs, teachers in the classroom, those that students seek first when there are problems.

Business and industry are slowly realizing that power is not confined to the board room, but is organic and active at the lowest and/or most visible level. When Joyce Clifford was hired as vice president of nursing for Beth Israel Hospital in Boston, she turned the power structure on its head. The health care industry was known for the power held by boards and physicians. Everyone served the administration or those with M.D. on their badges. Clifford successfully reformed the thinking of Beth Israel, helping employees from top to bottom understand that if patient care is the goal, then the nurses are those with the most power. They are the front liners who see patients every day and also form the largest group of a hospital's employees.

To some degree higher education already follows this philosophy. At most institutions educators are the front line folks with power over their content, their classes, and institutional governance. Faculty deliver a vote of no confidence and a college president falls. Faculty make a subjective decision to waive an attendance policy or curve a grade and a failing student passes the class. Faculty vote to add a new major and a fledgling department has the chance to flourish. At most of our colleges, faculty have direct access to the provost and even president if they so desire. But power can be deceptive and educators with both informal and formal power find themselves in what

C. S. Lewis refers to as the "Inner Ring," the invisible place where official hierarchy of an organization coincides with its actual workings. Lewis describes the Ring as an unavoidable necessity:

> There must be confidential discussions, and it is not only not a bad thing, it is (in itself) a good thing that personal friendship should grow up between those who work together. And it is perhaps impossible that the official hierarchy of any organization should quite coincide with its actual workings. If the wisest and most energetic people invariably held the highest posts, it might coincide; since they often do not, there must be people in high positions who are really deadweights and people in lower positions who are more important than their rank and seniority would lead you to suppose. [3]

Lewis asserts that the Ring itself is not evil, but the desire to be a part can become one's nemesis. This chapter will not delve into motivation or desire for power, but simply advise that a new educator be aware of the Inner Rings (there are many in any organization), learn from those who belong, and focus his or her motivation on what is best for the college and Christ's kingdom.

Understanding the concept of "relational power" helps one leverage existing power and find one's place of influence in an organization. Relational power is realizing that underneath the individualism of academia there is an appreciation of collaborative work. As Christians we are called to a community of connections. John Bennett, in *Academic Life*, writes that in relational power,

> Sharing with and learning from each other are seen as primary values. Competition is understood in terms of value added. Others are viewed as bearers of intrinsic value that can enrich the self, and vice versa. Relational power is honored and celebrated; the ability to incorporate and reflect contributions from others is judged as a mark of strength, not a lack of power.[4]

Successful leadership, whether as educators leading a class, committee members influencing policy, or department heads managing other employees, depends on allowing others to have significant input. We are reminded in Philippians 2:1-4 that we are to do nothing from selfish ambition or conceit, but in humility regard others as better than ourselves, looking not to our own interest, but to the interests of our students and colleagues. In our view true power is being ready to submit our individual will for the collective will of others. Paraphrasing Richard Foster, it is the freedom to lay down the terrible burden of always having to have our own way, thus finding the freedom to value and serve others.

Finding Joy in Self

A good friend gave this advice to her son: "If you want a different life, live a different life." The advice can be modified to new educators: "If you want positive, joyful work, work positively and joyfully." Humans are by nature critical and cynical, but as Christians we are called to joy, to seeing our work as good, meaningful and transformational. Keeping a joyful heart takes spiritual discipline and the foresight to make good choices. It means seeking the positive in frightening processes like tenure and promotion. It means finding perspective when you receive your course or program evaluations and it means investing time in building social capital, relationships built on trust that will help you professionally and personally when the details of work inevitably steal your joy. Parker Palmer writes:

> Successful leadership, whether as educators leading a class, committee members influencing policy, or department heads managing other employees, depends on allowing others to have significant input.

> what will transform education is not another theory or another book or another formula but a transformed way of being in the world [and in the institution, we would add]. In the midst of the familiar trappings of education—competition, intellectual combat, obsession with a narrow range of facts, credits, credentials—we seek a life illumined by spirit and infused with soul.[5]

Promotion and Tenure

Almost nothing in academic life darkens the soul more than dread about the process of promotion and tenure. The route toward promotion and tenure often seems like some purgatorial mountain that must be climbed, often without the aid of a sympathetic Virgil as one's guide. All of us will hear tales about how good people have perished in the petty rivalries and campus politics that settle, like an ominous cloud, over a review process. And it is often a cloud: the criteria in many personnel reviews can still be opaque and misty.

Admittedly, the stakes for the tenure review are especially high. The possibility that one could be denied tenure—almost always leading to the end of one's job—not only threatens one with the loss of income but also undermines one's sense of worth. For a faculty member who has spent years pursuing a Ph.D., often at great sacrifice of time and resources, tenure becomes the long-awaited affirmation that one belongs in the academy. Yet tenure is a weighty matter for institutions. It is, in most cases, a million-dollar choice: a decision to invest more than six figures in future compensation to secure a faculty member as a lifelong colleague.

Tenure does not always fare well in the popular press: too often it is satirized as a politicized means of protecting deadweight teachers and allowing scholars to either sleep or chase the irrelevant. But such common tales—although not without some shades of truth—vastly misrepresent reality. Not only has tenure contributed profoundly to the intellectual health of American higher education, but personnel reviews at most institutions, especially at Christian ones, tend to be humane and reasonable. Admittedly, there will always be angst about undergoing a review, but in most cases anxieties can be reduced by knowledge. And, while colleges will make efforts to keep new educators aware of the landmarks along the promotion and tenure roads, it is wise to be proactive about getting the map straight on the journey. A few guidelines may help.

First, speak well, not fearfully or suspiciously, of the promotion and tenure processes. You want to belong to an institution that has high standards: if you are going to invest your career in an institution, you'll want colleagues who have proven their mettle. Additionally, you want to belong to an institution that encourages the freedom and trust that tenure offers. Colleges with a tradition of several strong, tenured faculty members generally have a culture of open dialogue and a spirit of mutual respect between educators and administrative leaders.

Second, study the process well—both the written process and the oral tradition. That requires, of course, carefully reading handbooks, speaking with colleagues, and proactively filling some holes that are not readily covered by the written materials. When it comes to defining the criteria for tenure, institutions do vary. Some spell out the criteria and procedures with aeronautic detail; other colleges have less developed handbooks or prefer to keep the criteria more broadly and philosophically pitched, rather than define every iota. No matter the level of details, however, you are likely to have some questions about exact expectations. It is wise to get your questions answered in advance by speaking with the relevant administrator (department chair, dean, or provost).

One of the reasons for this conversation, of course, is to understand the weight given to each portion of the review. Almost all Christian colleges emphasize three aspects of professional work during a tenure review: teaching, scholarship, and service to the institution. Some colleges or universities have additional expectations, such as involvement with the sponsoring denomination. Candidates often wonder about baseline expectations: How many published articles are necessary? What is the minimal score needed on the student evaluations? How many committees must one serve on? The answers to these questions vary by institution and by discipline, and it is unlikely that any institution can give one a quota for each category. Yet an administrator should be able to help educators assess what is relevant for their fields; furthermore, most schools will make models of successful applications available to untenured candidates to review. Having such conversations early in one's career—not in the nervous first week or two, but sometime in the first couple of years—will help insure that one is devoting one's energy to the essential matters from the outset. Many schools have third-year or mid-point reviews during the pre-tenure process to provide faculty such perspective. Even if your school does not, it would be worthwhile to ask for something equivalent to that on your own.

Educators also need to remember that institutions cannot chart every expectation with clinical precision. Promotion and tenure reviews are not, as it were, just the compulsory portion of a figure-skating competition. They are the free style as well. Demonstrating that you have complied with basic expectations in each category will not, in and of itself, impress the judges. Somewhere in your work there must a few triple axels, a salchow now and then. Colleges often are intentionally more general in their description of tenure criteria for the very reason that they do not want the review to be a matter of minimal compliance with an encyclopedic list of standards; rather, they want educators to demonstrate what they have accomplished with the freedom they have been granted. They want to see not just competence, but creativity, energy, and courage.

In this respect, remember that tenure is about looking forward, not simply about documenting the past. Although most schools employ similar procedures for tenure and promotion reviews, there is a vital distinction between them. Promotion, by and large, is an affirmation of what has been achieved. Tenure is a vote of confidence in one's future. Indeed, that vote is often based in part on an assessment of past performance, but it is not difficult to imagine individuals who have compiled strong records—lots of publications and even high teaching scores—who will not make good lifelong colleagues. A strong application, though, demonstrates something more: maturity and wisdom, as well as a nuanced, progressive collegiality. Too many educators allow their cases to rest on what they have accomplished in their guilds. Also, the best teachers tend to be self-aware: they know what works and where they might improve in their teaching. In their promotion and tenure applications they can discuss their work in ways that inspire their colleagues' confidence that they will be educators who will strive, with intrinsic ardor rather than just external pressure, to become better and better at what they do.

Increasingly, Christian colleges are requiring faculty to submit "integration" papers as part of the tenure review process. The rationale is compelling: before granting you the lifelong gift of tenure the institution expects you to demonstrate the ability to explore the interrelationship between faith and learning. These papers can be seen as the synthesis of a candidate's pre-tenure years—as attempts to harvest what educators have learned from teaching, late-night talks with colleagues, and extensive reading, and then to cook up a hearty meal. In other respects these tenure essays are also ways that review committees and trustees can assess the disposition of the candidate's mind. If we grant the faculty member tenure, they ask, what kind of inquiries and scholarly ventures will this scholar bring into the intellectual and spiritual discourse of the campus? Keep both perspectives in mind as you start to think about your paper. If your college keeps models of excellent previous papers, be sure to ask to see them.

Nothing steals your joy faster than reading program and course evaluations. No matter how long you work, the moment when you unseal the envelope and begin perusing student comments is always filled with dread.

While preparing a tenure paper or working on other forms of scholarship you should try to find a happy synthesis between teaching and scholarship. There is no doubt that research and teaching can often be at odds, competing for your time and loyalty. But with some thoughtful foresight and dialogue, you and a department chair can find as much common ground as possible between teaching and scholarship. Many deans or chairs are adept at working with colleagues to arrange teaching and workloads that draw upon the research interests of the educator. This is not mere convenience: conversations about synthesizing your research and teaching endeavors are also ways in which colleges can help faculty and student development educators enrich the learning experience for students by drawing them closer to cutting-edge scholarly pursuits.

Program and Course Evaluations

Nothing steals your joy faster than reading program and course evaluations. No matter how long you work, the moment when you unseal the envelope and begin perusing student comments is always filled with dread. Tenured faculty members who have received outstanding teaching awards can awaken in the middle of the night mentally reviewing that one caustic comment. Student development professionals toss and turn due to evaluations of a program they have poured their heart and soul into. No amount of rationalization relieves them of the feeling, "They don't like me."

Chris Argyris, in his article, "Teaching Smart People How to Learn," argues that most successful people don't know how to process criticism or failure when it occurs. Using the terms "single-loop learning" and "double-loop learning," Argyris believes that because successful leaders rarely experience failure they don't know how to learn from their mistakes and often put the blame on others—single-loop. He advocates double-loop learning where people learn how to reason about their behavior, avoiding defensiveness and examining what might have caused the failure (or in our case, student comments). Argyris discusses two metaphors: the "doom loop" and "doom zoom."[6] According to Argyris, because successful employees rarely fail and are so used to doing their jobs well and receiving accolades, they go into a doom loop of despair when confronted with any kind of negative feedback. And, says Argyris, they don't ease into it, they zoom into it. The program and course evaluation, for example, with its focus on improvement, is tailor-made to send intelligent, diligent educators zooming into the quagmire of doom and gloom.

Fortunately, there are ways for new and veteran educators to sustain joy even in the midst of student criticism. We encourage you to first learn to interpret the quantitative results you receive. Teachers receiving a 3.5 on a 5 point scale might think they are doing well, certainly above average, until they learn that the average for teachers in their department is a 4.3. Numbers mean very little without context. Some institutions publish course evaluation results so you can see where you fit into the bigger picture, and chairs and deans can help you interpret quantitative measures. It is helpful to compare where your results fall on the broad continuum, in your department, your division and the college as a whole.

With the rise of an assessment culture in higher education, more and more programs are being evaluated. From new student orientation to lecture series to intramural sports, students are asked for feedback. Keeping this feedback in context, evaluating percentage of responses, and realizing that every criticism is not a personal one can help educators process student input.

Negative qualitative comments are more difficult to digest. Students, even at our Christian institutions, can be mean-spirited in their remarks. Educators are often shocked by the less than grace-filled way students respond to questions. If you receive comments you perceive as unfair, remember to put them in perspective. Chances are they are a small percentage of the overall feedback you have received and, more often than not, the criticism is invalid. To help you determine how seriously to take those negative comments, ask yourself two questions: "Is the criticism really about me and my teaching" (or is it more about the students' lack of motivation or overall class attitude)? and "Have I received similar criticism from more than one student?" Mentors and trusted colleagues can also serve as sounding boards for educators wounded by course and program evaluations.

Harsh student comments, even if unjustified, can be painful to read and can put us on the defensive, but it is good to remember why student evaluations are important. Sometimes, out of defensiveness, we dismiss or belittle student criticism as naïve or off kilter. But allowing students to comment and advise is an important part of underscoring their dignity within a community of learners and also demonstrating that we have the humility to learn and grow in our work. Student evaluations, remember, are not the final word about teaching or programming; they need to be supplemented by counsel from peers and self-criticism. Yet our work is largely about motivating students and connecting to what they know and perceive. Good educators can calibrate their strategies to connect more fully next time.

On the other hand, when student reviews are very positive you have reason to celebrate—but also to be cautious. Popularity should never be mistaken for excellence. Far too many new educators, enjoying the encouragement of their students, stop maturing in their pedagogy and even feel some sense of superiority over veterans. The best teachers—those who win awards for their craft—see student evaluations as prompts for improvement.

Social Capital

As administrators, when we review promotion and tenure portfolios and as we serve on committees alongside student development professionals and other campus educators, we are reminded of the mental capacity of our colleagues. Christian colleges, rich with intellectual capital yet often poor in financial capital, rarely consider a very important aspect of successful college life: social capital. Much of the important work of teaching and learning, co-curricular programming, and interdisciplinary and interdepartmental initiatives relies on how much social capital an employee has banked. Social capital can be defined as building relationships based on trust and mutual respect, where each person in the relationship is willing to pull together for a common good. Those with social capital make good departmental and institutional citizens.

Social capital can be defined as building relationships based on trust and mutual respect, where each person in the relationship is willing to pull together for a common good. Those with social capital make good departmental and institutional citizens.

Social capital involves the hard work of building authentic relationships that are intentional, purposeful, and based on openness. Authentic relationships are often antithetical to the personality and training of teacher/scholars, with their islands of independence that go against working in harmony and building community.

Educators begin building social capital by intuitively understanding individual and group dynamics and by acquiring the skills of social intelligence. Social intelligence, a relatively new concept, extends emotional intelligence; it involves interacting in groups and is based on the latest findings in biology and brain science that reveal we are "wired to connect." This need to connect or "call to community" influences the way we think, the way we work, and the way we think about our work. Daniel Goleman, originator of the ideas of emotional and social intelligence, organizes the concept of social intelligence into two broad categories: social awareness—what we sense about others; and social facility—what we then do with that awareness.

Social awareness refers to one's ability to understand feelings and thoughts and to "get" complicated social situations. It includes primal empathy (feeling with others), sensing nonverbal emotional signals, attunement (listening with full receptivity), empathetic accuracy (understanding another person's thoughts, feelings, and intentions), and social cognition (knowing how the social world works). Social facility is building on social awareness to allow for smooth, effective interactions. Social facility includes synchrony (interacting smoothly at the nonverbal level), self-presentation (presenting ourselves effectively), influence (shaping the outcome of social interactions), and concern (caring about the other's need and acting accordingly).

Social intelligence comes easily to some educators, but takes work and effort for others. New educators will want to find a trusted colleague to help assess how well they are adapting socially to the institution. For example, consider Professor Simmons, an associate professor who has taught for twenty years at a Christian university. Professor Simmons longs to be recognized as a valuable faculty member and hopes to be nominated for Outstanding Faculty Member. He fantasizes about receiving a teaching award or actually having one of his papers accepted at a regional conference. He realizes he is not part of the "inner ring" and even feels like an outsider in his own department. Dr. Simmons's chair has tried to help him each year during their annual evaluation meeting, but despite numerous conversations, the chair feels that Dr. Simmons is just "clueless." And he is. Even though his tenure is long and his personality is not overly obnoxious, he has not been able to click with any of his colleagues. His blunt comments in committee meetings and his over-attentiveness to minute details have prevented him from gaining credibility on campus. The bottom line is that Dr. Simmons falls short on every aspect of the social facility spectrum. He doesn't interact with others well nonverbally, he doesn't present himself effectively, he is unable to influence positively any social interactions, and he is so self-absorbed he is unable to care about his colleagues.

One's social ability can have a direct tie to one's ability to achieve professionally and is often tied to retention, promotion, and tenure decisions. Robert Boice writes: "Decisions against retention/tenure/promotion (R/T/P) are just as often made subjectively, on the basis of sociability (Can we get along with this person; will he treat students humanely?) and citizenship (Is she likely to carry her share of departmental duties?) as on productivity numbers or teaching ratings."[7] The case can be argued that for one to fail because of quantifiable promotion and tenure criteria one has to prove oneself incompetent beyond doubt. However, to fail because of social problems one only has to be perceived as uncooperative or an outsider in the department.

Studying social networks and developing an understanding of social contexts and expectations within an institution will save more time and angst than it takes. Aligning with positive faculty and staff who are committed to the institution and avoiding naysayers who are skeptical about institutional practice and policies and tend to extend excessive emotional energy on rumors and innuendo helps the new educator maintain a positive attitude about the new job.

The social goal for all new educators should be to avoid becoming what Boice calls a middle-aged, disillusioned colleague (MADC). Becoming a MADC can happen to even the most optimistic, idealistic person if choices, friendships and behaviors go unchecked. MADCs are characterized as those who qualify in five of eight of the following categories:

1. Socially isolated from colleagues
2. Regularly unfriendly to chair [or supervisor]
3. Disruptive in departmental meetings
4. Inactive as scholars/researchers
5. Frequent source of student complaints
6. Shirks student advising
7. Explosive with students and colleagues
8. Commonly suspicious/paranoid[8]

Departmental social capital is critical for influencing change in an organization, developing programs and curricula, requesting resources, and overall peace and harmony in the institution. Developing social capital is not a selfish endeavor because the success of a department relies on how much goodwill has been established across campus. A department can only have as much social capital as its individual team members have acquired. Therefore, each faculty and staff hire has a responsibility to see his or her actions as contributing positively to a greater good that not only influences the reputation of the department, but also of the college.

One of the ways to begin attaining social capital is choosing a good mentor. Research shows that a strong mentoring relationship is a powerful predictor of self-satisfaction and job satisfaction. The old paradigm, where educators work behind closed doors, seldom seeking advice and afraid to ask questions, does not work in the new academic environment that prizes interdisciplinary teaching and research, collaborative and shared governance, and an emphasis on building relationships with students.

> Developing social capital is not a selfish endeavor because the success of a department relies on how much goodwill has been established across campus.

Mentoring relationships happen both formally and informally and many debate the pros and cons. However, for educators new to an institution, a planned institutional mentoring program is important until they can learn the various personalities and expertise of colleagues and then select their own mentors. Caroline J. Simon, in her book *Mentoring for Mission*, warns, "Unless a college institutionalizes its commitment to becoming a mentoring community, overworked educators are unlikely to make time either to be mentors or to be mentored. Assuming that mentoring will 'just happen' may leave those who need it most without a resource that could help them become more effective teachers and scholars. New faculty [and staff] members are too valuable to allow their development to occur haphazardly."[9] If the institution does not provide a mentoring program, the educator should ask his or her supervisor to suggest potential mentors.

Valuable mentoring partnerships do not just happen. We encourage new hires to think reflectively about what they want from the relationship and consider thoughtfully the kind of person they need. As you prepare for mentoring consider what you both want and need from the relationship. What are your teaching, scholarship, and service goals? What parts of the job do you anticipate causing you the most stress? It is important for you to feel a connection with your mentor, but selection of a good mentor involves more than compatibility. Some characteristics to consider in finding the best person who fits your needs include age, academic discipline, personality, research interests, and hobbies.

Not all colleagues make good mentors. It is often difficult for new educators to know who will give strong mentorship. We suggest that you choose a mentor who

- Understands and shares the mission and values of college.

- Pursues his or her own professional development and encourages colleagues to do likewise.
- Exemplifies a strong teaching commitment and provides an environment that fosters creativity and curiosity.
- Perceives his or her work as a "calling" that involves loving God with all their heart, soul, mind, and strength, which inspires one to consider the foundations of his or her discipline from a biblical worldview.
- Embraces knowledge as good with the confidence necessary to pursue truth and beauty knowing that he or she is advancing the vision of God.
- Seeks involvement in the college community through institutional service (i.e., serving on committees, advising student groups) and attendance at campus wide events (special lectures, fine arts events, athletics); while holding biblical principles as priority in balancing his or her time and energy.
- Pursues student relationships.
- Demonstrates mature discipleship of Jesus Christ by growing in obedience to the Scriptures and manifestation of the fruits of the Spirit described in Galatians 5:22.

A 1988 study of faculty mentors shows that new faculty members work best with mentors who are direct, honest, and willing to share their knowledge, allow growth, and give positive, critical feedback.[10] The most important trait in a mentoring relationship is trust. Finding someone you can trust in your new academic environment will probably be your most valuable resource.

The average search for educators at Christian colleges takes approximately two years. For many positions, search committees sift through numerous applications looking for appropriate academic credentials, a history of or potential for successful scholarship, and a statement of faith. Hours are spent debating the pros and cons of candidates, further information is requested, references checked, phone interviews conducted and finally the pool is weeded to the two or three candidates who are invited to campus. Administrative assistants work feverishly arranging the logistics of flights and housing, organizing complicated interview schedules, and assembling important information about the college. A vast amount of time and resources are spent on what is arguably the most important task of higher education, finding the best fit for each institution and each position, the right person to enhance teaching and learning.

Finding the right person presents complex challenges from the viewpoint of the institution as well as for the faculty or staff member hired. Administrators involved in hiring recognize the reality that a new hire is the most expensive investment made and, hopefully, suggests a long-term commitment to the institution. The candidate also realizes the importance of the interview process, but often is distracted during the interview by competing pressures: completing graduate work, teaching a full load or holding down a full-time job outside of education. Studying the institution, reading online and print publications, interviewing faculty, staff, and alumni of the college are luxuries often pushed to the back burner.

No dice were rolled, no coins tossed. Your appointment was not by happenstance. You were called and you accepted the call.

After the whirlwind of the hiring season, new hires return the signed contracts, breathe sighs of relief at having landed jobs, and immediately begin the task of wrapping up loose ends and planning their moves. There is little thought beyond a cursory understanding of the Christian and perhaps denominational commitment of the institution, the location of the college, and some particulars of the job assignment. The new educators often arrive on campus one week before the academic year begins with little time to think about anything more than learning the job, meeting students, planning classes and activities, finding the mailroom, and getting their e-mail working.

As you begin your journey as educators, we hope you will adjust quickly and embrace the institution that has hired you. We encourage you to find joy in the fact that you were chosen. Hiring you was not a flippant decision. No dice were rolled, no coins tossed. Your appointment was not by happenstance. You were called and you accepted the call. It is a calling that will change lives—not only lives of students but of colleagues. And it will change *your* life. Let your joy be full because you have good work to do.

Discussion Questions

1. Choose either your current institution or one with which you are familiar. Discuss the culture of the institution, considering the following questions:

    a. What are the core beliefs?

    b. What are the shared values?

c. How would you describe (in 3 sentences or less) the organizational identity?

d. What are the prevailing attitudes about teaching? Scholarship? Faith? Community?

e. What is the current working climate of the institution? Of your department? Is it collaborative, healthy, positive?

f. Every organization has a pivotal value around which all other values revolve. What is your college's pivotal value?

g. Colleges and universities have norms, standards of expected behavior, speech, and "presentation of self." What are the distinctive norms of your institution?

h. The ideology of an institution is the dominant set of interrelated ideas that explain to members of a community why the important understandings they share "make sense." An ideology gives meaning to the content of a culture. Discuss the ideology of your college or university.

2. Answer the questions you can from the list below. For the unanswered questions, discuss where you can find the information that will lead to a good answer.

What is the history of the college?

What is the history of the department?

Who are the college's heroes? The department's heroes?

What documents are used to drive decision making?

Is there a strategic plan?

What measures/surveys are used to assess the department? The college?

Where are the results of national survey data found?

What are the demographics of the students?

Where do I find student profiles?

What are the unwritten expectations?

3. Describe a time when you served on a highly functional, productive committee. What happened during the committee meetings that made this committee successful? What were the roles of the leaders? Of the members? How can you duplicate the success of this committee in your new role as an educator?

4. Write down your three greatest fears about your new job. Choose one to discuss with the group. What can you do to combat those fears? Who can help you overcome your fears?

5. Discuss what success will look like for you after you complete your first year at your institution. Then consider what success will look like after you complete three years. How does the description of your success differ from those in your group? How is it similar?

For Further Reading

Argyris, Chris. "Teaching Smart People How to Learn." *Harvard Business Review*, May-June 1991, 5-15.

Holmes, Arthur. *The Idea of a Christian College.* 1st ed. Grand Rapids, Mich.: Eerdmans, 1974.

Russo, Richard. *Straight Man.* 1st ed. New York: Random House, 1998.

Palmer, Parker. *The Courage to Teach.* 1st ed. San Francisco, Calif.: Jossey-Bass, 1998.

Chapter 8

Meet George Newfellow

Sabbath Existence as a Way of Life

Todd C. Ream and Brian C. Clark

George Newfellow was a young student development professional with significant potential. In addition to his considerable talents, George was blessed with the opportunity to serve as a residence director at a Christian college in Southern California after finishing his master's degree. This college not only possessed vast resources but also a forward-looking administrative culture which placed a heavy emphasis on professional development. With the support of his colleagues in both student development and academic affairs, George earned his Ph.D. at one of Southern California's highly regarded research universities. Upon completion of his dissertation, George was well prepared to move quickly through the ranks in student development. Several other Christian colleges subsequently showed interest in bringing George to their campus as a mid-level or even a senior-level student development officer.

Following a series of on-campus interviews at a number of Christian colleges, George agreed to serve as the chief student development officer at a Christian college in the upper-Midwest, Heartland Christian College. This college possessed neither the resources nor the administrative culture present at George's previous community. Regardless, George detected a strong sense of camaraderie among his new colleagues and thought he had found a fulfilling place to serve. A month or so into his tenure, George began to feel professionally disoriented. He began to sense that the goals and assumptions which guided the work at his previous institution were not in place where he now found himself. The hours grew longer, and the solutions he found himself pursuing seemed more short-sighted. Day after day the same problems returned only to be met by the same limited range of answers. For George, no end appeared in relation to these problems. As a result, the sense of joy he once found in his vocation began to disappear.

In a moment of despair, he found himself admitting to his wife, Sally, that he wondered if taking this position and moving away from Southern California was a mistake.

While we hope George's predicament is atypical, we wonder if it might prove to be more normative. Despite the impressive mission statements carried by many of our institutions, the daily details of many of our lives are often monopolized by maximizing revenue, increasing student retention, and contending with deferred maintenance. While such details are important, our sense of joy—the joy which George Newfellow at first experienced in his vocation—ebbs away when these details become the defining purpose or end of our existence. When we become people preeminently consumed with maximizing revenue, increasing student retention, or contending with deferred maintenance, our individual and our institutional ends become disoriented. In this chapter we argue that the end of our existence as individuals and that of the institutions we serve is defined by the Sabbath. Failure to recognize a Sabbath existence as a way of life invites the declining sense of joy we see in the life of George Newfellow and perhaps in ourselves. We explore such an existence by detailing these interrelated topics: the presence of competing ways of life in the academy, the significance of the Sabbath as a single day, the significance of the Sabbath as a way of life, the role of worship, and the establishment of an end or purpose for our lives.

Competing Ways of Life

In *Theology and the Public Square: Church, Academy, and Nation*, Gavin D'Costa suggests that the mission of the Christian college is "oriented toward a single vision of the meaning of human life as fulfilled in praise to God."[1] While few administrators or faculty members would challenge this assertion, we face many pressures each day which decrease our ability to carry forward with a single vision. A complete list of these pressures is long, so we will offer three examples at this point.

First, while the state of secularization in our institutions is debatable, its effects nonetheless are still evident. In eloquent detail, works such as James T. Burtchaell's *The Dying of the Light*, George Marsden's *The Soul of the American University*, and Douglas Sloan's *Faith and Knowledge* present the various ways secularization works its way into both the curricular and co-curricular fabric of Christian institutions.[2] At times secularization presents itself as the logical evolution of Christianity. At other times secularization whittles away the essentials of a Christian identity under the guise of broadening appeal. Scholars such as C. John Sommerville now contend that secularity is in decline.[3] However, the effects of the historical record are still intact. In simple terms, campus worship services and course requirements in areas such as philosophy and theology are fewer than they were 100 years ago. The formative demands we place on students are also fewer, so our capacity for the integration of faith and learning is also reduced.

Second, with modernity came the steady pressure for fragmentation within the university. In *The Making of the Modern University,* Julie Reuben presents the story of how matters of morality and intellect were eventually separated from one another.[4] With morality becoming difficult to justify based upon evolving standards of truth, faculty secured control over the emerging array of academic disciplines. The moral questions, pushed out of the classroom, continued to persist and were given over to the emerging class of professionals who came to be known as student development. Ironically, the lines of fragmentation continued to grow and were not limited to the divide emerging between faculty efforts and the efforts of student development professionals. Within the faculty's domain, fault lines surfaced between academic disciplines. As these disciplines continued to proliferate, finding a common identity or aspiration between them became more difficult. In *The Uses of the University,* Clark Kerr goes so far as to pronounce that "multi-versity" may prove to be a more apt description for today's institutions of higher learning than "university."[5]

Third, over the course of the past decade the logic of the market economy has called into question both the nature of the student vocation and that of the academic vocation. In *Universities in the Marketplace,* Derek Bok offers that "What is new about today's commercial practices is not their existence but their unprecedented size and scope."[6] The nature of academic work and its surrounding relationships were once thought to be immune to market pressures. Within even the modern university, those market pressures making their way past campus gates and into the halls of Old Main were dismissed in time. Since the early 1990s, market pressures proved to be more numerous, persistent, and influential for higher education. As a result, academic cultures are now less able to shake these pressures. Some institutions even uncritically embrace them. While for-profit universities have grown in popularity, non-profit universities have become more sensitive to pressures placed upon them by a host of constituencies including students, parents, and corporations—all presenting themselves as consumers.

In an educational environment facing the pressures created by secularization, fragmentation, and commercialization, sustaining a focus on the educational mission can prove difficult. Invariably, these pressures weave themselves into the cultural fabric of Christian institutions. Some institutions, recognizing such pressures quickly, are more readily able to critically encounter them. Other institutions succumb before ever recognizing these pressures exist in their institution. On one level, for colleges and universities as a whole, greater margin provides a greater ability to pursue their respective educational missions. Margin in this sense refers to any number of factors ranging from the size of an endowment to the size of the applicant pool—all of them relate to market pressures and thus bear the subtle yet persistent message that mission is made possible by margin. On another level, for Christian colleges and universities, the very nature of our Christian identity may offer an alternative. Gavin D'Costa asserts that "Rather than human ends at the center, we have God's glory, and from that follows the purpose of humankind."[7] In the next section we propose that a Sabbath existence reflects the placing of God's glory at the center of Christian life.

The Sabbath as a Single Day

Though most Christians readily agree that their lives should glorify God, most balk at the idea of setting aside an entire day each week for the purpose of worship and rest. Their lives are too busy and their work too important to leave for even a few hours. The difficulty lies in a ubiquitous problem. If most people are too busy for their friends and family, how can they realistically devote an entire day each week to rest and worship? Resigning ourselves to the impossibility of the proposition, most of us hurriedly wedge a few minutes of worship into our hectic schedules on Sunday morning, and an afternoon nap if we are lucky, hoping that these experiences are somehow adequate. At some point Christians lost the simple beauty and critical importance of keeping a Sabbath day. We turned worship into a 9:30 service on Sunday morning, Sabbath rest into an afternoon nap, and the observance of an entire Sabbath day into a pre-Industrial Revolution oddity. We must rediscover the significance of the Sabbath day lost by our negligence and make the Sabbath holy once again.

Most balk at the idea of setting aside an entire day each week for the purpose of worship and rest.

The Sabbath day is significant first of all because of its divine precedence. Inseparable from Genesis's creation narrative, the concept of a day of rest is a reminder of God's labor. For six days God created and at the end of the sixth day God deemed his creation good, though not complete. The culmination of God's creative work is not the creation of humanity, as is often assumed, but rather the rest of God. The conclusion comes on the seventh day when God rests from his work of creation, providing an unexpected climax to his awesome display of creative power. The act of creation is not complete until God rests. Norman Wirzba describes this rest as being the creation of "*Menuha*, the rest, tranquility, serenity, and peace of God."[8] This "rest" and "peace of God" extends beyond God's ceasing to continue the initial process of creation. On the seventh day God rests from his labor, and creates a day of rest that he shares with creation. When God rests after creating, he celebrates the first Sabbath with his new creation, and the Sabbath day becomes a divine precedence.

Not something to be forgotten, the first Sabbath day's rest enjoyed by God and his creation is preserved in the Hebrew Sabbath celebration. The Hebrew Sabbath continues the practice of rest begun at creation, allowing the Hebrew people to remember God's act of creation while honoring the Sabbath day. The author of Exodus painstakingly connects celebration of creation and continuation of the first Sabbath rest with the Hebrew observance of a Sabbath day, thus emphasizing the Sabbath's relationship to rest. In such passages, "the seventh day is a Sabbath to the LORD your God . . . for in six days the LORD made the heavens and the earth . . . but he rested on the seventh day. Therefore the LORD blessed the Sabbath day and made it holy."[9] This passage boldly assumes that Sabbath worshipers participate in the rest of God through remembrance and worship when keeping the Sabbath day. The Hebrew Sabbath, therefore, combines action and memory to re-create a living history of the works of God, fusing past and present, while preserving God's rest.

If the remembrance of and participation in the rest of God are not reason enough to identify the Sabbath day as a vital component of human life, the fact that Sabbath keeping is worship offered to God compels us to give the Sabbath this honor. Worship is something we must do because worship is the act for which we are created. When we keep a Sabbath day, we offer one day in seven to God for rest, remembrance, and worship. This act of faithfulness shows that we recognize that our lives both begin and find completion in worship. Understanding the necessity for humans to worship, Norman Wirzba says that "Sabbath, being the climax of creation, is thus the goal toward which all our living should move."[10] Since Sabbath is worship, our lives will gravitate toward it, if we are to fulfill our purpose of worship. The Sabbath is both the last day of the week and the first. It begins our week and is the day toward which our week progresses. When we keep the Sabbath day, we recognize that the essence of our lives is worship.

Worship is something we must do because worship is the act for which we are created.

The Christian equivalent of the Sabbath day of worship is Sunday, which combines the Hebrew understanding of Sabbath rest with a Christian insistence on participation in Christ's resurrection. Sunday unites a Hebrew understanding of remembrance with the Christian experience of hope. Sunday is the day where past, present, and future are joined. It serves as the day where worshipers praise God in the present, while the past looks on and the future brings anticipation of the day when God is glorified and creation is brought to incorruptible perfection. Robert Taft claims that "Sunday was . . . everything" for the early church, a claim recognizing that Sunday incorporates and condenses observance of the whole Christian faith into a single day of the week.[11] Sunday is the day when Christians participate in the liturgy and assemble the body of Christ—remembering creation and participating in the resurrection.

The Sabbath as a Way of Life

The importance of the Sabbath does not end where the day stops. Sunday's close is not the completion of worship. The Sabbath goes far beyond any single day because its illuminating holiness radiates throughout the entire week. The Sabbath is more than twenty-four hours at the end of our week or an island of surrender in the vast, tempestuous ocean of daily life. While keeping the Sabbath day is of vital importance, of equal importance is discovering the Sabbath's significance for the rest of our lives. One must not assume that Monday is any less special than Sunday or that traces of the holy cannot be found throughout the week. The Sabbath is more than a day. Sabbath existence is a way of life.

Practicing the Sabbath way of life takes us far beyond the participation in and remembering of creation that takes place on the Sabbath day. When God created the physical world in Genesis 1, God does much more than simply make water, earth, and sky. God creates patterns for work, worship, and rest. As part of a God-given pattern, they are intended for continual practice. Rather than being simply repeated, work, rest, and worship take on a special significance every time they occur. This understanding of time is expressed by Bruce Chilton when he observes that "the recurrence that time brings is never simply repetition . . . whatever recurs happens in a new context and bears a new meaning."[12] Repetition tends to imply monotony but, in reality, the opposite is true. The pattern of creation infuses the Sabbath life, bringing meaning and freshness to all of human existence. The Sabbath way brings continual renewal to our work and worship, giving them new meaning every time they take place.

While keeping the Sabbath day is of vital importance, of equal importance is discovering the Sabbath's significance for the rest of our lives.

A life informed by the Sabbath recognizes that rest is an integral part of existence and that it necessarily follows work. Humans are created in the image of God and they possess a compulsion to create. Geoffrey Wainwright calls this compulsion becoming "co-creative with God."[13] This human compulsion to create is evident in work modeled after God's act of creation. The Sabbath life participates in the pattern of work and rest found in creation. When we live our lives as a Sabbath, we learn to rest from our work as God rests in Genesis. Because rest follows work it gives purpose to yesterday's accomplishments and prepares us for tomorrow's labor.

> A life informed by the Sabbath recognizes that rest is an integral part of existence and that it necessarily follows work.

The Sabbath life's importance stems from its ability to transcend a single day's celebration and define not only tomorrow but all of the ensuing week. When the Sabbath life is fully grasped, it transforms and reorders us, becoming a lens through which we view the coming week. Our work is given new purpose, as Marva Dawn suggests, because "we remember that we work out of rest rather than in order to deserve it."[14] The effects and benefits of Sunday worship do not end at midnight, but continue throughout the week, forming and informing, defining and divining. When we live the Sabbath life, we are defined by worship and learn to fulfill our created potential. Echoing the words of Augustine, Rodney Clapp writes, "What we worship or ultimately adore is what we live and die for."[15] Sabbath worship prepares us for life, while becoming our life. Eventually the two merge, and our fragmented, sinful selves become whole.

Once our lives find their created purpose and wholeness, the Sabbath becomes a way of life. Our lives become a Sabbath for the Sabbath. The entire week, not just Sunday, becomes Sabbath oriented, anticipating the worship, rest, remembrance, and pattern of the Sabbath day. Six days of the week prepare us for the Sabbath's rest and worship. These days, though not the Sabbath, imitate or mimic the Sabbath and its practices. When our lives become truly Sabbath oriented, our lives move inexorably toward the Sabbath. We look forward to its joy and anticipate its calm. We match the Sabbath's rhythm, and are nourished by the grace God placed in it. Like the ocean's tide washing back and forth across the sand, so too our lives are swept into the Sabbath day by the force of our weekly anticipation and pulled back out into the week by the force of the ebbing tide bringing with us a piece of the Sabbath.

Defined by Worship: The Liturgy

Humans are created for worship. While worship takes place at many times and in many places, at no time is worship more powerful, holy, or natural than in the church's structures of worship on the Christian Sabbath. We are defined by how we worship and by whom we worship. For this reason God jealously keeps Israel for his own in the Old Testament, meeting the Israelites' repeated insistence on idolatry with awesome and terrible displays of divine wrath. Rightly ordered worship preserves humanity's basic identity, but failure to worship God or incorrect worship leads to charges of apostasy and heresy. As a result, the liturgy is an event of great power and consequence. Not something to be taken lightly, this form of worship or liturgy is the focal point of Sunday observance, sustaining our life's worship and safeguarding the sacraments in our worship.

The Sabbath takes on a whole new meaning for Christians when its observance is moved to Sunday, a change signaling more than a change of venue. Christians practice the liturgy on Sunday because, as Justin Martyr observes, "it is the first day on which God, having wrought a change in the darkness and matter, made the world; and Jesus Christ our Saviour on the same day rose from the dead. For He was crucified on the day before that of Saturn (Saturday); and on the day after that of Saturn, which is the day of the Sun, having appeared to His apostles and disciples."[16] Sunday is the day when creation is commemorated and Christ's return anticipated. Sunday worship is not confined to the person or community engaging in it; rather it joins earthly worshipers in the present with vast clouds of past witnesses and the hosts of heaven crying out in unison for the coming perfection. Far more significant than any single day, Sunday bridges all time—past, present, and future.

While possessing peculiar anachronistic qualities connecting us to a community much larger than the present one on earth, the source of Sunday's anachronism is not the day but the liturgy which is the apex of the day. Liturgy defines Sunday, and Sunday defines our lives. Liturgy, then, is the culmination of Sunday, and one cannot understand Sunday's significance without understanding the liturgy. Mark Searle contends that Sunday "stands in continuity with the rest of time and emerges out of it to point to the ultimate meaning of time itself. Like all the sacraments, it is part of the fabric of human life and yet it points beyond it."[17] Sunday is a holy day, but its real significance is derived from participation in the life-sustaining worship preserved in the liturgy. Liturgy is the culmination of our week because liturgy is the purest expression of our created purpose of worship. Christian liturgy unites worship, remembrance, and repetition to preserve our identity. Rodney Clapp defines the liturgy as "a rehearsal of the Christian story" and compares the rehearsal to a dance, saying that the more we do it the better "we learn the dance."[18] Liturgy is worship at its finest and the more we perform it the more we become ourselves. Since we are created for worship we find our true selves on Sunday when we participate in the liturgy.

The liturgy is a life-giving event gaining its power from the sacraments it sustains. When the various parts of the liturgy (prayer, Scripture reading, singing, and preaching) slowly build to a crescendo, the congregation is drawn into participation in the Eucharist. Following in the rich heritage of Christ, the Eucharist unites its participants in remembrance and makes available to all a share in the grace of God. Those members participating in this sacrament are transformed into and renewed as the body of Christ which is the church. Communion is the epitome of worship, so it concludes the liturgy, and defines the day. As a result, Sunday is many things and defined in many ways. Sunday is a day of rest and remembrance, hope and worship, a day defined by liturgy and sacraments, by the church and its head, who is Christ.

A Doxological *Telos*

In his *Doxology: The Praise of God in Worship, Doctrine, and Life,* Geoffrey Wainwright writes that "the sacraments, and Christian worship as such, are the gift and opportunity of new life in anticipation of the final kingdom."[19] In essence, the sacraments correct our view of life. They offer us a way of seeing ourselves and others as God created all of us to be seen. Life, however, offers us a host of alternatives. In higher education, many of these alternatives are driven by larger concerns such as secularization, fragmentation, and commercialization. We easily come to think of our students as mere consumers and ourselves as mere purveyors of services. Our view of life is altered to accept that the highest good is to offer services to more and more consumers. The sacraments correct this view, teaching us to live in anticipation of the life to come. Echoing similar thoughts, John Henry Newman, author of *The Idea of a University,* had inscribed on his memorial tablet, "'*Ex umbris et imaginibus in veritatem*'. Out of unreality into Reality."[20] The sacraments form within us the ability to see Sabbath existence as a way of life—to see the reality residing beyond the unreality persisting all around us.

In essence, the sacraments correct our view of life. They offer us a way of seeing ourselves and others as God created all of us to be seen.

For Christians this sense of reality has what philosophers identify as a *telos* or end purpose. Such an understanding has a long history reaching back to the ancient Greeks. Drawing upon the work of Aristotle and Plato, Thomas Aquinas helped bring this understanding to life for Christians. According to John Milbank and Catherine Pickstock, a Christian understanding of *telos* "is the ecstatic attaining to 'something else' that is yet one's goal, one's rest."[21] Without an understanding of "something else," Christians lack clear goals and thus the rest afforded to us by God. By identifying the purpose of our lives, a *telos* provides us with a means of ordering and evaluating our lives. While many modern philosophers may have little regard for the notion of *telos*, one could argue that all persons consciously or subconsciously possess a perception of their end. Without such an understanding, we lack the ability to justify the particular choices or decisions we make. In essence, all persons consciously or subconsciously perceive their end purpose even if that purpose has succumbed to alternatives such as secularization, fragmentation, and commercialization.

By contrast, a Sabbath existence defined by the sacraments brings Christians into contact with the reality that our *telos* is doxological. In a literal sense, a doxology is a hymn crafted with the intent of offering praise to God. But in a broader sense, our lives are also to have a doxological end or *telos* reflective of efforts to praise God. We learn that all components of the created order were created, redeemed, and sustained not by our own efforts but by God. As a result, the only appropriate response we can offer God is our praise. Alternatives such as secularization, fragmentation, and commercialization lead us into thinking that we, by virtue of our wills, are responsible for creating, redeeming, and sustaining our own existence. For Christians, nothing is less accurate. James K. A. Smith goes so far as to claim that "Truth, therefore, resides in things insofar as things participate in God. . . . As a result, no secular account of things could possibly be true.[22] "Participation" according to Smith, as well as "ecstatic attaining" according to Milbank and Pickstock, are capacities demanding not force of will but resignation and acceptance of God's sovereignty over our lives. As a result, we are left with no other proportional course of action but to offer praise to God. Each Sunday the sacraments bring us back to the point of praise in the hope that the sacraments' lessons will provide us with the doxological *telos* we need to see clearly the significance of our lives' more ordinary details.

For most of us Christian colleges and universities provide us with places where we can think through even these ordinary details of our lives. A doxological *telos* will not remove the challenges our institutions face. However, by knowing who we were created to be and thus what end purpose we are to serve, these challenges appear with greater clarity. The underlying anxiety we face about the larger significance of our decisions is greatly diminished. What is left for us to face includes the smaller details which cumulatively fall in line with a larger doxological *telos*. Administrators such as George Newfellow will still face challenges. Some days will still prove to be difficult; but they will not near the professional disorientation he was beginning to face. With a doxological *telos*, comfort comes in knowing that not only does the end justify the means but also the beginning.

Returning to George Newfellow

Despite the sense of professional disorientation he occasionally faced, George was beginning to feel at home at Heartland Christian College. Most students proved to be a real blessing and he was starting to make headway with students populating the shadow cultures of alcohol and drugs. These students were beginning to see George as someone who was going to uphold the Christian expectations of the institution but also as someone interested in reaching out to them as individuals. He listened to their stories and sought to engage them in ways which were truly redemptive. Some of the students who wrestled alcohol addiction even came to him and asked if he would be willing to help them establish an Alcoholics Anonymous chapter on campus.

In addition, George began to establish meaningful and productive relationships with the faculty. Over the years the curricular and co-curricular components of the life of Heartland Christian had never proved adversarial. But they were never close—and certainly never approached the ideal of being integrated in any significant fashion. George made time to listen to the faculty. He talked to as many of them as he could, ranging from the leaders who had given their lives to the institution to the newest of colleagues. He heard their stories of success about students who had graduated and gone on to do great things. He also heard their stories of failure when students faded away for often inexplicable reasons and never lived up to their potential. Together, George and the faculty began to dream about how they could come together, the curricular and the co-curricular, to foster an environment where all students are challenged and no one simply fades away without significant intervention.

Adding to his growing perception of community was the sense of integration he and Sally were beginning to feel in relation to the church. Both George and Sally found the worship and the biblical study to be transformative. In addition, they also developed several significant friendships with people from the church and, in particular, the Sunday school class they were now attending. When Sally and George had their first child, Ann, several members of their church were overwhelmingly supportive. People Sally had only known for a matter of months threw her a baby shower. In addition, they brought Sally and George meals, even offering to do things around the house for them like yard work. Although George and Sally did not know a single person in this community when they moved, they were beginning to feel at home thanks to their church.

Despite these developing relationships, George felt from time to time a sense of strain between himself and the provost, Dr. Steven Wakefield, whom he served. Like George, the provost was relatively new to Heartland Christian. Prior to his arrival Dr. Wakefield served as the dean of a growing business school at a rival institution.

Although he never proved to be popular with many of the faculty, Dr. Wakefield developed a reputation for initiating programs which attracted students. The primary complaint launched by the faculty at his previous institution was that they lacked sufficient resources to serve all of these students and serve them well. However, the provost to whom Dr. Wakefield reported at that time was overwhelmingly appreciative of the ways he had increased the enrollment by populating new majors.

For almost five years the enrollment at Heartland Christian had decreased. At first the decrease was only ten students. However, the year George arrived at Heartland Christian the enrollment dropped by forty-five students. Since Heartland Christian only had 1,300 students at its largest point (four years prior to George's arrival) and an endowment of $22 million, revenue from tuition was critical. In George's second year the president charged the provost to come up with a plan to end the decrease in enrollment and, at minimum, return the enrollment to 1,300. Since George was responsible for overseeing student persistence, his input proved to be critical in the development of the provost's plan.

One of the most distinctive features of Heartland Christian is its core curriculum. Several years prior a group of theology professors worked with their other colleagues in the humanities to develop an integrated core curriculum, reflecting the highest ideals of liberal learning. Although the classes were demanding, various assessment efforts confirmed that students not only developed a deep appreciation for the humanities but also a deep appreciation for how a Christian worldview draws together the lessons offered by previously disparate disciplines. The level of rigor involved in these courses as reported by several students led Dr. Wakefield to consider whether the core curriculum was partly responsible for Heartland Christian's declining enrollment. After several contentious meetings with the faculty, Dr. Wakefield was prepared to propose that students in various professional fields such as business, education, and nursing, be given the option to take an abbreviated version of the core curriculum. In essence, Dr. Wakefield believed that the core curriculum was outdated for the needs of the majority of today's college students. He was willing to tolerate it for students in the humanities, but for students in the professional fields he contended that the core curriculum was impractical.

After analyzing data from a key student satisfaction survey, George learned that the level of effort students were asked to expend in relation to the core curriculum actually proved to have positive gains for retention. This finding held true regardless of major. While some students complained about these courses, the core curriculum instilled within the majority of students a distinct appreciation for Heartland Christian. On a couple of occasions George tried to share this information with Dr. Wakefield. However, at their most recent meeting, Dr. Wakefield told George that he was prepared to present his proposal to the faculty senate and that he expected George to publicly offer his support for the plan. George left Dr. Wakefield's office quietly that day, unsure whether he was going to be able to offer his support. On one level, George believed that efforts such as Heartland Christian's core curriculum provided the foundation for a Christian education. On another level, George was unsure how he could offer support for a plan when the data he reviewed proved that the provost's position was wrong. However, George knew that offering Dr. Wakefield anything less than his full support at the faculty senate meeting on Monday would be deemed insubordination.

Conclusion

George and Sally's church provided great preaching, baptized new members, and took Eucharist each Sunday. These practices reminded George that his vocational goal had become confused. George realized that the sense of professional disorientation he felt since leaving California was partly due to the fact that he was now more focused on keeping his job than on doing his job. Ultimately he was reminded that the end or *telos* of his vocation was not only for him to offer praise to God but also to help his students develop a comparable understanding. In his opinion, the core curriculum was one of the distinct ways Heartland Christian helped its students develop a doxological *telos*. In addition, George wondered how offering his support to Dr. Wakefield's proposal would serve as an expression of his own doxological *telos*.

When George got home he sat down with Sally and shared with her what he felt he needed to do on Monday morning. He explained that he was going to communicate to Dr. Wakefield prior to the faculty senate meeting that he could not offer his support for his plan. While he did not want Dr. Wakefield to be caught off-guard by his response, he also wanted to be clear with Dr. Wakefield about his position. George acknowledged to Sally that in his current institutional culture this move may be viewed as insubordination and, for better or worse, he served at the pleasure of the provost. Although his decision may create a hardship for his young family, he also offered that he could not take Eucharist as he had done that morning and yet lead a divided existence. If needed, he was prepared to resign his position.

We will leave you to ponder how Dr. Wakefield may have responded to George's communication. Responses could range from thanking George for his input to dismissing him from his position for not offering his support. Regardless, a Sabbath existence as a way of life is not one absent of challenges. However, as Parker Palmer contends, "no punishment anyone lays on you could possibly be worse than the punishment you lay on yourself by conspiring in your own diminishment."[23] The diminishment Palmer has in mind is the divided life we find within ourselves when we lack a sufficient *telos*. For George Newfellow, as for all Christian college and university administrators, our *telos* is doxological. The question we all face is one of faith—will we follow its leading not only in times of great prosperity but also in times of great strain?

Discussion Questions

1. Within the academy what other forces work their way into our lives and shape our priorities? How do they make their presence known to us? How do they shape our sense of purpose?

2. How might one order a Sabbath existence if unable to observe a Sabbath on the day of worship?

3. What spiritual disciplines can be practiced throughout the week that will aid in the creation and upkeep of the Sabbath lifestyle?

4. Can one claim the title of Christian educator if he or she does not participate in the liturgy in any kind of consistent manner? To what extent does the liturgy define our Christian identity?

5. How often do you think about the end or purpose of your life? In what ways can a doxological *telos* help you to critically engage other forces which work their way into your life and shape your priorities?

6. Is George's situation unique? Is the kind of conflict George faced always so readily apparent to us?

For Further Reading

Bass, D. C. *Receiving the Day: Christian Practices and the Gift of Time*. San Francisco, Calif.: Jossey-Bass, 2000.

Clapp, Rodney. *A Peculiar People: The Church as Culture in a Post-modern Christian Society*. Downers Grove, Ill.: InterVarsity Press, 1996.

D'Costa, G. *Theology in the Public Square: Church, Academy, and Nation.* Malden, Mass.: Blackwell Publishing, 2005.

Palmer, Parker. *The Courage to Teach: Exploring the Inner Landscape of a Teacher's Life*. San Francisco, Calif.: Jossey-Bass, 1998.

Wirzba, N. *Living the Sabbath: Discovering the Rhythms of Rest and Delight*. Grand Rapids, Mich.: Brazos Press, 2006.

CHAPTER 9

NEGOTIATING LEADING AND BEING LED

Mark J. Troyer

As Christian student development and faculty educators, we have the privilege of impacting colleagues and students in diverse ways, and this privilege should not be taken lightly. Scripture reminds us about the weight of an educator's role. As a preface to his discussion on the power of the tongue, James warns that "not many of you should presume to be teachers, my brothers, because you know that we who teach will be judged more strictly."[1] As educators we have been called to a community in which our words, actions, and attitudes can have significant impact.

It is imperative for new student development and academic affairs educators to think strategically and intentionally about issues of leadership. We are called to follow Christ's model of servanthood, as portrayed in the Gospels. But what does that look like on our campuses today? Scholarly writing and popular literature is exploding with theories and models of leadership. The old industrial, top-down models of leadership are giving way to more collaborative, transformational models that, frankly, are more difficult to navigate but better reflect what Scripture teaches. This chapter explores aspects of leadership and issues a challenge to grow in our leadership skills.

This chapter is divided into four main sections. Section one explores models of leadership that are important for the Christian college environment. Sections two and three explore "context" in leadership and being intentional about development of leadership skills. Finally, section four provides practical applications.

Let's look first at the work of two men of faith who have written small but powerful books that provide a context for this initial discussion. Francis Schaeffer's book *The Mark of a Christian*, based upon John 13:34-35, illustrates Jesus' point that the distinguishing mark of a Christian is the love shown to others.[2] Dietrich Bonhoeffer makes a similar point in *Life Together*, where he discusses Christian community. Bonhoeffer, who became a martyr at the hands of the Nazis in 1945, writes of the importance of

Christian fellowship and of the incomparable joy and strength Christians can receive through the physical presence of other believers.[3] The words of the Gospel writer John, Bonhoeffer, and Schaeffer help set the important context of relationships in which we view the nature of leadership.

The way believers approach leading and being led should be different. We should live our lives together in such a way that our love for one another is obvious and engaging. Theories of leadership and power should be understood and applied within this New Testament approach that includes a commitment to community. Non-believers should recognize that we are Christ's disciples by the love that we have for each other, regardless of the power structures or contexts in which our leadership is exhibited.

DEFINING LEADERSHIP

Let's take a step back and explore the contemporary definitions of leadership. If anyone perused the local bookstore or Googled the term *leadership*, he or she would have noticed a growing number of authors. This list would include writers from the Christian community, the political arena, and the business sector, all trying to take advantage of the recent interest in leadership. Unfortunately, as Bernard Bass states in his *Handbook of Leadership*, "there are almost as many definitions of leadership as there are persons who have attempted to define the concept."[4] This chapter does not explore the history of leadership studies, but it does survey some of the influential principles that have shaped today's leadership theory.

In Matthew 20, the mother of James and John asked Jesus if one of her sons could sit at Jesus' right hand and the other on the left, basically requesting positions of prominence or leadership for her sons. Jesus responded in a very interesting way. He did not deny that someone could be in those positions; instead, he refocused the discussion by talking about the rulers of the Gentiles, who demonstrated a worldly approach to leading, as opposed to the one he encouraged the disciples to take. Eugene Peterson's paraphrase of the New Testament gives a fresh look at this passage in Matthew 20:24-28:

> When the ten others heard about this, they lost their tempers, thoroughly disgusted with the two brothers. So Jesus got them together to settle things down. He said, "You've observed how godless rulers throw their weight around, how quickly a little power goes to their heads. It's not going to be that way with you. Whoever wants to be great among you must first be your slave. That is what the Son of Man has done: He came to serve, not to be served. . . . "[5]

It is interesting to see a parallel between some current leadership models and this passage in Matthew. Here, Jesus was giving an opinion concerning the practices of the rulers of the day and their top-down, "lord it over" approach. Though they may have had positional authority, their style and approach to interacting with others was not consistent with the way Jesus viewed effective leadership.

Joseph Rost, in his book *Leadership for the Twenty-First Century*, made the case that the approach to leadership prior to the mid-twentieth century was based on an industrial model or a top-down approach where a positional leader made the decisions, set the goals, and determined the vision. He argued that the industrial approach to leadership was focused more on a positional authority and less on the relationships between leaders and followers.

Much of today's literature suggests a change. Bernard Bass and Joseph Rost have reviewed over five thousand works on the topic of leadership.[6] Their works point to some common themes in leadership definitions, which now include such terms as "relationships," "interaction," and "change." Additionally, John Gardner wrote about a process of leadership that includes a leadership team working toward shared objectives.[7] Concurrently, Ron Heifetz, who taught the first Harvard class dedicated to leadership development, wrote in his book *Leadership without Easy Answers* that leadership should be viewed as an "activity" and that leadership can "happen from multiple positions in a social structure."[8] In all of these noted works, leadership is viewed as a "functional role in a group, which may be taken up later by another individual depending on the needs and tasks of the group."[9] This suggests a growing realization that leadership is more than something that a person in authority has or does. Jesus taught this concept to the disciples nearly two thousand years ago. Serving and putting others' interest first is a concept that enhances society.

A leadership model based upon social change was developed in the mid-1990s by an ensemble of higher education practitioners led by Helen and Alexander Astin at the University of California, Los Angeles. This model of leadership development, which minimized the positional approach, will be explored more fully later in the chapter. But what is important to note here is that for them "A leader is not necessarily a person who holds some formal position of leadership or who is perceived as a leader by others. Rather, we regard a leader as one who is able to effect positive change for the betterment of others, the community and society."[10] I believe this is what Christian higher education should be about. The gospel message can and should effect positive change. Contemporary views of leadership are beginning to look more and more like the servanthood approach that Christ espoused in the New Testament.

Contemporary views of leadership are beginning to look more and more like the servanthood approach that Christ espoused in the New Testament.

When we view leadership as a process or an interaction, by default the relational component becomes more prominent. Joseph Rost, after reviewing hundreds of works on leadership, crafted a definition that many see as the most recent turning point in leadership theory. In his post-industrial paradigm, "Leadership is an influence relationship among leaders and their collaborators who intend real changes that reflect their mutual purposes."[11] Rost advocated the notion that leadership "does not require a position out of which to operate," but that "leadership occurs within a dynamic system and group as they work toward real change."[12]

If we embrace the more relational, process-oriented, others-centered definitions of leadership, then as new educators we have a responsibility to develop our leadership capacities regardless of our position. In addition, we are called to develop the leadership skills in those around us so that the "process" of leadership can operate more successfully. We have an opportunity in Christian higher education to model leadership relationships that are loving, honoring, and Christ-like. The world is hungry for these types of interactions.

LEADERSHIP IN CONTEXT

Context of Place

When we begin our work at a university, one of our first tasks is to get acclimated to the new environment. It is easy to think first of locating the bookstore, checking out the new office, finding the coffee shop, or discovering a favorite place for informal interaction with colleagues. But we are not as apt to spend time learning the history of the institution and the current challenges that it faces. Other significant questions tend to go unasked, like: What are the important components of the university's mission statements and founding documents? What is the history of my department? How long has it operated under its present organization, and what are the newest innovative programs?

The answers to these questions expose how leadership works on a particular campus, and these answers will shape how you move forward and shape the future. For example, I examined the history of a particular college's no-debt policy, a policy that had been voted into place by a board of trustees more than fifty years before. After interviewing administrators and reading historical documents, I began to understand and appreciate why these decisions were made. My study shed light on the school's historical financial pressures. This contextualized the past decisions and informed the current leadership on how to navigate the future.

When we understand our institution's history, we begin to appreciate and connect to it in a deeper way. Leadership involves influence, influence requires relationships, and relationships take time and energy. Too often, we live in silos—just paying attention to our own areas and not building relationships on and off campus. Effective leadership involves doing the hard work of understanding your community.

Leadership involves influence, influence requires relationships, and relationships take time and energy.

In his research, James O'Toole found that organizational leadership factors were more important performance drivers than simply a strong individual at the helm.[13] Specifically, he found that the better organizations were ones that had institutionalized key tasks and responsibilities of leadership into the systems, practices, and cultures of the organization. Taking his principle to heart, we must be familiar with our institution's systems to be able to effect change. O'Toole also found that organizations that had a high LQ (Leadership Quotient) operated in ways where people acted more like owners and entrepreneurs: they took initiative to solve problems, willingly accepted accountability for meeting commitments and for living the values of the institution, shared a common philosophy and language of leadership which included tolerance for contrary views, and maintained adherence to systems that were designed to measure and reward appropriate behaviors.[14] The degree to which your institution or department incorporates these operational practices will be important clues to how you should adjust your own leadership style.

Context of People

In any institution you will have influence with a circle of people. In some instances, your circle will be comprised mainly of student staff; in others it will involve fellow professionals. Perhaps your circle may even include graduate students or off campus colleagues in a particular field of study. As important as it is to understand the context of place, it is equally if not more important to understand the people with whom God has granted us community. For effective leadership to take place, we must understand those with whom we are in relationship. It is easy, though inaccurate, to assume that the people we work with are similar to us in how they set goals, make decisions, work on projects, or deal with conflict.

God is a creative God. He has given each of us specific talents and weaknesses. First Corinthians 12 is a great reminder of the complexity of humanity and the creativity of God. After Paul's discussion of spiritual gifts, he uses the metaphor of the body to describe the diversity of the believer's community. He states that the body isn't just a single part. It's a combination of diverse parts arranged and functioning together. He writes,

> if Foot said, "I'm not elegant like Hand, embellished with rings; I guess I don't belong to this body," would that make it so? If Ear said, "I'm not beautiful like Eye, limpid and expressive; I don't deserve a place on the head," would you want to remove it from the body? . . . No matter how significant you are, it is only because of what you are a part of. An enormous eye or a gigantic hand wouldn't be a body, but a monster. . . . You are Christ's body—that's who you are! You must never forget this. Only as you accept the role that your part of that body plays does your "part" mean anything.[15]

In order for us to be effective in our leadership, we must do the hard work of getting to know those colleagues, students, direct reports, and supervisors in our circle of influence. Clarifying questions help us understand who they are: Are they initiators or responders? Do they make decisions based on facts or feelings? Are they more task-oriented in their approach to work or are they more people-oriented? Do they play the role of the hand as Paul described in 1 Corinthians or are they a limpid eye? In addition to these clarifying questions, several assessment instruments can help. For example, you may wish to use personality profile tests or personality type indicators to name but two. These tests can help us assess ourselves and others with respect to behavioral tendencies and approaches to leadership. The important point is that we must continually examine ourselves and others in regard to leadership capacities and tendencies.

The Social Change Model of Leadership Development mentioned earlier is based on the idea that there are a variety of different values and concepts important in developing student leaders. The model is used as a way to examine one's own leadership approaches and capacities, as well as to provide a grid for helping to develop leadership skills in the people with whom you are associated.[16] Unlike other approaches, the model focuses on individual capacities, group dynamics, and the influence of the larger community on leadership. I believe this represents sensitivity to "kingdom" values.

Specifically, this approach examines leadership development from three different perspectives that include a total of seven values or "C"s of leadership. The arrows indicate that each perspective or value informs and influences the others.

The *Individual* circle addresses personal values and qualities we are encouraging those around us to incorporate. *Consciousness of Self*, *Congruence*, and *Commitment* make up those individual circle values. Consciousness of self is defined as how well I recognize the values, beliefs, and attitudes that encourage me to take action. Congruence refers to behaving with consistency, authenticity, and honesty toward others. Commitment implies a passion and energy that motivates one to serve.

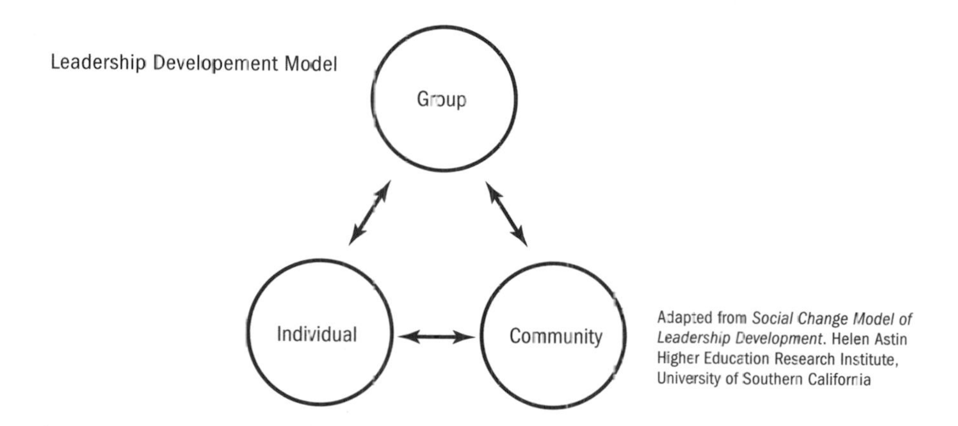

The *Group* circle addresses how *Collaboration, Common Purpose,* and *Controversy with Civility* can be fostered to accelerate positive change. Collaboration becomes the cornerstone of the group process by empowering others through trust; it capitalizes on the multiple talents, abilities, and gifts of the group. Common purpose means to work with shared vision and values. And once established continual communication becomes vital. Finally, conflict with civility allows the recognition that differences in viewpoints are a normal part of the leadership process. Conflict is inevitable, but how we handle it speaks volumes about our walk with God and our love for each other.

The Community/Kingdom circle incorporates *Citizenship*. This is the seventh "C" of this model and calls us to be full participants in the community in which we work and live. I like to think of this area as kingdom values. It asks the question, "How am I leaving it better than I found it?" Intentionally participating in and working for positive change in our institutions and community should be a mark of a Christian leader. By examining ourselves in light of this model and by using it as a tool to supervise and influence others, we can enhance or create a healthy culture of leadership development.

Leadership Power and Conflict

A significant aspect of leadership is how one manages conflict. As Christian educators we have pursued positions in higher education for a number of reasons: the passion for developing others, interest in a particular field of study, or because of a sense of calling. Unfortunately, in our daily operation these differences can sometimes create situations where conflict arises. How we approach and address these issues of power and conflict will go a long way in making our leadership experience successful.

Sometimes the frustrations within our chosen workplace surprise us. Bonhoeffer's book, *Life Together,* provides a refreshing yet convicting reminder of how we should frame our actions within the community to which we are called.

> Because God has already laid the only foundation of our fellowship, because God has bound us together in one body with other Christians in Jesus Christ, long before we entered into common life with them, we enter into that common life not as demanders but as thankful recipients. We thank God for what He has done for us. We thank God for giving us brethren who live by His call, by His forgiveness, and his promise. We do not complain of what God does not give us; we rather thank God for what he does give us daily. And is not what has been given us enough: brother, who will go on living with us through sin and need under the blessing of His Grace: Is the divine gift of Christian fellowship anything less than this, any day, even the most difficult and distressing day? Even when sin and misunderstanding burden the communal life, is not the sinning brother still a brother, with whom I, too, stand under the Word of Christ?[17]

Reframing relationships with colleagues the way Bonhoeffer describes can help us to graciously practice patience, which is a hallmark of a good leader.

Janet Hagberg, in her book *Real Power,* discusses the stages of personal power as 1) Powerlessness, 2) Power by Association, 3) Power by Achievement, 4) Power by Reflection, 5) Power by Purpose, and 6) Power by Wisdom. She identifies stage three, Power by Achievement, as the stage where many of us reside because of positional influence. As Hagberg puts it, "this is the most externally oriented of the stages, the stage where most of our power comes from outside ourselves, from making things happen, and from external recognition."[18] A new position at a university brings with it the trappings and privileges of power based on our achievements. It is important to be careful with that newfound influence. In some cases we are given more credit than we deserve; in others more blame. Such is the challenge of leadership.

Conflict and power issues are real even in a place where most would say they are Christ-followers

It is essential to think critically about influence, especially when we realize that even our communications have impact for today and for many years to come. Our statements and policies have a profound effect on staff and colleagues; and as our influence increases we should exercise even more care. It is important to ask questions like, "How would I like to be treated?" and "What are the implications of my influence from an organizational, interpersonal, political, and spiritual perspective?" Looking at issues through multiple lenses is vital.

Hagberg's model stresses the importance of a commitment to personal reflection, establishing purpose, nurturing your spiritual life, and allowing yourself to be led by the Holy One, as keys to developing true personal power, not just position or achievement power. Having someone in your life to assist with reflection, to bounce ideas off of, and to listen to you is essential. God has made us relational beings, and once we earn the position of faculty member, chair, dean, or director we are not automatically provided with all the answers. Being aware of our place, being intentional in our reflections, and being honest with our shortcomings will help us appropriately manage our influence.

There will be times when each of us will be powerless to influence change or to solve a problem. In those times we must remind ourselves that change often comes more slowly than expected. During those times, being a person of integrity, doing the best possible job with the resources given, being thankful, and growing in intimacy with Christ will allow you to "be content in whatever the circumstances," as the Apostle Paul put it.[19] Ironically, this contentment and intimacy will lead to more personal power.

Conflict with colleagues, with students, and with subordinates is an issue that all of us face. A plaque in the lobby of the Chapel at Asbury College displays a quote from E. Stanley Jones, an early 1900s evangelist, that says, "Here we enter a fellowship, sometimes we will agree to differ, but always we will resolve to love and unite to serve."[20] God calls us to love one another, but he does not call us to avoid conflict. Conflict occurs most often when communication has lapsed or when our goal and someone else's are not being met or are incompatible. These situations force each one of us to ask the questions: "Do I deal with it head on, do I let it go, or do I avoid it?" and "How do I communicate—e-mail or face to face?" Matthew 18 deals specifically with conflicts between brothers. Matthew states that we should first talk privately with the person with whom we are in conflict. This can seem unnatural, as it is too easy to involve others in the conflict for the purpose of gaining support.

The information age has ushered in technology for instant messaging, e-mail, personal Web sites, and text messages. This in effect allows us to avoid face to face interactions. I would propose as a leadership principle that we should be careful and think critically about the modes of communication we use in dealing with others in conflicts. Quentin Schultz, in *Habits of the High-Tech Heart*, puts it this way: "Although we have more technologically aided communication than ever, the individual in society is feeling increasingly isolated and is searching for new ways to experience meaningful togetherness."[21] I am aware of students using instant messaging to communicate with each other in their room while having an argument! Although this is extreme, I am also aware of faculty members who have had a heated e-mail argument but who avoid acknowledging that it took place when interacting publicly.

In James 3 the writer defines real wisdom as a "holy life characterized by getting along with others." He then described a healthy, robust community as one that "lives right with God and enjoys its results only if you do the hard work of getting along with each other, treating each other with dignity and honor."[22] We should commit to each other to work through challenges face to face. A colleague established a rule for himself that I believe has merit for all of us: once an e-mail exchange involving conflict passes three interactions, he stops and makes sure that the issue is dealt with face to face.

We should think very carefully about the modes of communication we are willing to use in dealing with others in disagreements, conflicts, and even discussions

As a professional in higher education, you will experience conflict. It will be very important to think about how you will approach your colleagues, how you will deal with students, and what parameters for conflict resolution you will set with your staff. Time together is very important. In my area we use the term "face time" for encouraging the direct interaction that is so important in building and leading a community. Take advantage of the walk across campus to have that short discussion with a faculty member or go to the student union and track down a student. Could it be done quicker through e-mail? Probably. Does e-mail provide the same human connection that may be beneficial later when a larger issue arises? Probably not. Let us all think critically about the ways we communicate.

In the following section, I encourage us to think about the practical applications of leadership within academic and student affairs.

Academic Affairs Applications

Leadership in the academic arena is sometimes complicated. Circles of influence range from the students in the major to colleagues in the department. The circles also include divisional differences and specific committees assigned in the organizational structure of the campus. Faculty members are also involved in advising students and student organizations, a role for which they may have little or no experience.

Leadership opportunities as a new faculty member fall into a couple of different contexts. The first is developing relationships of influence with colleagues. The second is developing similar relationships with students. As stated earlier in the chapter, it is important to be a "student" of the institution. Learn the history of your particular department, the structure and organization of the faculty senate and other governing bodies, noting the formal and informal power structures. Understanding what the previous battles have been, what the current visions and goals are, and how the leadership structures on campus are organized will be fundamental for establishing influence.

Seek to understand, then seek to be understood.

Emerging leadership models speak much of the networks and webs of relationships that form the fabric of an institution. As an educator within a specific discipline, it would be easy to become isolated and separated from others across campus as you prepare for classes, grade papers, conduct research, and advise students. Being purposeful in meeting others and entering into collaborative projects that involve your passions and expertise will enhance the impact you can have on a campus. It is within these experiences that the leadership opportunities, formal or informal, will present themselves. Be involved in the life of the institution both within the decision-making structures and in the lives of the students.

Developing open communication with department chairs, deans, and those within the academic administration is important. If people do not know your interests, then they are not able to include you in discussions and decisions. Leading effectively in an educational structure that values autonomy and engagement in off-campus organizations means on-campus communication is even more important.

A faculty member's influence on students is a significant power issue. Students are at a formative time in life, and our influence on them is much stronger than we imagine. In leading students, whether in a formal organization such as a club advisor or through academic advising, we should exercise care. Set parameters and openly communicate about what others can expect from you. Students who invite faculty to be a part of their groups sometimes have very different expectations than the faculty who get involved.

Recently I had a conversation with two student leaders who were frustrated with the campus organization's faculty advisor. As we explored their frustrations, it became evident that they and the faculty member had a significantly different opinion about the leadership role of the advisor. When asked if they had discussed the issue with the faculty member, they responded, "We just assumed." Assumptions about the roles and expectations of faculty leadership are often misguided. Communicating openly with students (and with colleagues on committees) about leadership and influence issues can help minimize conflict and maximize effectiveness.

As faculty it is easy to be caught up with the discipline of study and become isolated from the rest of the campus. Our focus tends to be how policies and directives impact our area rather than the whole campus. Patrick Lencioni, in *The Five Dysfunctions of a Team*, highlights the ubiquitous temptation to place our departments, career aspirations, or ego ahead of the collective well-being of the institution.[23] As believers we are not immune to those tendencies. The stresses of research, tenure, and staying ahead in the field are real, but the rewards of being involved in leadership relationships with students and colleagues are rich.

I have encouraged you to seek out leadership opportunities, but in your busyness be careful to nourish the soul. Hagberg describes the leaders who have reached the higher stages of personal power as those who have "taken the inner journey" and "have a peace even in chaos, they are clear and undiluted, they are compassionate, they are courageous, and they listen to their calling."[24]

STUDENT DEVELOPMENT APPLICATIONS

As with the academic faculty, student development educators face leadership contexts on multiple levels. In addition, many positions in student development include a "staff" of students such as resident assistants, orientation leaders, and student admissions counselors. Student development educators find themselves in leadership roles that have unique challenges in navigating relationships with students, colleagues, and supervisors.

As a new professional recognize that you will develop an informed opinion on the workings of your area. When you communicate your opinion, do it carefully. It is a biblical principle to learn how to be quick to listen, slow to speak, and slow to anger. Take time understanding the department, the college, the expectations, and the culture of your place before you "enlighten" your colleagues with your informed opinion.

In one of my first positions in student development, I moved to a school where I immediately decided that, "If I'm here more than a few years, that policy needs to change." My vice president, seeing my zeal and ideological enthusiasm, wisely advised me to wait for a year and then see if I still felt the same way. That was great advice. After a year I understood the history of the institution, the context of the policy, and the culture of the school; taken together these reversed my original conclusion.

Seek to understand and then to be understood, goes the common adage. Student development educators sometimes feel that they have to fight to be respected, that as practitioners and not scholars they are assigned a different value. I have found that respect comes through open relationships and excellence in work. Take the opportunity to be involved in campus-wide collaborative projects and committees. When involved in those new leadership relationships, be aware of your own leadership tendencies. That first circle in the Social Change Model deals with consciousness of self—taking every opportunity to deepen your understanding of how God has gifted you and to recognize areas of needed growth. Supervisors love to have teachable staff. Be willing to ask the hard questions of those who are more seasoned; ask them their perception of your strengths and areas for improvement.

As you have opportunity to work with a staff, be it a professional staff or student staff, it is important to build an expectation of leadership growth. It is helpful to select a model or a paradigm of leadership and use that as a way to frame how your staff will work and grow together. Be intentional about verbalizing goals, objectives, processes for dealing with conflict, and processes for dealing with success. The expectation that we will be continually learning and growing together is a transformational approach to leadership that honors the people with whom we work.

It is important to acknowledge that not all the people on your staff are similar in decision making, work style, motivation, time management, and other leadership competencies. Creating an environment where group members not only understand themselves, but also understand how others on the staff operate will go a long way to enhance the staff's success. Many assessment instruments such as Myers-Briggs, Leadership Practices Inventory, DISC, and StrengthsFinder© are helpful to give structure to discussions about building a team and developing leadership capacities.

As you work with specific student groups or individual students, you should also understand the power and influence afforded you. Our language, our attitude, and our habits will be continually watched and evaluated. In 1 Corinthians 4 Paul urged the believers in Corinth to "imitate me."[25] Can you say that to the students with whom you work? Modeling the virtues that we espouse speaks louder than what we say. As we interact with students, we should be conscious of building systems, expectations, and relationships that are transformative. It is a compliment for someone to say, "Things would continue to operate smoothly, even if Jane left." The statement indicates that Jane's focus was on developing and encouraging leaders around her.

Navigating the leadership waters of higher education is a continually changing process. Being intentional about your own spiritual growth, about critically examining how you operate in the context of your institution, and about putting tools in your and others' toolboxes goes a long way in facilitating God's work.

Discussion Questions

1. How have I viewed leadership in the past and what constitutes good leadership?

2. What is the model of leadership that seems to function in my department?

3. What do I know about my own preferences and approaches to working with others and solving problems?

4. What are some of the historical milestones in my institution? In my department?

5. Of the seven "C"s of leadership in the Social Change Model of Leadership, what are the areas that I need to be more intentional in developing?

6. What am I and those in my circle of influence doing to be intentional about strengthening our influence relationships?

For Further Reading

Greenleaf, Robert. *Servant Leadership: A Journey Into the Nature of Legitimate Power and Greatness.* New York: Paulist Press, 1977.

Blanchard, Ken and Phil Hodges. *Lead Like Jesus: Lessons from the Greatest Leadership Role Model of All Time.* Nashville, Tenn.: W Publishing Group, 2005.

Sanders, Oswald. *Spiritual Leadership.* Chicago, Ill.: Moody Press, 1994.

Manz, Charles. *The Leadership Wisdom of Jesus: Practical Lessons for Today.* San Francisco, Calif: Berret-Koehler Publishers, 1998.

Chapter 10

Choosing to Engage the Culture

Eileen Hulme and Paul Kaak

With the emergence of the Industrial Revolution and the subsequent significant emphasis on scientific objectivism, religion in public and non-sectarian private higher education has been relegated to the sideline. The doctrine of separation of church and state during the twentieth century has had a chilling effect on academic dialogues that recognize the role of faith in human existence. And the increased access to institutions of higher education by a more diverse, pluralistic constituency has created a highly sensitized climate to any epistemological underpinnings that might alienate those who hold opposing views.

Simultaneously, American higher education has experienced a dramatic rise in enrollment at most faith-based institutions. A recent study conducted by the Council for Christian Colleges and Universities (CCCU) reports a dramatic 71 percent increase in enrollment since 1990. Enrollment at public institutions grew just 12.8 percent during the same period. The increase in student interest in religion and Christian values, more effective and robust faith-based institutional marketing efforts, and the rise of a significant Christian conservative political agenda may have contributed to this surge in enrollment. New faculty and staff positions have been added at almost all institutions represented by the CCCU. Yet this influx of Christian educators into Christian colleges and universities has not generated a similar influence within the larger academy.

Christian thought has become increasingly cloistered in journals and conferences that represent a selected audience of like-minded individuals. Journals and magazines such as: *Growth: The Journal of the Association for Christians in Student Development, Social Work and Christianity,* and *Christianity and Theater Magazine*; professional associations such as Christians in Political Science, Christian Association for Psychological Studies, and the Affiliation of Christian Geologists; and conferences including the Annual Conference of the Christian Association for Psychological Studies and the Association for Christians in Student Development have emerged over the last 25 years to provide an outlet for the Christian faith to be discussed and challenged. These venues have provided important outlets for the emergence of significant Christian scholarship and faith-oriented student development theory. However, this new strain of scholarship and professional development has served to diminish the Christian worldview from the general academic and professional dialogues.

Christian doctrine, however, demands that the Christian faith be lived in the greater marketplace of ideas. "You are the salt of the earth. But what if salt goes flat? How can you restore its flavor? You are the light of the world. A city set on a hill cannot be hidden. You do not light a lamp and then put it under a bushel basket. You set it on a stand where it gives light to all."[1] The Christian academy would be in direct conflict with the Scriptures if it allowed itself to be understood as a fringe element of higher education and thus only recognized by those who are of the same belief.

This chapter is designed to stir conversation about the biblical responsibilities of Christians in higher education to the general academy by expounding upon the biblical metaphor of salt and light. Additionally, suggestions regarding the practical application of our mandate to be salt and light to higher education will be provided.

BIBLICAL RESPONSIBILITIES OF CHRISTIANS IN HIGHER EDUCATION

After Christ challenges Christians to engagement with the world through the beatitudes,[2] he uses the timeless images of salt and light to provide a graphic depiction of that engagement. As recorded in the Scriptures, light was the first element mentioned in the creation story. "In the beginning . . . and God said 'Let there be light,' and there was light."[3] Light came into being before the other physical elements including water and land. And although the discovery of salt is not recorded, it seems reasonable to assert that it was put to use early in human history because of its preservative nature and enrichment function. Both elements are essential for sustainable life. They appeal to the senses of sight and taste as well as providing a valuable metaphor for purposes of comparison and illustration. The following sections delve into the nature of salt and light and provide practical applications for Christians called into academic endeavors.

1. As Salt Delays the Decay of Food, People of Faith are Concerned with the Decay of Societal Virtues.

Salt sustains life because of its ability to forestall decomposition. Sailors, for example, could sail longer and further into unknown territory because the survival time of salt-saturated meat onboard could be extended. In a similar way, families, education, and the rule of law serve humanity by preserving certain values and virtues. Jesus' words in the beatitudes make clear that Christian disciples are essential for the safe-keeping of Earth's myriad cultures. Dallas Willard refers to the important role of the Christian disciple when he notes, "These 'little' people, without any of the character or qualifications humans insist are necessary, are the only ones who can actually make the world work."[4]

Secular institutions are often limited in their ability to provide a cultural critique. As Robert Coles observed of his own university, there is a "disparity between intellect and character." He confessed a perception that "our schools and colleges these days don't take major responsibility for the moral values of their students, but, rather, assume that their students acquire those values at home."[5] The Christian university, in contrast, should make a significant contribution to the linking of mind and morality.

We know from history that ideas disseminated from the academy at-large are the ideas that shape subsequent generations.

> Ideas have consequences. The Marxists have grasped this fact, and they have tried to reconstruct every academic discipline in terms of Marxian presuppositions. The evolutionists have tried to reconstruct the thought of modern man along evolutionary lines. The Fabians virtually wrote England into socialism. John Maynard Keynes, the most influential economist of the twentieth century, ended his General Theory with the statement that 'the ideas of economists and political philosophers, both when they are right and when they are wrong, are more powerful' is commonly understood. Indeed the world is ruled by little else. Practical men, who believe themselves to be quite exempt from any intellectual influences, are usually the slaves of some defunct economist. The triumph of Keynesianism is a living testimony to the truth of Keynes's theory of ideas: even wrong ideas are enormously powerful. Christians, however, have been content to sit on the academic sidelines, waiting for the end.[6]

Essential to the calling to become a Christian scholar and administrator serving in higher education is the mandate to present clear and compelling critiques of the ideas that will inevitably lead to cultural decline.

2. As Salt, Christian Faculty and Administrators Should Intensify the Good Taste of What They Perceive to be the Beauty and Truth of Cultural Ideas and Behaviors.

Salt plays an important role among the array of spices used to enhance the flavor of certain foods. Christian faculty and student development educators, who recognize truth and beauty in the vast array of human endeavors, have the opportunity to enhance the lives of their students by exposing them to these concepts. Sadly, however, many Christian faculty members immediately dismiss secular scholarship when they discover that the authors aren't committed to the Bible as their authority. Additionally, student development educators often fall into the trap of believing that secular institutions and professional associations have little to offer because of their stance on particular social issues. To be salt, however, is to recognize a good idea in the writings of someone who doesn't share the same theological perspective. Good ideas don't need to come from redeemed people in order to have their source in God. All truth is God's truth, and it should be affirmed with a generous spirit. If people of the Christian faith are known only for what they oppose and not for what they affirm, they miss the opportunity to provide seasoning to enrich thoughts, ideas, and programs. Scripture encourages Christians to the following focus: "Finally, brethren, whatever things are true, whatever things are noble, whatever things are just, whatever things are pure, whatever things are lovely, whatever things are of good report, if there is any virtue and if there is anything praiseworthy—meditate on these things."[7] When psychological researchers state, for example, that "*Agape* is a spiritual love that reflects selflessness and altruism. . . . Our view is that we could use our strengths to be more giving and to build relationships founded on selflessness,"[8] Christ-followers should reply with a resolute agreement while also making a robust connection to the Christian worldview.

To be salt is to recognize a good idea in the writings of someone who doesn't share the same theological perspective.

The truth that all people are created in the image of God compels scholars and professionals to honor and engage the work of people from various faith traditions. God rains good ideas on those who know him and those who don't.[9] It is this conviction that allows Christian law professor and evolution antagonist Phillip E. Johnson to affirm the work of agnostic molecular biologist Michael Denton in his critique of Darwinian naturalism.[10] Faith-based higher education's challenge is to find an academic language that is unapologetically embedded in Christian narrative and God's truth as well as broad enough to speak to people of all faiths.

3. As Light, Christian Scholars and Administrators Seek After Wisdom, Not Simply Knowledge.

What must distinguish Christian scholars is not primarily their knowledge, but rather their wisdom. From the Old Testament book of Proverbs, wisdom may be defined as skillful living. Such wisdom contains minimal inconsistency between thought and action. It is oriented toward the good of others, full of integrity and sincerity. It is gracious—though fair; full of peace—but committed to righteous outcomes. As darkness approaches, the need for the light that is borne out of wisdom from God increases. Ephesians 5:8-15 (NKJV) states,

> For you were once darkness, but now you are light in the Lord. Live as children of light (for the fruit of the light consists in all goodness, righteousness and truth) and find out what pleases the Lord. Have nothing to do with the fruitless deeds of darkness, but rather expose them. For it is shameful even to mention what the disobedient do in secret. But everything exposed by the light becomes visible, for it is light that makes everything visible. This is why it is said: 'Wake up, O sleeper, rise from the dead, and Christ will shine on you.' Be very careful, then, how you live—not as unwise but as wise, making the most of every opportunity, because the days are evil.

Wisdom also affords those who seek after God the ability to judge the accurate proportions of salt and light that are required by the situation. Both salt and light are welcome in the right proportions. The correct amount of salt enhances the flavor of certain foods; however, too much salt assaults the taste buds. Light is also best when it is not overpowering. A light shone directly into someone's eyes creates temporary blindness, rather than illumination. Richard Mouw, president of Fuller Theological Seminary, says, "Through the centuries of church history, many Christians have been cruel and reckless speakers. Sometimes we have even thought of our uncivil speech as an exercise in Christian virtue. So some of us have some unlearning to do if we are going to enter the public square with confidence, as persons of good manners."[11]

The work of Christians in the higher education academy should be inviting rather than repelling, subtle rather than blunt. Other researchers, students, and teachers may choose to disagree ardently and oppose faith-oriented scholarly work or student life initiatives. However, it should not be because those adhering to Christian beliefs have been arrogant, spiritually oppressive, or overly anxious to correct perceived false doctrine. Paul speaks of this truth in Romans 2:3, 4: "The kindness of the Lord brings us to repentance" (NKJV). It is the kindness expressed through the wisdom of Christian scholars and administrators that will impact the prevailing thoughts and actions found in the larger higher education community.

4. As Light, Scholars and Administrators in Faith-based Schools Provide an Environment for Authentic Relationships.

The evening invites rest, while daylight calls forth engagement. Similarly, the Christian faith encourages relational engagement. Christian academics are compelled to forsake the comfort of the ivory tower. Jesus says that, as light, his blessed ones are not to get trapped under a bushel[12] or retreat to the safe environs of families and communities of faith. Rather, the call is to live lives of authenticity and openness to others. At the conclusion of his study in which he denounces the "moral and judgmental credentials" of the intellectuals who have advised humanity over the last 300 years, Paul Johnson says:

> One of the principal lessons of our tragic century, which has seen so many millions of innocent lives sacrificed in schemes to improve the lot of humanity, is—beware intellectuals . . . we must at all times remember what intellectuals habitually forget: that people matter more than concepts and must come first. The worst of all despotisms is the heartless tyranny of ideas."[13]

In the face of academic pursuits, Christian educators should never lose sight of the truth that people are God's priority.

Persons of faith are painfully aware of the reality that authenticity requires an open struggle between beliefs and actions. Paul captured this tension when he wrote: "For what I am doing I do not understand. For what I will to do, that I do not practice; but what I hate, that I do."[14] Ironically, as Christians shine the light of Christ on their own struggles, they illuminate the way for others to be known. Fear of being perceived as inadequate, misguided, or simply wrong often results in a self protective arrogance. Christian administrators and scholars must be the first to admit when they are wrong in thought or action. This humble admission may light the way for others to discover the truth found in Christ and to enter into authentic Christian community.

Persons of faith are painfully aware of the reality that authenticity requires an open struggle between beliefs and actions.

It should also be noted that Jesus warns his followers that to be his disciples authentically and unapologetically will involve persecution.[15] If Christ and his glory are the driving goals of the work of Christian administrators, researchers, and scholars, they will be mocked[16] and insulted.[17] Christian scholars and administrators' contributions will often be perceived as foolishness.[18] However, people of faith in the academy must take heart in knowing that this foolishness is the power and wisdom of God. The next sections provide practical suggestions on how to apply these concepts of salt and light in the higher education academy.

Application

Standard of Excellence

Faith-based institutions are called to be purveyors of transformational teaching, compassionate service, rigorous scholarship, and educationally intentional student programming. The argument could be made that these are the aspirations of all colleges and universities. While the outcomes may appear similar, the motivation to achieve distinction as a faith-based institution that is academically top-ranked is rooted in the desire to glorify God. Matthew 5:16 (NKJV) states, "Let your light shine before men in such a way that they may see your good works, and glorify your Father who is in heaven." If the work of Christian professors and administrators is substandard or lacks depth of understanding of the central questions of their fields and disciplines, then their voice is diminished and perhaps silenced. Henceforth, this requires that faith-oriented scholarship be enbued with the highest standards of rigor and that the teaching and learning process engage and transform each student. Student development educators must produce clear outcome statements for their programs and employ specific, rigorous ways to measure those outcomes. The stakes for producing excellence in faith-based education are high and compelling.

While the outcomes may appear similar, the motivation to achieve distinction as a top-ranked academic institution for faith-based institutions is rooted in the desire to glorify God.

Relevant Application

For Christian scholars and student development professionals to have a voice in the larger academy of higher education, they must seek to make their work significant and relevant. To be relevant does not mean that the Christian perspectives should blend into the greater prevailing thought. Relevancy has been erroneously equated with compromise. Scripture would make the case that relevance is critical to gaining a voice with unbelievers. Paul stated:

> For though I am free from all men, I have made myself a servant to all, that I might win the more; and to the Jews I became a Jew, that I might win Jews; to those who are under the law, as under the law, that I might win those who are under the law; to those who are without law, as without law (not being without law toward God, but under law toward Christ), that I may

> win those who are without law; to the weak I became as weak, that I might win the weak. I have become all things to all men, that I might by all means save some.[19]

The light that Christians bring should illuminate the pertinent questions of the day or biblical faith will be perceived as being irrelevant.

Christ provided a significant cultural critique during his life. He did not spend the majority of his time with those who were considered the religious leaders of his day. Rather, he ventured into the arenas of human need that were without the religious façade. Christian academic communities are vital for "building up of the saints"[20]; but they cannot become fortresses where walls are built to keep students removed from the secular academic dialogue. Christ provided an example of this when he prayed for his disciple in the following manner: "I do not pray that You should take them out of the world, but that You should keep them from the evil one. They are not of the world, just as I am not of the world. Sanctify them by Your truth. Your word is truth. As You sent Me into the world, I also have sent them into the world."[21] Faith-based institutions should firmly locate themselves in the center of their academic guilds and professional organizations, thereby giving them a voice of cultural critique for all to hear.

If the only expertise that Christian student development professionals bring is one of faith development, then they will have little to say to the majority of the members in their field who are struggling with issues ranging from the increase in mental health concerns to civic engagement. Recent discussions on spirituality in college students are often misinformed or incomplete because of the lack of integration of Christian theology. Today spirituality is often disassociated from the practice of organized religious activities and a commitment to a particular doctrine, although it can be argued that the most spiritually oriented students are also the most religious.

Christian academicians should be concerned with the great questions of their disciplines. Ken Bain, author of *What the Best College Teachers Do*, describes highly successful teachers in the following manner: "First, they have an unusually keen sense of the histories of their disciplines, including the controversies that have swirled around within them, and that understanding seems to help them reflect deeply on the nature of thinking within their fields. They can use that ability to think about their own thinking—what we call "metacognition"—and their understanding of the discipline qua discipline to grasp how other people might learn."[22] For faith-oriented colleges and universities to produce educated individuals who can impact their world for Christ, they must present the relevant questions of the day, while maintaining a firm foundation in Scripture.

A Voice in the Academic Marketplace

Scripture not only provides admonishment for faculty and staff to thoughtfully consider involvement in secular academic guilds and professional organizations, but it also paints a clear picture of the impact of noninvolvement on a person's faith. Matthew 5:13 (NKJV) depicts this state of nonactivity: "You are the salt of the earth; but if the salt loses its flavor, how shall it be seasoned? It is then good for nothing but to be thrown out and trampled underfoot by men." Christian scholars present a worldview that has the potential to illuminate a discipline or field. That light is too often hidden under the belief that the academy will not recognize, value, or understand a Christian perspective. Many national organizations have agendas that may be perceived as antagonistic to certain Christian perspectives. Without the courage to bring Christian beliefs to the academic marketplace, scholars and practitioners run the risk of allowing their "salt to lose its taste"[23] and becoming stale in their own academic work. Without the healthy immersion of Christian thought into the overall academic conversation, the higher education community will be incomplete and people of faith will languish.

Christian academics and student life professionals often face an inherent negative bias in the secular higher education academy. The basic credibility afforded most members of the academy is often withheld until the faith-oriented individual establishes his or her own reputation for academic trustworthiness. This is particularly difficult for new members of the Christian academy. Often the mistakes made by a secular scholar are understood as originating from inexperience while the mistakes of a young faith-oriented scholar are often viewed as errors of legitimacy. This type of scrutiny may compel Christian scholars and student development professionals to seek friendly venues for professional development and scholarly outlets. Faith-related professional and scholarly associations provide excellent conduits for the discussion of issues related to the unique education that faith-based institutions provide. The ultimate challenge is to produce academic products and student life initiatives that demand attention from the general higher education academy.

Embrace the Questions

To be active in an academic discipline or a professional field means allowing one's ideas and suppositions to be scrutinized by different worldviews. This type of scrutiny may create a desire for faith-based scholars and practitioners to publish and present only in venues where individuals understand the essence of the work. To be grounded in faith and to honestly pursue one's respective field of study provides a freedom to question. Wilkens, Shrier, and Martin argue:

> Many are inclined to interpret any form of questioning as doubt. . . . Often, it is not lack of faith in God or a theological tradition that we find behind questions, but a lack of faith in ourselves and a natural response to our fallenness. While faith-based institutions affirm the trustworthiness and completeness of God's truth, there is plenty of evidence that we should not have the same level of confidence about the accuracy and adequacy of our own ideas about God's truth. It would also be helpful to remember that whatever theological tradition you value arose as a result of someone questioning previously held belief systems.[24]

Submitting faith-oriented work for dialogue among the larger academic community provides an opportunity to illuminate the inaccuracies in existing beliefs. Christian scholars and professionals should welcome and seek out this type of criticism so as to be prepared to give a defense of their faith.[25] This does not negate the benefit of critique from a faith-based perspective. Faith-oriented journals and conferences play a valuable role in strengthening the Christian perspective within higher education. However, if the ultimate goal is to educate students to be effective citizens in a democratic society, the Christian academy must prepare them to face questions and doubt without losing their essential faith in God. We do this through modeling the courage to submit faith-oriented scholarship and student development programs to critical critique from the larger academy.

Humility Produces Great Teaching

The Christian faith is full of paradoxical wisdom. Believers are asked to "do justice, but to love mercy"[26] and to be "wise as serpents and harmless as doves."[27] In higher education people of faith are to be part of the intellectual elite that seeks to develop new knowledge and convey the highest ideals of Western culture. Yet, our place in the kingdom of God is always as a child of God firmly rooted in a sense of awe and humility. Christ rebuked his disciples for hindering small children from approaching him. He stated: "Let the little children come to me, and do not forbid them; for of such is the kingdom of God. Assuredly, I say to you, whoever does not receive the kingdom of God as a little child will by no means enter it."[28] Knowledge can be intoxicating, and academic ego is always knocking at the door of the soul.

Humility in the academy is often not easy to find. Yet Ken Bain, in his book, *What the Best College Teachers Do,* mentions it as a significant factor in what makes excellent college professors. As scholars and administrators grow in their field they are often struck by how little they know even after years of diligent work and study. It is tempting at that point to become arrogant about what one knows in order to compensate for the gnawing sense that one knows so little. However, if arrogance can be avoided, the teaching, counseling, and advising relationship is transformed. Bain, when describing the humility found in great teachers, wrote: "It appeared most frequently and prominently in people who had a sense of humility about themselves and their own learning. They might realize what they knew and even that their own knowledge was far greater than that of their students, but they also understood how much they didn't know and that in the great scheme of things their own accomplishments placed them relatively close to those of their students."[29] Scripture implores a childlike attitude that is found in a deep sense of humility. John 11:25 (NKJV) states: "At that time Jesus answered and said, 'I thank You Father, Lord of heaven and earth, that You have hidden these things from the wise and prudent and have revealed them to babes.'"

Conclusion

Many Christian universities emphasize primarily the teaching and administrative responsibilities of the faculty and staff. These vitally important roles have a significant influence on the students that choose a faith-based institution. In the twenty-first century students will seek graduate degrees in larger numbers and the role of preparing the next generation of college graduates will be extended to the preparation of students seeking advanced degrees. Students will gain a critical advantage in their next stage of preparation if our institutions are known nationally for quality teaching, learning, and co-curricular programming. It is no longer enough to be content with a local view of knowledge. The Christian academy must be globally minded and willing to advance faith-informed knowledge in the larger academic marketplace of ideas. The Christian academy must take up the command to be salt and light if Christianity is to expand into the technologically progressive first world market. Christian faculty members and student life professionals must engage students with a transformational intent that they might become Christ's agents of transformation when they leave the campus. It is incumbent upon those called by God as educators to model such engagement.

Discussion Questions

1. What factors created a movement among Christian scholars and practitioners to work in faith-oriented organizations as opposed to the larger academic community? How should those factors be addressed?

2. How can Christian scholars and professionals be active in their disciplines if the academic community is not receptive to a Christian worldview?

3. How does a Christian embrace the questions while remaining uncompromisingly committed to the essentials of the Christian faith?

4. How do Christian scholars and practitioners develop wisdom as they grow in the knowledge related to their field and discipline?

For Further Reading

Hughes, Richard T. *The Vocation of a Christian Scholar.* Grand Rapids, Mich.: Eerdmans, 2005.

Jacobsen, Douglas & Ruth H. Jacobsen. *Scholarship and Christian Faith.* New York:Oxford University Press, 2004.

Marsden, George M. *The Outrageous Idea of Christian Scholarship.* New York: Oxford University Press, 1997).

Wilkins, S., P. Shrier & R. Martin. *Christian College, Christian Calling.* Lanham, Md.: AltaMira Press, 2005.

Endnotes

Introduction

[1] This list of texts is obviously not exhaustive of the relevant books on Christian Higher Education: Mark Cosgrove, *Foundations of Christian Thought: Faith, Learning, and the Christian Worldview* (Grand Rapids: Kregel Publication, 2006); Duane Litfin, *Conceiving the Christian College* (Grand Rapids, Michigan: Eerdmans, 2004); George M. Marsden, *The Outrageous Idea of Christian Scholarship* (New York: Oxford University Press, 1997); and, *The Soul of the American University* (New York: Oxford University Press, 1994); Cornelius Plantinga Jr., *Engaging God's World: A Christian Vision of Faith, Learning, and Living* (Grand Rapids: Eerdmans, 2002); and Harry Lee Poe, *Christianity in the Academy: Teaching at the Intersection of Faith and Learning* (Grand Rapids: Baker Academic, 2004).

[2] Daniel Goleman, *Emotional Intelligence: Why It Can Matter More Than IQ* (New York: Bantam Books, 1995).

Chapter 1

[1] This essay is a revision of an address to the faculty of Pepperdine University, delivered October 6, 2006.

[2] Daniel Yankelovich, "Ferment and Change: Higher Education in 2015," *Chronicle of Higher Education* November 25, 2005: B8.

[3] Harry R. Lewis, *Excellence Without Soul: How a Great University Forgot Education* (New York: PublicAffairs / Perseus Books, 2006).

[4] C. John Sommerville, *The Decline of the Secular University* (Oxford: Oxford University Press, 2006), 21.

[5] Yankelovich, "Ferment and Change," B6.

[6] Ernest L. Boyer, "The Scholarship of Engagement" in *Selected Speeches 1979-1995* (Princeton, NJ: Carnegie Foundation for the Advancement of Teaching, 1997), 85.

[7] Nathan Hatch, "Christian Thinking in a Time of Academic Turmoil" in *Faithful Learning and the Christian Scholarly Vocation*, eds. Douglas V. Henry and Bob R. Agee (Grand Rapids: Eerdmans, 2003), 88.

[8] Anthony T. Kronman, "Why Are We Here?" *The Boston Globe* September 16, 2007. (www.boston.com/news/education/higher/articles/2007/09/16) 9-18-07. See also Anthony T. Kronman, *Education's End: Why Our Colleges and Universities Have Given up on the Meaning of Life* (New Haven: Yale University Press, 2007).

[9] Stanley N. Katz, "Liberal Education on the Ropes," *Chronicle of Higher Education* April 1, 2005: B6.

[10] Lewis 264.

[11] David L. Kirp, *Shakespeare, Einstein, and the Bottom Line* (Cambridge: Harvard University Press, 2003), 259; Sommerville 21.

[12] Sommerville, 8. See also Sommerville, "The Exhaustion of Secularism," *The Chronicle of Higher Education*, June 9, 2006.

[13] Parker Palmer, quoted in Jaroslav Pelikan, *The Idea of the University: A Reexamination* (New Haven: Yale University Press, 1992), 18.

[14] Frank H. T. Rhodes, *The Creation of the Future: The Role of the American University* (Ithaca, N.Y.: Cornell, 2001), 47.

[15] Edward E. Jr. "The University under the Microscope," *Books and Culture*, May/June 2005. <http://www.christianitytoday.com /bc/2005/003/14.10.html>.

[16] Alexander W. Astin, Helen S. Astin et al., *Meaning and Spirituality in the Lives of College Faculty: A Study of Values, Authenticity, and Stress* (Los Angeles: Higher Education Research Institute, 1999).

[17] Anthony Kronman, "Why Are We Here?"

[18] Daniel Yankelovich, "Ferment and Change," B8. Surprising new voices are arguing that religion, after all, should play a significant role in the academy. For example, secular philosopher and sociologist Jürgen Habermas in a recently published dialogue with Joseph Ratzinger (Pope Benedict XVI), argues that those who hold to a strictly scientific view of reality "do not in the least enjoy a *prima facie* advantage over competing world views or religious understandings." Indeed, Habermas writes, "philosophy has good reasons to be willing to learn from religious traditions." Both the religiously and the philosophically inclined must "reflect on their own respective limits." Habermas argues that reason owes its existence to something other than reason: "when reason reflects on its deepest foundations, it discovers that it owes its origin to something else. And it must acknowledge the fateful power of this origin, for otherwise it will lose its orientation to reason in the blind alley of a hybrid grasp of control over itself. The model here is the exercise of a repentance that is carried out (or at least set in motion) by one's own power, a conversion of reason by reason. . . ." See Joseph Ratzinger and Jürgen Habermas, *Dialectics of Secularization: On Reason and Religion*, ed. Florian Schuller, trans. Brian McNeil (San Francisco: Ignatius Press, 2006), 23, 40, 42, 51.

[19] Ibid., B9.

[20] Robert Benne, *Quality with Soul: How Six Premier Colleges and Universities Keep Faith with Their Religious Traditions* (Grand Rapids: Eerdmans, 2001), 6.

[21] Carlin Romano, "One University, Indivisible, Under a Coherent Idea," *Chronicle of Higher Education* 26 July 2002: B10.

[22] Dennis O'Brien, *The Idea of the Catholic University* (Chicago: University of Chicago Press, 2002), 25.

[23] Harry Lewis, 268.

[24] Michael Hamilton, "A Higher Education," *Christianity Today* June 6, 2005: 31.

[25] James T. Burtchaell, "Notre Dame and the Christian Teacher," *Notre Dame Magazine*, December 1972: 14.

[26] Robert Benne, 6.

[27] Philip Jenkins, *The Next Christendom: The Rise of Global Christianity* (New York: Oxford University Press, 2002) and *The New Faces of Christianity: Believing the Bible in the Global South* (New York: Oxford University Press, 2006).

[28] Robert Louis Wilken, *The Spirit of Early Christian Thought* (New Haven: Yale University Press, 2003), xiii.

[29] Benedict XVI, "Faith, Reason, and the University: Memories and Reflections," Lecture at

the University of Regensburg, September 12, 2006. www.vatican.va/holy_father/benedict_xvi/speeches/2006.

[30] It is time to declare our intellectual and spiritual poverty and to rediscover Augustine, Origen, Justin, Irenaeus, Basil, Chrysostom, Ambrose, and Gregory of Nyssa. I can't help feeling we would be miles down the road if we absorbed the learning of just one or two books—like Rowan Williams's *The Wound of Knowledge*—and then conducted a campus-wide discussion of what we had read. Rowan Williams, *The Wound of Knowledge: Christian Spirituality from the New Testament to Saint John of the Cross* (Cambridge: Cowley, 1990).

[31] Lee Shulman, "More than Competition," *Chronicle of Higher Education*, September 1, 2006: B9-10.

[32] Various church historians and theologians have noted that a deep ambivalence about the past pervades these American "restoration" movements. On the one hand, its leaders appealed to the sacred past, focusing intently upon the Bible and, to a lesser extent, the ancient world in which the Bible was written. But on the other hand, the influence of modernity often prompted the same leaders to treat the intervening history with cavalier indifference. See Richard T. Hughes and C. Leonard Allen, *Illusions of Innocence: Protestant Primitivism in America, 1630-1875* (1988; new edition, Abilene, Tex.: Abilene Christian University Press, 2008).

[33] *Heart* is a term of honor, for Jesus loved the heart and sought its transformation. See Bruce J. Malina, *The New Testament World: Insights from Cultural Anthropology*, 3rd ed. (Louisville: Westminster John Knox, 2001), 68.

[34] Ibid., 68-75.

[35] "A Prayer for Old Age." *The Collected Works of W. B. Yeats*. Volume I: *The Poems*. New York: Scribner, 1996.

[36] Jean Leclercq. *The Love of Learning and the Desire for God: A Study of Monastic Culture* (New York: Fordham University Press, 1982).

[37] Robert S. Root-Bernstein and Michèle Root-Bernstein, "Learning to Think with Emotion," *Chronicle of Higher Education* January 14, 2000: A64; Robert S. Root-Bernstein and Michèle Root-Bernstein, *Sparks of Genius: The Thirteen Thinking Tools of the World's Most Creative People* (Boston: Houghton Mifflin, 1999).

[38] Joel Carpenter, quoting Peter Berger in Carpenter, "The Christian Scholar in an Age of World Christianity," in Douglas V. Henry and Michael D. Beaty, eds. *Christianity and the Soul of the University* (Grand Rapids: Baker Academic, 2006), 68.

[39] *On the Divine Images* (Crestwood, N.Y.: St. Vladimir's Seminar Press, 1980), 16.

[40] Simone Weil, *Waiting for God* (New York: Harper & Row, 1951), 178.

[41] Parker J. Palmer, *The Courage to Teach* (San Francisco: Jossey-Bass, 1998), 36, 56.

[42] See Brian McLaren, *A Generous Orthodoxy* (Grand Rapids: Zondervan, 2004).

[43] See Jenkins, *The Next Christendom*; and Carpenter, "The Christian Scholar in an Age of World Christianity," 85-99.

[44] Wilken, viii.

[45] John Henry, Cardinal Newman, *University Sketches* (London: Walter Scott Pub. Co., 1902), 73.

[46] Burtchaell, "Notre Dame and the Christian Teacher," 15-16.

[47] Douglas Jacobsen and Rhonda Hustedt Jacobsen, *Scholarship and Christian Faith* (Oxford: Oxford University Press, 2004), 60.

[48] Kirp, 259. See Clark Kerr, *The Uses of the University* (Cambridge: Harvard University Press, 2002), vii, ix, 1, 31.

[49] Ibid., 263.

Chapter 2

[1] A discussion of John Calvin's philosophy of education is found in Cornelius Plantinga Jr., *Engaging God's World: A Christian Vision of Faith, Learning, and Living* (Grand Rapids: Eerdmans, 2002), x-xi.

[2] George Marsden, *The Soul of the American University* (New York: Oxford University Press), 33-47.

[3] Frederick Rudolph, *The American College and University: A History* (New York: Vintage Books, 1962), 18-20.

[4] Henry Zylstra is quoted in Henry Beversluis, "Toward a Theology of Education" (Calvin College Papers, February 1981), 10.

[5] Jonathan Edwards's approach to learning is discussed in Mark Noll, *The Scandal of the Evangelical Mind* (Grand Rapids: Eerdmans, 1994), 50-51.

[6] Edmund Morgan, "The American Revolution Considered as an Intellectual Movement," in Arthur Schlesinger Jr. and Morton White, eds., *Paths in American Thought* (Boston: Houghton Mifflin, 1963), 11.

[7] William Ringenberg, *The Christian College* (Grand Rapids: Baker Academic, 2006), 58.

[8] The Old-Time College is described in Ringenberg, 61-84.

[9] Michael Hamilton and James Mathison, "Faith and Learning at Wheaton College," in Richard Hughes and William Adrian, eds., *Models for Christian Higher Education* (Grand Rapids: Eerdmans, 1997), 268-269.

[10] Rudolph, 96-99.

[11] Ringenberg, 59.

[12] Marsden, 167-172.

[13] Statistics concerning nineteenth-century higher education can be found in Rudolph, 486.

[14] Wayland's remark is quoted in Rudolph, 220. Henry Adams's quip comes from Mark Noll's introduction to an earlier edition of Ringenberg's *The Christian College* (Grand Rapids: Eerdmans, 1984), 17.

[15] Noll, 107.

[16] The best accounts of the late-nineteenth-century transformation of American colleges and universities are Marsden's *The Soul of the American University* and George Marsden and Bradley Longfield, eds., *The Secularization of the Academy* (New York: Oxford University Press, 1992).

[17] Hedge is quoted in Marsden, *The Soul of the American University*, 186. James Burtchaell's *The Dying of the Light* (Grand Rapids: Eerdmans, 1998) is the most thorough account of this process.

[18] T.C. Horton is quoted in the *Ozark American* (September 1922), 11.

[19] Virginia Brereton, *Training God's Army: The American Bible School, 1880-1940* (Indiana University Press, 1990), 115. Brereton's book is the best analysis of the fundamentalist Bible colleges.

[20] See Noll, *Scandal*, especially chapter 5, "The Intellectual Disaster of Fundamentalism," 109-145.

[21] Ringenberg, 183-202; see also Michael Hamilton, "We're in the Money: How Did Evangelicals Get So Wealthy and What Has It Done to Us?" *Christianity Today* (June 12, 2000), 36-43.

[22] Kuyper's statement is quoted in James Bratt and Ronald Wells, "Piety and Progress: A History of Calvin College," in Hughes and Adrian, eds., *Models for Christian Higher Education*, 143.

[23] Holmes, *The Idea of a Christian College* (Grand Rapids: Eerdmans, 1975).). See, for example, Douglas Jacobsen and Rhonda Hustedt Jacobsen, *Scholarship and Christian Faith: Enlarging the Conversation* (New York: Oxford, 2004).

[24] The wardrobe metaphor is adapted from Beversluis, "Toward a Theology of Education."

Chapter 3

[1] This statement is similar to a quote spoken by Ann Druyan, the wife of Carl Sagan, during an interview on *Live with Regis and Kathy Lee*, ABC TV, Hollywood, California.

[2] Genesis 1:26, Holy Bible, New International Version, NIV, copyright 1973, 1978, 1984 by the National Bible Society. Grand Rapids: Zondervan.

[3] Arthur Holmes, *The Idea of a Christian College*, Revised Edition (Grand Rapids: Eerdmans, 1987), 7.

[4] Harry Lee Poe, *Christianity in the Academy: Teaching at the Intersection of Faith and Learning* (Grand Rapids: Baker Academic, 2004), 53.

[5] George M. Marsden, *The Outrageous Idea of Christian Scholarship* (New York: Oxford University Press, 1997); idem, *The Soul of the American University* (New York: Oxford University Press, 1994).

[6] Douglas Sloan, *Faith and Knowledge: Mainline Protestantism and American Higher Education* (Louisville: Westminster John Knox Press, 1994).

[7] Mark Cosgrove, *Foundations of Christian Thought: Faith, Learning, and the Christian Worldview* (Grand Rapids: Kregel Publication, 2006). The puzzle illustration of integration is a common one; Cosgrove incorporates the model well in his introductory chapters, 13-27.

[8] Marsden, *The Soul of the American University* (New York: Oxford University Press, 1994).

[9] George Kuh, *Student Success in College: Creating Conditions That Matter* (San Francisco: Jossey-Bass, 2005).

[10] V. James Mannoia, *Christian Liberal Arts* (New York: Rowman & Littlefield, 2000).

[11] Ibid.

[12] Cornelius Plantinga Jr., *Engaging God's World: A Christian Vision of Faith, Learning, and Living* (Grand Rapids: Eerdmans, 2002).

[13] Ibid.

[14] Holmes, *The Idea of a Christian College*, 18.

[15] Donald Palmer, *Does the Center Hold? An Introduction to Western Philosophy* (Toronto: Mayfield Publishing Company, 1996), 425.

[16] Ibid.

[17] Robert Harris, *Integration of Faith and Learning: A Worldview Approach* (Eugene, Ore.: Cascade Books, 2004), 31.

[18] Cosgrove, *Foundations, 55-59.*

[19] Ibid., 55.

[20] Ibid., 55-56.

[21] Ibid., 56.

[22] Stephen Jay Gould, *Rocks of Ages: Science and Religion in the Fullness of Life* (New York: Ballantine Books, 1999), 6.

[23] Cosgrove, *Foundations*, 56.

[24] Ibid, 56-57.

[25] Ibid, 57.

[26] Ibid.

[27] Ibid, 57-58.

[28] Ibid, 58.

[29] Douglas Jacobsen and Rhonda Hustedt Jacobsen, *Scholarship and Christian Faith: Enlarging the Conversation* (Oxford: Oxford University Press, 2004), 24.

[30] Ibid, 28.

[31] Rick Ostrander, "The Integration of Faith and Learning: An Introduction," in *The Gateway Seminar in Christian Scholarship Coursepack* (John Brown University, Fall 2006).

[32] Richard T. Hughes, *How Christian Faith Can Sustain the Life of the Mind* (Grand Rapids: Eerdmans, 2001).

[33] Roger Ebertz, "Beyond Worldview Analysis: Insights from Hans-Georg Gadamer on Christian Scholarship," *Christian Scholar's Review,* 36:1 (Fall 2006).

[34] Hughes, *How Christian Faith*.

[35] Ebertz, "Beyond Worldview Analysis," 28.

[36] William Hasker, "Faith-Learning Integration: An Overview," *Christian Scholars Review* (March 1992), 234-248, 242.

[37] David L. Wolfe, "The Line of Demarcation Between Integration and PseudoIntegration," in Harold Heie and David L. Wolfe, eds., *The Reality of Christian Learning: Strategies for Faith-Discipline Integration* (Grand Rapids: Christian University Press, 1987).

[38] Ronald R. Nelson, "Faith-Discipline Integration: Compatibilist, Reconstructionalist and Transformationalist Strategies," in *The Reality of Christian Learning*. It appears that Nelson originated this classification of integrative strategies.

[39] Harris, *Integration,* 221-247.

[40] Ibid, 224.

[41] Ibid.

[42] Ibid, 225.

[43] Ibid.

[44] Wolfe, as cited in Hasker, "Faith-Learning," 239.

[45] Harris, *Integration*, 225-226.

[46] Ibid., 226.

[47] Nelson, as cited in Hasker, "Faith-Learning," 241.

[48] Harris, *Integration*, 227.

[49] Hasker, "Faith-Learning," *241.*

[50] Harris, *Integration*, 227-228.

[51] Andrew Chambers, "Why Integrate Faith and Learning?" Missouri Baptist University, 2006, available from http://www.mobap.edu/academics/fl/whyofintegration.asp#f1

[52] David Claerbaut, *Faith and Learning on the Edge: A Bold New Look at Religion in Higher Education* (Grand Rapids: Zondervan, 2004).

[53] Council for Christian Colleges and Universities Resource Center, available from http://www.cccu.org/resourcecenter/resID.1002,parentCatID.215/rc_detail.asp

[54] Judy Vander Woude, "Statement on the Integration of Faith and Teaching," Calvin College Communication Arts and Sciences, available from http://www.calvin.edu/academic/cas/faculty/faith/jvw.htm. Professor Vander Woude attributes these ideas to Nicholas Wolterstorff.

[55] Harold Heie, *Integration of Faith & Learning in the Classroom: Posing Integrative Questions* (Wenham, Mass.: Center for Christian Studies at Gordon College, 2005).

[56] Harold Heie, "Examples of Integrative Questions by Discipline," Council for Christian Colleges and Universities Resource Center, available from http://www.cccu.org/resourcecenter/resID.2241,parentCatID.215/rc_detail.asp

[57] Richard Light, *Making the Most of College* (Cambridge: Harvard University Press, 2001), 8.

[58] Arthur Chickering and Linda Reisser, *Education and Identity*, 2nd Edition (San Francisco: Jossey-Bass Publishers, 1993).

[59] Arthur Holmes, "Wanted: Christian Scholars," Breakpoint 2004, available from http://www.breakpoint.org/listingarticle.asp?ID=2520.

[60] Mark Noll, *The Scandal of the Evangelical Mind* (Grand Rapids: Erdmans, 1995).

Chapter 4

[1] Association of American Colleges and Universities, *Greater Expectations: A New Vision for Learning as a Nation goes to College* (Washington, D.C.: Association of American Colleges and Universities, 2002).

[2] Ernest Boyer, *Scholarship Reconsidered: Priorities of the Professoriate* (New York: The Carnegie Foundation for the Advancement of Teaching, 1990), xii.

[3] Derek Bok, "Seizing the Initiative for Quality Education," *Trusteeship*, Volume 14 no. 2 (March/April 2006).

[4] Peter Ewell, "Grading Learning: Progress and Prospects," in *Measuring Up: The National Report Card on Higher Education* [cited October 14, 2006]. Available from http://measuringup.highereducation.org/commentary/gradinglearning.cfm

[5] Elyse Ashburn, "The Spellings Report: Commission Calls Colleges Self-Satisfied and Risk Averse," *The Chronicle of Higher Education*, Volume 53 no. 2, September 1, 2006.

[6] James Freedman, "A Theological Education," *The Chronicle of Higher Education*, Volume 51 no. 43, July 1, 2005, B9.

[7] Robert Barr and John Tagg, "From Teaching to Learning: A New Paradigm for Undergraduate Education," *Change*, Volume 27 no. 6 (November/December 1995), 12.

[8] John Gregory, *The Seven Laws of Teaching*, revised ed. (Grand Rapids: Baker Books, 1997), 19.

[9] Ibid.

[10] Larry Spence, "The Case Against Teaching," *Change*, Volume 33 no. 6, 106.

[11] Arthur Chickering and Zelda Gamson, "Seven Principles for Good Practice in Undergraduate Education," *AAHE Bulletin* 39 (March 1987), 3-7.

[12] Marvin Lazerson, Ursula Wagener, and Nichole Shumanis, "What Makes a Revolution?" *Change*, Volume 32 no. 3 (May/June 2000), 14.

[13] Thomas Naylor and William Willimon, "The Essential Mission: Teaching Undergraduates," *Academic Questions*, Volume 9 no. 4 (Fall 1996), 45.

[14] Boyer, *Scholarship*, 55.

[15] Carnegie Foundation for the Advancement of Teaching (January 29, 2007). *Carnegie Academy for the Scholarship of Teaching and Learning*, available from http://carnegiefoundation.org/programs/sub.asp?key=21

[16] Alexander Astin, "Student Involvement: A Developmental Theory for Higher Education," *Journal of College Student Development*, Volume 40 no. 5 (September/October 1999), 519.

[17] Shouping Hu and George Kuh, "Maximizing What Students Get out of College: Testing a Learning Productivity Model," *Journal of College Student Development,* Volume 44 no. 2 (March/April 2003), 188.

[18] George Kuh, "What We're Learning about Student Engagement from the National Survey of Student Engagement: Benchmarks for Effective Educational Practices," *Change,* Volume 35 no. 2 (March/April 2003), 25.

[19] William McKeachie, *Teaching Tips: Strategies, Research, and Theory for College and University Teachers* (Boston: Houghton Mifflin, 1999), 53.

[20] Lion Gardiner, "Redesigning Higher Education: Producing Dramatic Gains in Student Learning," in *ASHE-ERIC Higher Education Report* (Washington, D.C.: ERIC Clearinghouse on Higher Education and the Association for the Study of Higher Education, 1994), 45.

[21] Ibid.

[22] National Research Council, Suzanne Donovan, John Bransford, and James Pellegrino, eds., *How People Learn: Bridging Research and Practice* (Washington, D.C.: National Academy Press, 1999).

[23] Gardiner, "Redesigning," 73, 76.

[24] Ernest Pascarella and Patrick Terenzini, *How College Affects Students: Findings and Insights from Twenty Years of Research* (San Francisco: Jossey-Bass, 1991), 90.

[25] National Research Council, "How People Learn," 20.

[26] George Kuh, *Student Success in College: Creating Conditions That Matter* (San Francisco: Jossey-Bass, 2005).

[27] Kuh, "Student," 302.

[28] American Association for Higher Education, *Powerful Partnerships: A Shared Responsibility for Learning: A Joint Report* (Washington, DC: American Association for Higher Education, 1998), 3.

[29] Ibid.

[30] George Kuh, "Guiding Principles for Creating Seamless Learning Environments," *Journal of College Student Personnel,* 37 no. 2 (March/April 1996), 137.

[31] Peter Ewell, "A Brief History of Assessment," in *Building a Scholarship of Assessment,* Trudy Banta, ed. (San Francisco: Jossey-Bass, 2002), 7.

[32] It should be noted that several of the definitions used in this table were developed by Dr. Steve Bird, Taylor University.

[33] C.S. Lewis, *The Abolition of Man* (San Francisco: Harper Collins, 1947).

[34] Neil Postman, *The End of Education: Redefining the Values of School* (New York: Vintage, 1995).

Chapter 5

[1] Richard T. Hughes, *The Vocation of a Christian Scholar: How Christian Faith Can Sustain the Life of the Mind* (Grand Rapids: Eerdmans, 2005), and George M. Marsden, *The Outrageous Idea of Christian Scholarship* (New York: Oxford University Press, 1997).

[2] Ibid., 106.

[3] M. L. Peterson, *With All Your Mind: A Christian Philosophy of Education* (Notre Dame, Ind.: University of Notre Dame Press, 2001), 206.

[4] Ibid., 218.

[5] Hughes, *Vocation of a Christian Scholar*, xiv.

[6] Duane Litfin, *Conceiving the Christian College* (Grand Rapids: Eerdmans, 2004), 216.

[7] Ibid., 64-65.

[8] Hughes, *Vocation of a Christian Scholar*, 71.

[9] Ibid.

[10] Parker Palmer, *The Courage to Teach: Exploring the Inner Landscape of a Teacher's Life* (San Francisco: Jossey-Bass, 1998), 11.

[11] Ernest Boyer, *Scholarship Reconsidered: Priorities of the Professoriate* (Princeton, NJ: Carnegie Foundation for the Advancement of Teaching, 1990).

[12] Ernest Boyer, "Creating the New American College," *The Chronicle of Higher Education*, A48 (1994, March 9).

[13] Ibid.

[14] Taylor University, *2006-2007 Catalog* [University Pamphlet] Upland, Ind., 7.

[15] Boyer, *Scholarship Reconsidered*, 17.

[16] Ibid., 81.

[17] Ibid., 77.

[18] Ibid., 18.

[19] Arthur Holmes, *The Idea of a Christian College* (Grand Rapids: Eerdmans, 1975), 18.

[20] Ernest Boyer, *College: The Undergraduate Experience in America* (New York: Harper & Row, 1987), 297.

[21] W. James Mannoi, *Christian Liberal Arts: An Education that Goes Beyond* (Lanham, Md. Rowman & Littlefield, 2000), 128.

[22] Ibid., 126.

[23] Ibid., 127.

[24] Hughes, *Vocation of a Christian Scholar*, 98.

[25] Arthur Chickering and L. Reisser, *Education and Identity*, 2nd Edition (San Francisco: Jossey-Bass, 1993).

[26] Alexander Astin, "Student Involvement: A Developmental Theory for Higher Education," Journal of College Student Personnel, 25: 4 (1984), 297-308, and Astin, *What Matters in College? Four Critical Years Revisited* (San Francisco: Jossey-Bass, 1993).

[27] James Fowler, *Stages of Faith: The Psychology of Human Development and the Quest for Meaning* (San Francisco: Harper, 1981).

[28] Boyer, 21.

[29] P. R. Loeb, *Soul of a Citizen: Living with Conviction in a Cynical Time* (New York: St. Martin's Griffin, 1999), 307, 308.

[30] Ibid., 345.

[31] Ibid., 313-314.

[32] Boyer, *Scholarship Reconsidered*, 23, 24.

[33] Peterson, *With All Your Mind*, 215.

[34] C. S. Lent, "Becoming a Great Catholic University," in T. Hesburgh, ed., *The Challenge and Promise of a Catholic University* (Notre Dame, Ind.: University of Notre Dame Press, 1994), 146.

[35] Taylor University Center for Teaching & Learning Excellence, *Mission and Purposes* [Online Blackboard Course Site, 2006], Upland, Ind.

[36] Hughes, *Vocation of a Christian Scholar*, 89.

[37] Ibid., 103

[38] Ibid., 98.

[39] George Kuh, "Guiding Principles for Creating Seamless Learning Environments for Undergraduates," *Journal of College Student Development* 37, no. 2 (March 1996), 135-148.

[40] Arthur Holmes, *Shaping Character: Moral Education in the Christian College* (Grand Rapids: Eerdmans, 1991), 72.

[41] Ibid., 72.

[42] Ibid.

Chapter 6

[1] Noah benShea, *Jacob the Baker (New York: Ballantine Books, 1989), 79-80.*

[2] Nancy J. Evans, Deanna S. Forney, and Florence Guido-DiBrito, *Student Development in College: Theory, Research, and Practice* (San Francisco: Jossey-Bass, 1998), 25, 26.

[3] Patricia M. King, "Putting Together the Puzzle of Student Learning," *About Campus* 4:1 (1999), 2-4.

[4] Philippians 2:1-2.

[5] I. J. Marinez-Moyano, "Exploring the Dynamics of Collaboration in Interorganizational Settings," in *Creating a Culture of Collaboration: The International Association of Facilitators Handbook*, ed. Sandy Schuman (San Francisco: Jossey-Bass, 2006), 83.

[6] Ibid.

[7] American College Personnel Association, *The Student Learning Imperative: Implications for Student Affairs* (Washington, D.C.: American College Personnel Association, 1994), 1.

[8] American Association for Higher Education, *Powerful Partnerships: A Shared Responsibility for Learning: A Joint Report* (Washington, D.C.: American Association of Higher Education, 1998).

[9] *Student Learning Imperative,* 1.

[10] Ibid., 3.

[11] Ibid., 3-5.

[12] David L. Potter, "Where Powerful Partnerships Begin," *About Campus* 4:2 (1999), 11-16.

[13] Donna M. Bourassa and Kevin Kruger, "The National Dialogue on Academic and Student Affairs Collaboration," *New Directions for Higher Education* 116 (2001), 9-38.

[14] James Martin and James E. Samels, "Lessons Learned: Eight Best Practices for New Partnerships," *New Directions for Higher Education* 116 (2001), 89-100.

[15] Adrianna Kezar, "Documenting the Landscape: Results of a National Study on Academic and Student Affairs Collaborations," *New Directions for Higher Education* 116 (2001), 47.

[16] Ibid., 48.

[17] Elizabeth S. Blake, "The Yin and Yang of Student Learning in College," *About Campus* 1:4 (1996), 4-9.

[18] Bourassa and Kruger, "National Dialogue," 13.

[19] Ibid., 13.

[20] Trudy W. Banta and George D. Kuh, "A Missing Link in Assessment: Collaboration Between Academic and Student Affairs Professionals," *Change* 30:2 (1998), 40-46.

[21] Thara M. A. Fuller and Adrian K. Haugabrook, "Five Facilitative Strategies in Action—Thoughtful Collaborations Between Student and Academic Affairs Enhance the Student Learning Environment," *New Directions for Higher Education* 116 (2001), 85.

[22] Ibid., 86.

Chapter 7

[1] James T. Burtchaell, *The Dying of the Light* (Grand Rapids: Eerdmans, 1998), 828.

[2] Joan Didion, "On Going Home," in *Slouching Towards Bethlehem*, Modern Library (New York: Simon & Schuster, 2002), 149.

[3] C. S. Lewis, "The Inner Ring," in *The Weight of Glory* (San Francisco: HarperSanFrancisco, 1976), 2.

[4] John R. Bennett, *Academic Life* (Bolton, Mass.: Anker Publishing, 2003), 40.

[5] Parker J. Palmer, "The Grace of Great Things: Reclaiming the Sacred in Knowing, Teaching, and Learning," *The Holistic Education Review* 19 (1997), 12.

[6] Chris Argyris, "Teaching Smart People How to Learn," *Harvard Business Review*, May-June 1991, 5-15.

[7] Robert Boice, *Advice for New Faculty* (Needham Heights, Mass.: Allyn & Bacon, 2000), 203.

[8] Ibid., 217.

[9] Caroline J. Simon, *Mentoring for Mission* (Grand Rapids: Eerdmans, 2003), 1-2.

[10] Pamela L. Knox and Thomas V. McGovern, "Mentoring Women in Academia," *Teaching of Psychology* 15 (1988), 39-41.

Chapter 8

[1] Gavin D'Costa, *Theology in the Public Square: Church, Academy, and Nation* (Malden, Mass.: Blackwell, 2005), 94.

[2] James.T. Burtchaell, *The Dying of the Light: The Disengagement of Colleges and Universities* (Grand Rapids: Eerdmans, 1998); George M. Marsden, *The Soul of the American University: From Protestant Belief to Established Nonbelief* (New York: Oxford University Press, 1994); D. Sloan, *Faith and Knowledge: Mainline Protestantism and American Higher Education* (Louisville: Westminster John Knox Press, 1994).

[3] C. John Sommerville, *The Decline of the Secular University*. (New York: Oxford University Press, 2006).

[4] Julie A. Reuben, *The Making of the Modern University: Intellectual Transformation and the Marginalization of Morality* (Chicago: University of Chicago Press, 1996).

[5] Clark Kerr, *The Use of the University* (Cambridge: Harvard University Press, 2001).

[6] Derek Bok, *Universities in the Marketplace: The Commercialization of Higher Education* (Princeton, NJ: Princeton University Press, 2003), 2.

[7] D'Costa, *Theology in the Public Square*, 189.

[8] Norma Wirzba, *Living the Sabbath: Discovering the Rhythms of Rest and Delight* (Grand Rapids: Brazos Press, 2006), 33.

[9] Exodus 20:10-11.

[10] Wirzba, *Living the Sabbath*, 33.

[11] Robert Taft, "Sunday in the Eastern Tradition," in *Sunday Morning: A Time for Worship*, ed. M. Searle (Collegeville, Minn.: Liturgical Press, 1982), 51.

[12] Bruce Chilton, *Redeeming Time: The Wisdom of Ancient Jewish and Christian Festal Calendars* (Peabody, Mass.: Hendrickson Publishers, 2002), 7.

[13] Geoffery Wainwright, *Doxology: The Praise of God in Worship, Doctrine, and Life* (New York: Oxford University Press, 1980), 26.

[14] Marva Dawn, *The Sense of the Call: A Sabbath Way of Life for Those Who Serve God, the Church, and the World* (Grand Rapids: Eerdmans, 2006), 123.

[15] Rodney Clapp, *A Peculiar People: The Church as Culture in a Post-modern Christian Society* (Downers Grove, Ill.: InterVarsity Press, 1996), 121.

[16] Justin Martyr. *The First Apology of Justin*, vol. 1 of *The Ante-Nicene Fathers: Translations of the Writings of the Fathers down to A.D. 325*, ed. A. Roberts and J. Donaldson (Grand Rapids: Eerdmans, 1956), 186.

[17] Mark Searle, *Sunday Morning: A Time for Worship* (Collegeville, Minn.: Liturgical Press, 1982), 8.

[18] Clapp, *Peculiar People*, 118.

[19] Wainwright, *Doxology*, 406.

[20] I. T. Ker, *John Henry Newman: A Biography*. (New York: Oxford University Press, 1990), 745.

[21] J. Milbank and C. Pickstock, *Truth in Aquinas* (New York: Routledge, 2001), 34.

[22] James K. Smith, *Introducing Radical Orthodoxy: Mapping a Post-secular Theology* (Grand Rapids: Baker Academic, 2004), 159-160.

[23] Parker Palmer, *The Courage to Teach: Exploring the Inner Landscape of a Teacher's Life* (San Francisco: Jossey-Bass, 1998), 171.

Chapter 9

[1] James 3:1.

[2] Francis A. Schaeffer, *The Mark of a Christian* (Downer's Grove, Ill.: Intervarsity Press, 1970).

[3] Dietrich Bonhoeffer, *Life Together: A Discussion of Christian Fellowship* (New York: Harper & Row, 1984).

[4] Bernard M. Bass, *Bass & Stodgill's Handbook of Leadership* (New York: Free Press, 1990), 11.

[5] Eugene Peterson, *The Message* (Colorado Springs: NavPress Publishing Group, 2003).

[6] Joseph C. Rost, *Leadership for the Twenty-First Century* (Connecticut: Praeger, 1993), 102.

[7] John Gardner, *On Leadership* (New York: Free Press, 1990), 1.

[8] Ron Heifetz, *Leadership without Easy Answers* (Cambridge: Harvard University Press, 1997), 20.

[9] Ibid., 1.

[10] Helen Astin and Alexander Astin, *A Social Change Model of Leadership Development Guidebook* (Los Angeles: Higher Education Research Institute, 1996), 16.

[11] Rost, *Leadership*, 99.

[12] Ibid., 13.

[13] James O'Toole, "When Leadership is an Organizational Trait," in *Building Leadership Bridges 2001* (College Park, Md.: University of Maryland, International Leadership Association, 2001).

[14] Ibid., 20.

[15] 1 Corinthians 12:14-16, 18-19, 27, *The Message*.

[16] James MacGregor Burns, *Leadership* (New York: Harper & Row, 1978), 4.

[17] Bonhoeffer, *Life Together*, 28.

[18] Janet Hagberg, *Real Power: Stages of Personal Power in Organizations* (Salem, Wis.: Sheffield Publishing Company, 2003), xv.

[19] Philippians 4:11.

[20] E. Stanley Jones, quote from a plaque in back of Hughes Auditorium, Asbury College, Wilmore, Ky. 2007.

[21] Quentin J. Shultz, *Habits of the High-Tech Heart* (Grand Rapids: Baker Academic, 2002), 166.

[22] James 3:17-18, *The Message*.

[23] Patrick Lencioni, *The Five Dysfunctions of a Team* (San Francico: Jossey Bass, 2002), 7.

[24] Hagberg, 304.

[25] 1 Corinthians 4:16.

Chapter 10

[1] Matthew 5:13-15, New King James Version.

[2] Matthew 5:1-12.

[3] Genesis 1:1, 3 NKJV.

[4] Dallas Willard, *The Divine Conspiracy* (San Francisco: HarperCollins, 1998), 125.

[5] Robert Coles, "Point of View," *The Chronicle of Higher Education*, September 22, 1995.

[6] Gary North, *Foundations of Christian Scholarship* (Vallecito, Calif.: Ross House, 1976), 332.

[7] Philippians 4:8, NKJV.

[8] C. R. Snyder and Shane Lopez, *Positive Psychology* (Thousand Oaks, Calif.: Sage, 2007), 74.

[9] Acts 14:15-17.

[10] Michael Denton, *Evolution: A Theory in Crisis* (Bethesda, Md.: Adler & Adler, 1986).

[11] Richard Mouw, *Uncommon Decency: Christian Civility in an Uncivil World* (Downers Grove, Ill.: InterVarsity Press, 1992), 50.

[12] Matthew 5:15.

[13] Paul Johnson, *Intellectuals* (New York: Harper & Row, 1988), 2:342.

[14] Romans 7:15 NKJV.

[15] Matthew 5:12-13.

[16] 2 Peter 3:3.

[17] 1 Peter 2:21-23.

[18] 1 Corinthians 1:18-25.

[19] I Corinthians 9:19-22, NKJV.

[20] Ephesians 4:12, NKJV.

[21] John 17:15-18, NKJV.

[22] Ken Bain, *What the Best College Teachers Do* (Cambridge, Mass.: Harvard University Press, 2004), 25.

[23] Matthew 5:13, NKJV.

[24] Steve Wilkens, Paul Shrier, and Ralph Martin, *Christian College, Christian Calling* (Lanham, Md.: AltaMira Press, 2005), 6.

[25] 1 Peter 3:15, 16.
[26] Micah 6:8, NKJV.
[27] John 10:16, NKJV.
[28] Mark 10:14-15, NKJV.
[29] Bain, *Best College Teachers,* 142.

are you playing the Devils advocate or God's advocate re: globalization & limited ~~resources~~ ~~ecology~~ ?

Liberals liberal (D. Prager)

Rachel Madow? (sp)
Keith Oberman